COCKTAILS FOR TWO

COCKTAILS FOR TWO

THE MANY LIVES OF GIANT SONGWRITER SAM COSLOW

ARLINGTON HOUSE·PUBLISHERS
NEW ROCHELLE, NEW YORK 10801

Library of Congress Cataloging in Publication Data

Coslow, Sam, 1902-
  Cocktails for two.

  Autobiographical.
  Discography: p.
  1. Coslow, Sam, 1902-   2. Composers—United States—Biography. I. Title.
ML410.C825A3   780'.92'4[B]   77-6822
ISBN 0-87000-392-5

Manufactured in the United States of America

We are grateful for permission to quote the lyrics from the following songs:

KITTEN ON THE KEYS
by Zez Confrey and Sam Coslow
Copyright © 1921, 1922 by Mills Music, Inc.
Copyright renewed

DOWN THE OLD OX ROAD
by Sam Coslow and Arthur Johnston
Copyright © 1933 by Famous Music Corporation
Copyright renewed 1960 by Famous Music Corporation

A LITTLE WHITE GARDENIA
by Sam Coslow
Copyright © 1934 and 1935 by Famous Music Corporation
Copyright renewed 1961 and 1962 by Famous Music Corporation

COCKTAILS FOR TWO
by Arthur Johnston and Sam Coslow
Copyright © 1934 by Famous Music Corporation
Copyright renewed 1961 by Famous Music Corporation

LEARN TO CROON
by Sam Coslow and Arthur Johnston
Copyright © 1933 by Famous Music Corporation
Copyright renewed 1960 by Famous Music Corporation

THE LONESOME ROAD
by Gene Austin and Nathaniel Shilkret
Copyright © 1927 and 1928 by Paramount Music Corporation
Copyright renewed 1954 and 1955 and assigned to
Paramount Music Corporation

TO FRANCES

I am indebted to Sherry Hill and Nancy Sidebotham
for the long and arduous hours they spent in typing
the manuscript of this book.

Sam Coslow

CONTENTS

A CAST OF THOUSANDS, INCLUDING . . .

Gene Austin, a Western Yodeler
Irving Berlin, a Ragtime Composer
Eddie Bracken, a Comic
Carl Brisson, a Great Dane
Eddie Cantor, a Standup Comic
Earl Carroll, a Beautician
Lew Cody, a Screen Heavy
Russ Columbo, a Radio Crooner
Con Conrad, a Dynamo
J. Fred Coots, a Songsmith
Bing Crosby, an Orange Grower
Bebe Daniels, a Movie Actress
Cecil B. DeMille, a Bible Salesman
Peter DeRose, a Songwriter
Buddy DeSylva, Another Songwriter
Marlene Dietrich, a German Vamp
Tommy Dorsey, a Trombone Player
The Duncan Sisters, a Sister Act
Jimmy Durante, a Fashion Plate
Thomas A. Edison, an Inventor
Duke Ellington, a Jazz Piano Player
Nathaniel Finston, a Musical Executive
Rudolf Friml, a Hungarian Musician
Greta Garbo, a Scandinavian Bombshell
George Gershwin, a Genius
Abel Green, a *Variety* Cub Reporter
D.W. Griffith, a Pioneer
Charles K. Harris, a Tearjerker
Phil Harris, a Drummer
Larry Hart, a Dreamer
F.B. Haviland, a Pop Publisher
Hecht and MacArthur, a Gag-Writing Team
Arthur Johnston, a Collaborator
Al Jolson, a Minstrel
Spike Jones, a Cocktail Assassin
Frances King, a Chanteuse
Dorothy Lamour, a Sarong Model
Flo Lewis, a Vaudevillian
Carole Lombard, a Movie Queen
Guy Lombardo, a Schmaltz Dispenser
Vincent Lopez, a Righthanded Pianist

Ernst Lubitsch, a Dialectician
Herbert Marshall, a British Dude
Groucho Marx, Member of a Quartet
Jessie Matthews, a Dancing Doll
Louis B. Mayer, a Tycoon
Irving Mills, a Jazz Entrepreneur
Boris Morros, an FBI Counterspy
Esther Muir, a Comedienne
Evelyn Nesbit, a Bird in a Gilded Cage
Ray Noble, a Comedy Englishman
Mabel Normand, a Silent Movie Actress
Gabriel Pascal, Another Hungarian
Mary Pickford, America's Sweetheart
Martha Raye, a Scream
Leo Robin, a Rhymer
Buddy Rogers, America's Sweetheart's Sweetheart
Sigmund Romberg, a Tune Twister
James Roosevelt, a Member of Congress
Artie Shaw, a Marriage Counselor
Al Sherman, a Romanticist
J.J. Shubert, a Bird Watcher
Abner Silver, a Parodist
Sime Silverman, a Legend
Frank Sinatra, a Swooner-Crooner
Kate Smith, a Moon Crooner
Larry Spier, a Partner
Igor Stravinsky, a Giant
Preston Sturges, a Playboy
Rudy Vallee, a Vagabond Lover
Charles Vanda, a Press Agent
Jerry Vogel, a Music Merchant
Jack Votion, a Quickie Producer
Kurt Weill, a Foreign Composer
Mae West, a Sex Symbol
Paul ("Pops") Whiteman, a Big Bandleader
Richard Whiting, a June-Mooner
Flo Ziegfeld, a Chicken Inspector

Chapter One

THE TIN PAN ALLEY
THAT WAS

My very first glimpse of that crazy, cockeyed little world known as Tin Pan Alley was so vivid and unforgettable an experience that I can scarcely realize the Alley vanished from sight more than a generation ago. It was sheer bedlam I walked into. The year was 1919, World War I had recently ended, and I was a junior at Erasmus Hall High in Brooklyn.

With my first song manuscript clutched in my nervous hand, I emerged from the 49th Street subway station into a building that housed the establishment of Leo Feist Incorporated, New York's largest song publisher. One flight up from the street, I suddenly found myself in the middle of a nightmare of deafening noise, confusion, and feverish activity. Thoroughly unprepared for what I saw and heard, my first impulse was to turn around and run—back to the comforting embrace of the subway and Brooklyn. But my curiosity was stronger than my teenage shyness, so I stayed.

I had walked into a long corridor lined on both sides by rows of cell-like cubicles, about ten or twelve in each row. The glass doors revealed that all the cubicles were occupied by pianists and singers or dancers rehearsing pop songs. There was no sound-proofing in those days, and what made it so confusing was that I could hear all the songs at once—full blast and in different keys.

In the corridor, songpluggers and other employees were dash-

13

ing to and fro like the fast-moving people in oldtime films. I peeked into some of the glass doors, and nobody seemed to mind. I was then an avid and dedicated vaudeville fan, regularly sneaking off from school for a matinee at B. F. Keith's Flatbush Theater around the corner. And so I instantly recognized a few of the occupants of the little cells. There, for example, were Gus Van and Joe Schenck, who headlined the Palace bill that week. Joe was tinkling away at the piano while Gus was looking over his shoulder at a professional copy of a new song, reading the lyrics. Across the corridor, a songplugger was demonstrating a number to Emma Carus, who was listening with attentive approval. The great Emma Carus herself. Hefty, statuesque, as big as life. I was fascinated, thrilled out of my skull. A few rooms down the corridor, a pair of twins in leotards practiced a tap routine to "I'm Sorry I Made You Cry." It amazed me how they stuck to the waltz rhythm when right next door a ragtime pianist was pounding away furiously at "Ja Da."

Beyond the last glass door I spotted a small reception room presided over by a ravishing redhead. She was typing away in complete concentration, as if she couldn't hear any of the fifteen different songs that were all being played at once. The redhead guarded a door marked "Phil Kornheiser—General Professional Manager."

Phil Kornheiser! A name that was legend to everyone who wrote, played, or sang popular songs in that era. His ability to pick a song hit on hearing the first eight bars had been the subject of a recent Sunday newspaper feature story. Phil could make or break a songwriter—literally.

The redhead, oblivious to my presence, went right on typing. She finally finished her letter and looked up. Everyone's out to lunch, I was informed, although I hadn't even asked. I sat down on a bench and waited, trying to distinguish the Babel of tunes clashing with each other down the hall.

About thirty or forty choruses later a short, stocky individual with black, bushy eyebrows darted in, walking rapidly. When the redhead greeted him with a "Hi, Boss," I sprang to my feet. Phil, glancing at the large manila envelope I was practically waving at him, said, "C'mon in, kid." The redhead glared at me as I followed Phil into his sanctum.

It turned out that Phil had mistaken me for a messenger boy he was expecting with some papers to be signed. Otherwise, to get an appointment with him would have taken many weeks—if that soon.

When I told him I was there to play a song, he frowned at first, then laughed. He had heard fifteen or twenty new songs that morning and had vowed he'd had it for the day. But I had snuck in by a fluke, and it amused him. "I've never had a schoolboy up here with a song before," he said. "How old are you, thirteen?"

True to his reputation, Phil stopped me after the first eight bars. My budding masterpiece was a thing called "Jazzland." Phil tried to be as kind as possible. "Let me teach you something, kid," he said, "and you will thank me for it. That's a very pretty tune, but it isn't wedded to the lyric. The words are all about jazz, but there's nothing jazzy about the tune. It's too damn pretty. Remember that, next time you work on a song, and come back and see me again. You have it in you to write a good tune."

He was right, of course, about the nonmarriage, and I never again made the same mistake. I had had my first valuable lesson in the songwriting art.

I was frustrated, yet encouraged just enough to try again. If the great Kornheiser said I could write tunes, who was I to doubt his word? I dug hard for a new idea and a new melody. I just had to, because popular music was my whole life. I lived, breathed, ate and drank it. I could play by ear every popular song I had ever heard. What is more, I was a living encyclopedia on the subject. I could tell you who wrote the words or the music of every hit song I had ever heard sung, played, or whistled. They were magic names to me—Irving Berlin, Harry Von Tilzer, Wolfie Gilbert, Jerome Kern, Sigmund Romberg, Fred Fisher, Jimmy Monaco, Joe McCarthy, Jean Schwartz, Grant Clarke, Young and Lewis, and all the other giants of songdom. Mention any one of them, and I could play you a whole medley of his songs. I envied them and wondered what they were like. How they lived, worked, played, dressed, even what they ate and drank. I had never seen or met any of my little tin gods, the Big Names of Tin Pan Alley, but I vowed that one day I would be in that select circle myself. It had become an overpowering ambition.

Back in Brooklyn, a few more long sessions at the family baby grand produced another epic called "Heartsickness Blues." Blues, after a long period of neglect, were big items that year. W. C. Handy had become a national celebrity. His works were widely imitated, and I was one of the imitators. My tune was a mournful minor melody fashioned after "St. Louis Blues." The lyric was the heartrending, anguished plea of an unrequited love. Naturally, I knew all about it—never even having been out on a date at that age.

As in the case of "Jazzland," it took a number of weeks before I could gather up enough courage to bring Opus Number Two to the Alley. I had taught myself how to jot down a tune—lead sheet with chords—which was the way you went about it in those pre-cassette days. Painstakingly, I spent an evening getting my blues song down on paper—intro, both verses, and chorus.

I took the long subway ride to Times Square again, walking around for several hours debating with myself about which firm to try. It had dawned on me that Phil Kornheiser, hearing fifteen songs in a single morning, was too much of a longshot for a newcomer. I'd stand a better chance with a smaller firm, obviously.

I walked all over the Alley, trying to make up my mind. Tin Pan Alley, of course, was not an alley at all, or even a street. It was an area spread out within New York's theatrical district, and its boundaries reached from M. Witmark & Sons down on 38th Street and 6th Avenue to as far uptown as Broadway in the Fifties where some of the Western firms had branch offices. A few years before I began composing, most publishers had been downtown on 28th Street. The heavy concentration of firms all on one block sounded like a symphony of tin cans, with tinny, cheap pianos tinkling away in every brownstone house all day long. The theatrical press began referring to the block as Tin Pan Alley, although there are so many different versions of the story that no one really knows who first thought of the name. The older songwriting luminaries—Paul Dresser, Gus Edwards, Will Cobb, Percy Wenrich, Jack Norworth, and their contemporaries—had all been familiar figures on the block, and the current crop of vaudeville superstars were daily visitors.

By the time I appeared on the scene, the publishers had all moved to larger quarters uptown. 46th Street—the block between Broadway and 8th Avenue—was the most heavily populated. As on 28th Street, most of the buildings there were converted old brownstone homes, except for Jerome Remick and Company which occupied a large office building in the middle of the block. Across the street were McCarthy and Fisher, Stark and Cowan, and a number of others. In summer, when the windows were

16

open, it was as noisy a street as 28th Street had been a decade before.

Around the corner on 45th Street were Will Von Tilzer's Broadway Music Corporation, and Jack Mills, and a few more. On Broadway itself, the four corners on 47th Street housed four different firms, one on each corner of the intersection—Shapiro, Bernstein and Co., Charles K. Harris, Witmark's uptown professional office, and Waterson, Berlin and Snyder, where Irving Berlin was both partner and head songwriter.

Almost all the firms had cell-like cubicles similar to Feist's, ranging from three or four at the smaller houses to ten or fifteen at the larger publishers. Though spread all over Times Square and its side streets, it was still Tin Pan Alley and always referred to as such.

As I walked, I looked over the exteriors of the various firms, in a few cases taking a quick look inside. After passing up a dozen or so, I decided on one that was adjacent to the Lambs Club on 44th Street. The firm was F. B. Haviland, and from the street it looked small, cozy, and somehow less forbidding than the others. I knew the name well, for F. B. Haviland was the remaining partner of the great Paul Dresser's publishing firm, Howley, Haviland and Dresser. It had flourished around the turn of the century when it published "Banks of the Wabash" and other Dresser evergreens. Dresser, whose brother was the novelist Theodore Dreiser, had passed on years before and so had Pat Howley, the other partner. I had heard that the firm was now struggling under Haviland's guidance, barely managing a modest profit.

Inside, there were no cubicles, no noise, and very few employees. The sole piano, a small upright, was visible in Haviland's inner office through the open door. I found it astonishingly easy to get in to see F. B. himself. Something about the cordiality with which he greeted me told me that visits from songwriters had become rare events at Haviland's. He actually *wanted* to hear new songs!

F.B. listened attentively as I played and sang "Heartsickness Blues" with all the feeling and pathos I could muster up. After a verse and two choruses he said, very softly, "Play it again, Sam" —a phrase I was reminded of years later in the Humphrey Bogart film, *Casablanca*.

As I played a few more choruses, I was dismayed to see, out of a corner of my eye, that Haviland looked anything but enthused.

17

He was, in fact, frowning. He's not sold on it, I thought. "It needs a little work," he began, rather apologetically.

At that point, before Haviland had a chance to explain what he meant, a lucky interruption occurred—lucky because without it, my songwriting career might very well have been nipped in the bud right then and there. A bright-eyed, lively young man burst into the office and was greeted by F.B. most effusively, even affectionately. He was introduced to me as Jerry Vogel, head buyer for the Plaza Music Company, New York's largest sheet music wholesaler. Acknowledging the introduction, Jerry turned to me and said, "I was listening from outside the door. That's a hell of a number you've got there!"

That was all F.B. needed to make up his mind. His *largest customer* liked the song, a fact that insured the sale of thousands of copies. However, they then sat down and picked the song apart! It needed a new middle section or "release," and the minor melodic theme was a bit somber and heavy, needing a little relief, some light and shade to brighten it up.

Jerry came up with the solution. Why not put this kid together with a pro, he suggested—someone like your boy Peter DeRose? F.B. beamed. My spirits began to perk up.

Peter DeRose, who was later to achieve fame as the composer of "Deep Purple," "Wagon Wheels" and other great standards, was at that time an F.B. Haviland discovery—a nineteen-year-old veteran who had contributed most of the Haviland catalog for the past two years. By day, Peter worked in the New York retail branch of the Italian operatic publishers, G. Ricordi of Milan, in charge of counter sales—items like vocal scores of *La Boheme* and *Madame Butterfly.* Puccini, who was Ricordi's principal composer, was still alive at the time, working on his final work, the opera *Turandot,* and was Peter's personal hero. Evenings, Peter did his moonlighting, writing songs at home until far into the night.

Before I left F.B.'s office, I had been introduced over the telephone to Peter, had signed a royalty contract for the publication of "Heartsickness Blues," and received an advance royalty check of ten whole dollars. I left the office with a heart pounding with excitement and the conviction that I had found not only a publisher, but in Jerry Vogel a lifelong friend and booster. Jerry, incidentally, is still very much a part of the Tin Pan Alley scene. His business astuteness paid off later when, on launching his own publishing firm, he acquired all of the famous George M. Cohan copyrights during Cohan's lifetime. "Give My Regards to Broad-

18

way," "I'm a Yankee Doodle Dandy" and the rest of the Cohan perennials are now published by the Jerry Vogel Music Company.

I walked around the corner to Ricordi's, met Peter DeRose, and arranged to work at his house in Brooklyn that evening. I encountered the second lucky coincidence in a single afternoon when I learned that Peter's home was only four blocks from mine.

Peter and I hit it off instantaneously. He was short and wiry, dapper and exuberant—and his exuberance was matched by his talent. He lived with his parents, upper-class Italians who had emigrated to this country just before Peter was born. In that first evening, in a burst of inspired and feverish collaboration, not only did we "fix" the weaknesses in "Heartsickness Blues," we also dashed off three other songs, all of which were published in very short order by F. B. Haviland. It was, in fact, the start of a period of collaboration that lasted about two years and produced several dozen songs, most of which Haviland published.

"Heartsickness Blues" achieved the dubious status of a minor standard, chiefly by virtue of the fact that it was selected for recording by a celebrated jazz group, the Louisiana Five, on the old Emerson record label. As such, it has become an extremely rare collector's item among dedicated jazz freaks, and you couldn't buy the recording today—if you were lucky enough to locate one—for less than $25 or $50. Certainly it wasn't the song. It was the Louisiana Five, whose recordings have over the years become more and more scarce and valuable, their output linked with the work of such early jazz greats as the Original Dixieland Jazz Band. It was my very first recording—and I wish I had a copy of it today.

Unfortunately, none of the other DeRose-Coslow collaborations ever set the world afire, so their names—forgotten efforts like "Rambling Rose," "Beautiful Nights" et al.—would be a futile exercise to list. However, because of Haviland's "in" with the Woolworth stores and with Jerry Vogel's music jobbing firm, the songs did manage to sell a few thousand copies each and to land an occasional recording, so that I earned just enough to barely get by and keep my songwriting ambitions alive.

Nevertheless, I soon found myself becoming restless. I had dropped out of Erasmus Hall, convinced that Tin Pan Alley was to be my world and choosing not to go on to college to study classical music or anything else that might retard my progress among the pop songsters. A big mistake, of course, although I subsequently gave myself the semblance of a do-it-yourself musical education by studying theory and harmony on my own, and listening hour after hour to symphony and opera.

My restlessness was related to my reluctance to serve the necessary apprenticeship in the songwriting game. I was well aware, of course, that the average pop writer spent his first few years in the Alley struggling and starving, sometimes waiting many years for his first hit. But the fact that I had achieved publication so swiftly and easily led me to the illusion that Hitville was just around the corner, along with fame, acclaim and loads of money for Pierce Arrows, dinners at the Palais Royal, weekend jaunts to Atlantic City, hundred-dollar suits, and whatever else were status symbols in the early 1920's.

It didn't work out that way. There were some lean stretches in the long six-month wait between royalty statements, and during one of these stretches, mentally counting the number of weeks until my next Haviland royalty check, I decided I must find a job —in the Alley, naturally.

I could sing and play the piano at least as well as some of the songpluggers I had met, so I gravitated toward the larger publishing houses which always seemed short of staff. I tried Remick's first because a young fellow I had recently met named George Gershwin told me he had once worked there as a rehearsal pianist and had found it an easy place to land a job. George told me to go out and get a haircut and a manicure and come back to see Remick's professional manager, Mose Gumble, a fastidious gentleman who liked his songpluggers neat and well groomed.

Duly clipped, scented and manicured, I strolled over to Remick's, where the jovial Mose, all smiles, listened while I sang and played. Without breaking his smile, Mose said, "Kid, take some more lessons and when you can play like George, come back and see me."

On the subway ride back to Brooklyn, I thumbed through the pages of the theatrical weekly, *Variety,* which I had salvaged from the wastebasket in Mose Gumble's anteroom while waiting to see him. I thought I might find some news of the music publishing world, perhaps a clue to some kind of a job. I found nothing, not even a paragraph. But I did notice a few ads, new songs being called to the attention of vaudeville performers. I reflected upon that for a few minutes. Ads—but no news. Strange. Something clicked inside my head, and I got off at the next station, made a beeline to the opposite platform, and took the next train back to Times Square.

20

Chapter Two

THE ROAD TO HITVILLE

"Can I see the editor, please?"

I was inside the office of *Variety,* on 46th Street just off Broadway, speaking to the receptionist.

"Mr. Silverman is pretty busy. This is the day before we go to press. I'll have to tell him what you want to see him about."

Certain that the receptionist would not get my message across properly, I scribbled a short note and handed it to her.

"Can you get this note to him? I'll wait."

The note I had scribbled read: "Can you spare just three minutes to listen to a great idea for *Variety?*"

It worked. A few minutes later I was seated next to the desk of the legendary Sime Silverman, founder, owner, and editor of the country's leading theatrical weekly, the bible of show business.

Sime was pecking away at a typewriter. There were a dozen reporters typing at other desks in the large editorial office. Sime worked right along with them, writing many of the important news stories himself.

He glanced at me quickly, said "What's your great idea?" and continued typing as if he were still alone.

I told him I thought *Variety* covered everything in show business except one important branch—Tin Pan Alley. The world of music publishers and songwriters. I couldn't understand why they were excluded.

Sime kept right on typing, his eyes glued to the machine.

"Keep talking," he fairly snapped. "What else?"

"Well, I think if you added such a department, the music publishers would become interested and run more and bigger ads."

Sime stopped typing and looked up at me.

"You really think so?"

"Yes, I do, and I can cover all the publishers and dig up the news."

"Give me a sample. Let's see what it'll read like."

Next day, I submitted a column called "Music Chatter"—the news and gossip I had heard around publishers' offices recently. Berlin had signed to write another Ziegfeld score, "Love Nest" was the country's number-one seller, Benny Davis and Con Conrad had teamed up to write songs together—that sort of thing. Mostly short, crisp paragraphs, just the bare essentials.

Sime scanned the column at lightning speed and said, "Okay, use that empty desk over there. Twenty-five bucks a week," and went back to his typing.

My brainstorm, the single column of chatter, was the first time a theatrical paper had ever carried news about the music publishing scene. Sime soon realized that a column was not enough, and it was expanded to a full page of music news. The rival *Billboard* weekly, noting that *Variety* was now carrying a great many full-page song ads in each issue, began to add music news. (Through the years, *Variety's* music section has grown to a half dozen pages, while *Billboard* is now a pop music trade paper in its entirety.)

The desk next to mine was occupied by a studious-looking young man with large hornrimmed glasses. His name was Abel Green and he had joined the staff a few weeks before. We lunched together frequently, trading news items. Abel gave me news he had picked up about musical shows, and I reciprocated with items about new vaudeville acts I had run into at publishers' offices. My career as a reporter was destined to be a very brief one, but Abel went on to become editor-in-chief of *Variety* after Sime's death. We remained close friends throughout his fifty-odd years with the paper.

The important thing that the *Variety* job accomplished for me was to give me entree into the music publishing industry. I found

22

that publishers and writers were eager for publicity, and doors suddenly opened for me. Before long, I knew almost everyone in the business.

During my sojourn of six months or so at *Variety*, I continued writing songs in my spare time, placing a few here and there as I made my Tin Pan Alley rounds. It was, in fact, the reason I lost the job. One day I made the mistake of leaving an unfinished lyric in my typewriter. The following morning, when I arrived at work, the lyric was removed from the machine and placed on my desk, clipped to my weekly pay envelope. Inside the envelope was a short note in Sime's handwriting, as follows: "After reading your lyric, I think you are wasting your time here. This is your last paycheck. Good luck."

Sime didn't know it at the time, but he had just done me a great favor.

During my stint at *Variety,* one of the people I never failed to call on each week was the world-famous songwriter and publisher, Charles K. Harris. I found I was always welcome in the Harris office, and on most occasions he had saved up a story or two for me. He had also published a song I had written in collaboration with Abel Green called "Daddies," the title song of a David Belasco stage production.

When I first met Harris, I had expected to see the stern face with the fierce black mustachio that is so familiar to all collectors of old sheet music. That old photo was the trademark of his publishing firm, imprinted on the bottom of all of his publications. Instead, I found a grey-haired, mild-mannered gentleman of the old school imbued with great charm, good humor, and an eternal twinkle in his eye. Harris was, without a doubt, one of the most lovable and memorable characters I ever knew in the business. Although a quarter of a century had gone by since he wrote and published one of the most famous hits of all time, "After the Ball," he was still very active. "After the Ball" and the great Harris hits that followed like "Always in the Way" and "Break the News to Mother" had made Harris a multimillionaire, and he lived like one. An immaculate dresser, he lived with his wife and daughter in an East Side townhouse, lunched at the Lambs Club with cronies like Joe ("I Wonder Who's Kissing Her Now") Howard and Eddie ("Ida, Sweet as Apple Cider") Leonard, and was driven home in his limousine every evening by a uniformed chauffeur.

C.K., as I called him, was, like Irving Berlin, a one-finger piano

23

player, but regardless of how badly he played, the great, tuneful melodies that poured out of his brain sold millions of copies.

When I visited him, shortly after Sime had fired me, I found him very sympathetic and eager to demonstrate his friendship. "Did you save any money while you worked at the paper?" he asked me.

I told him I hadn't because I had received only $25 a week.

"Well, then, now that you have some free time, how about you and I writing some songs together? I have a couple of new tunes you might like."

It was a sweet and marvelous gesture, one that I have never forgotten. Here was one of the greatest names in the history of American popular music—offering to collaborate with a comparative newcomer who had only a few songs published and was yet to write his first real hit!

Neither Harris nor anyone else around Tin Pan Alley knew that I was only seventeen at the time. I looked a few years older. Most Alleyites thought I was nineteen or twenty.

I liked both of the new melodies Harris played for me. He was perfectly capable of writing his own lyrics and had in fact written both the lyrics and music to all of his great hits. Nevertheless, I spent several evenings working with him at his home, and supplied lyrics to both tunes. One was called "Someone Cares" and the other was "A Little Brook, a Little Girl, a Little Love." The sheet music covers of both songs read:

Words and music by Charles K. Harris and Sam Coslow.

They are great rarities, one of the very few occasions that Harris ever collaborated.

On the completion of each lyric, I found an envelope in my mail containing a royalty contract and a check for $100 in advance royalties, although I had asked for no advance. It was the sort of lift I needed at that particular time, and it kept me going. Although the songs barely managed to earn their advance royalties, selling less than 10,000 copies apiece, Harris kept encouraging me, telling me he thought I had a good deal of talent and would make my mark one day. He asked me to make my headquarters at his office, and to be sure and show him anything I wrote. On one occasion, he told Joe Howard he considered me the most promising protege he had ever found.

I became friendly with two of the pianists on the Harris staff of songpluggers. One was Vincent Lopez, who soon left to form a

24

five-piece dance band at a Chinese restaurant across the street, the Pekin. Within a year, the Lopez band was to expand to twelve men and become the second highest paid dance orchestra in the country, topped only by the Paul Whiteman band. Throughout his long career as a hotel maestro, Lopez seldom failed to include one of my songs in his broadcasts.

The other Harris pianist I was friendly with, Joe Gold, had just written his first tune, "Everybody Shimmies Now," to a lyric by Eugene West, and it was the biggest seller in the Harris catalogue that year, 1920. In introducing me to Joe, I am sure Harris never dreamed that it would lead to the fulfillment of his prediction about me, and that I was to write my first big hit as a result of the introduction.

It came about when Joe asked me to join him one evening at Healy's, a popular cabaret on 66th Street.

At Healy's Joe said, "Sam, you've got to do me a big favor. The leader of the band here, Joe Gibson, wrote a tune with the banjo player, Joe Ribaud, and it didn't sound quite right, so I fixed it up for them. We need a lyric for it, and we want to buy it outright, because the boys feel that to divide the royalties four ways would be a bit too much. So would you be a good kid and knock out a quick lyric for us—for twenty-five bucks? I promise I'll return the favor real soon. Okay?"

I was astonished at the proposal, and didn't say yes or no. All I said was, "Let's hear the tune."

The band played a few choruses of the melody, and it was undoubtedly very catchy. Soon, instead of just Joe Gold, I had three Joes at the table working on me, pleading to do them the favor.

I suppose that at seventeen I was still pretty naive, and I felt that maybe I ought to do the three Joes this favor. All the musicians I had ever met were nice guys, and I liked them. Besides, I figured out mentally that every song was a thousand-to-one shot, and that dividing the royalties four ways might not result in my share being as much as twenty-five bucks anyway.

They kept playing the song every other dance, all evening, and I soon hit on a title—"Grieving for You." All three composers liked the sound of it, and I wrote the entire lyric right there at the table, finishing it around the time the place was closing for the night. Joe Gibson wrote out a full release on back of an envelope, which I signed, and he handed me twenty-five dollars in cash. The envelope merely stated that I was selling my complete inter-

25

est in a song called "Grieving for You," outright, for the sum of twenty-five dollars.

"That's not bad for one evening's work, kid," commented Joe Number Three as I left. "Twenty-five bucks is more than I made tonight!"

The first jolt I received was about a week later, when Joe Gold told me that the song had been accepted by the firm of Leo Feist, Inc. I had sort of taken it for granted that Joe, being on the Charles K. Harris professional staff, would naturally offer the song to Harris first, and I made no bones about it.

"Look," I remonstrated, "Harris just made a big hit for you by promoting 'Everybody Shimmies Now.' I think it's pretty lousy that you wouldn't give him your next song."

Joe put the blame on the other Joes. Phil Kornheiser had dined at Healy's one evening and had heard the song, he explained. He hoped I wouldn't say anything to "the old man," Harris.

The second jolt came when I dropped over to Feist's one day and saw a professional copy of "Grieving for You." My name was not on it! Only the three Joes were listed as writers.

I went back to Healy's that night, fit to be tied. All three Joes were there, and we adjourned to the musicians' room behind the bandstand. I told them what I thought of them, pulling no punches. I didn't mind being talked out of my share of the royalties for a paltry twenty-five bucks, but it would have meant a lot to me to have my name on a Feist song!

Joe Number Two pointed to Joe Number Three and said, "He did it! He told Phil we wrote the lyric ourselves. I couldn't make a liar out of him." Sensing that I was accomplishing nothing, I walked out, disillusioned and disgusted.

The third jolt came when I picked up a copy of *Variety* and spotted a full-page Feist ad announcing that Al Jolson had just introduced "Grieving for You" at the Winter Garden with great success! The following day I read a publicity release from Victor Records announcing that the next recording by the Paul Whiteman Orchestra, America's top dance band, would be "Grieving for You" and that they expected it would be as great a recording as the first Whiteman record, "Whispering"!

As a result of Al Jolson's success with the song, Feist decided to make it their "number-one plug"—a phrase used in the trade to indicate that a firm was concentrating its promotional efforts mainly on one song. A number-one plug at Feist was the dream of every aspiring songwriter and my song was getting it—except that

26

my connection with it was a big secret. It was a most frustrating experience, especially when I observed that Feist's dynamic plugging campaign through their coast-to-coast network of offices was resulting in a meteoric rise for "Grieving." For the first time in my young career, I was beginning to hear one of my songs whistled on the streets. More records were released, one on every major label. Columbia got out a topselling vocal version by Marion Harris, the rising new singing star of the year. George Gershwin made the best of the various player-piano rolls—a rare collector's item because it was one of the few tunes he made that he didn't write himself.

The dumb error I had made in selling my interest in my first smash hit for $25 began to prey on my mind. When someone told me that Whiteman was featuring the number every night, I went to the Palais Royal, the swank supper club where the band was appearing, curious to hear their rendition. The headwaiter at the door told me I would have to pay a five-dollar cover charge and order the expensive meal, representing more money that I had with me at the time. The club was on the second floor of a building just off Times Square, the entrance being at the top of an imposing wide circular stairway. Determined to hear Whiteman's arrangement, I sat on the bottom step and waited an hour or so until the band got to it. I could hear it quite clearly from where I sat. A sympathetic doorman allowed me to sit there after I told him the reason.

The following night, in a further masochistic spree, I indulged in the price of a standing-room admission at the Winter Garden and heard the great Jolson bring the house down with his rendition. It was the first time I had ever heard an important star sing a lyric of mine, and I was thrilled and miserable at the same time. I mentally kicked myself out of the theater.

Back home in Brooklyn, my father sensed that something was bothering me. Although I was ashamed to tell him about it, he managed to wheedle the story out of me. A Russian-born immigrant, he was a textile salesman completely unfamiliar with the world of show business, but he loved dancing and actually knew the tune of "Grieving for You." When I played the Whiteman record for him, he commented, "Sure, I've danced to it many times. You mean you actually *wrote* that song?"

"Yes, Pop."

"I think I'll see a lawyer. They have no right to take advantage of a seventeen-year-old kid. We'll sue them!"

"It's no use, Pop. I signed all my rights away. Don't waste your time and money."

Nevertheless, Pop went up the very next day to the law offices of Nathan Burkan, accompanied by a friend who was a client of Burkan's. It was the right place to go, for Burkan was the attorney for the American Society of Composers, Authors, and Publishers (ASCAP) and represented many leading publishers and songwriters. A young attorney named Phil Hart, who had recently joined the law firm, was assigned to the case.

Pop came home that evening brimming with optimism. "The lawyer said the case is a cinch," he announced gleefully. "He said you are still a minor under the law and any agreement you signed to sell your interest isn't worth the paper it's written on!"

It took almost a year before the case hit the court calendar. After the first suspenseful court session, the attorneys for both sides reached a settlement. I was awarded one-fourth of the royalties and all legal costs including attorney fees. Later, my name was added to subsequent editions of the song.

We learned that some $24,000 in royalties had been earned to date, but Judge Bijur ordered that my one-quarter share, a little over $6,000, be placed in a trust fund since I was still a minor. It was to be doled out to me at the rate of $1,000 a year, and I was to receive the remaining balance, including further royalties that came in, when I reached 21.

My first thousand-dollar payment from the trust fund made me feel like a millionaire. I had never had that much money at one time before. I opened a checking account, splurged on a new wardrobe, and tried to make the rest of it last as long as I could.

A thousand dollars went much farther in those days than it does now, it is true, but nevertheless the time came when I ran out of money. The second payment, and my royalties at Harris and at Haviland, were not due for some months to come, and I realized I had to look for another job—preferably in the music business.

I was a subscriber to a weekly trade publication called *Music Trades,* and when the next issue arrived in the mail, I turned first to the classified ad section. It was there I saw the little Help Wanted ad that was to lead to one of the most memorable associations of my life.

Chapter Three

MY BOSS—THE
GREATEST MAN ALIVE

The ad was innocuous, yet so surprisingly worded that I stared at it in disbelief, wondering whether it was one of those phony "song shark" ads. It read, as closely as I can recollect:

> Popular composer-arranger wanted. Send details
> of experience and background.

It was followed by a post office box number in West Orange, New Jersey.

Who in the world would run a want ad for a pop composer? More curious than hopeful, I dashed off a note that evening, enclosing professional copies of a half-dozen songs I had written —my "experience and background."

A reply came a few days later. It was on the stationery of the Edison plant in West Orange, bore the signature of a man whose name I have forgotten, and consisted of a single sentence: "In reply to your letter, please come to our office for an interview any morning this week."

Still wondering what the catch was, I nevertheless rose early the next morning and made my way from Brooklyn to West Orange—a 90-minute trek via subway to Penn Station, commuter train to Newark, and street car to the Edison plant.

Inside the central building of Thomas A. Edison, Inc., a reception clerk directed me to the office of the man whose letter I was holding. The sender looked at me a bit dubiously, took my letter, and disappeared down the hall. A few minutes later he returned and said, "Wait outside of my office. Mr. Edison will see you as soon as he is free."

"Mr. Edison will see you"—I didn't believe what I was hearing. Years later, I still find it incredible. But that's what the man had said. I was so nervous I sat on the edge of the chair, trembling a bit and feeling generally shaky. I guess I was kept waiting long enough to calm down, for after about an hour I was ushered into Edison's private sanctum, ready for anything.

It was a large but sparsely furnished office—an ordinary looking desk, a few small chairs, a long work-table on which rested an assortment of notes, drawings, and unidentifiable gadgets and objects, a rather worn-looking rug, and several bookshelves. Not exactly a movie set, or even the conventional office of a minor executive.

A few moments later, a man entered the room and walked to his desk, very slowly and deliberately. It was the face I had seen in my history books at school, a face I had seen a thousand times in newspapers, magazines, and phonograph ads. It was actually true —I was in the presence of the greatest inventing genius of all time, Thomas Alva Edison. The man who had changed the entire world and the lifestyles of everyone, everywhere. If you think I was stunned to the point of naive, yokelish speechlessness, I was. I could not have been more impressed if I had suddenly found myself in the presence of Galileo, Shakespeare, Beethoven, or God Almighty. What in the hell was I—a kid from Brooklyn named Sam Coslow, not yet dry behind the ears—doing sitting alone with Thomas A. Edison, the man who invented the phonograph, motion pictures, the stock ticker, the transmission of sound by electrical current (which led to Bell's invention of the telephone), the electric battery, the electric light, and in fact the entire foundation for the science of electronics which revolutionized the civilized world?

The Great Man was then in his middle seventies, but looked older. I saw a tired, worn-looking face, but with eyes that were intensely alive and burned holes through you when they looked directly at you.

He appeared relaxed and very much at ease, never for a moment conveying the impression that he was busy, distracted, or eager to get to the pile of work on his work-table. So you are a popular

30

guts, naturally. To them, I was some kind of an upstart who had talked the boss into waxing a bunch of corny crap. But they recorded the stuff nevertheless, using a large house orchestra.

Once New York had satisfied the old man's whim, nothing more was ever done about the recordings. A few samples were pressed, and that was the end of it—no promotion, no advertising, not even a release date.

For some reason Haviland, who was still one of my publishers, was eager to get the adapted versions, and he gave the story to the trade papers about Edison hiring me to revolutionize the popular song business by reviving the hits of fifty years before. It sounded like a good name-dropping item, and *Variety* made it the front-page headline story that week. The following week, *Music Trades* published a rebuttal from A. L. Walsh, advertising manager for Edison Records in New York. To quote from the trade paper's rebuttal:

> A spectacular statement, recently published by a theatrical weekly *(Variety)* stated that Thomas A. Edison is at work on a plan to revolutionize the country's dance music and transmute the classics into a brand-new kind of synthetic jazz. The story, which was plastered all over the front page of the theatrical publication, stated that the first releases would be circulated on Edison Records. Sam Coslow, it was further alleged, was the fortunate man the great inventor had selected to turn out fox-trot arrangements of the classics.
>
> But here is what A. L. Walsh, advertising manager of Edison Records, says in reply to a query by a reporter of *Music Trades* requesting a confirmation or denial of the story: "We have heard nothing about Mr. Edison starting a movement to revolutionize the country's dance music. Thanks for telling us about it, nevertheless. It gave us a good laugh."

The article went on to imply that I had perpetrated some sort of a publicity hoax. Eventually, the New York recording division successfully buried the recordings, and Mr. Edison was told that the retailers were just not interested in oldtime songs.

When Edison learned that the revivals were not instant hit records, he was more determined than ever to prove that "those imbeciles in New York know nothing about picking song hits." He, Thomas A. Edison, had always had an infallible ear for a good tune, and by golly he would show them how to pick the hits! Out of his indignation came some new duties for me.

Knowing that I was acquainted with New York song publishers, Edison decided that I was to spend several afternoons each week making the rounds in Tin Pan Alley. I would hear all of the new song releases, weed them out, and then go over the most likely hit prospects with Edison at a weekly session at which he— and he alone—would personally decide on the final selections to be recorded at the New York studio. Thus I found myself suddenly transformed from "composer-arranger" to Mr. Edison's personal song scout. It seemed like an easy assignment. I didn't mind, because it also meant I could keep up with the Tin Pan Alley contacts I had been neglecting.

As a representative of what was then still one of the major recording companies, I received the red-carpet treatment in the Alley. Every large song publisher had a staff member designated as "mechanical man," whose function was to land as many new songs as possible on records and player-piano rolls, which in the Alley were termed "mechanicals." Any song selected for recording was worth at least several thousand dollars in royalties to the publisher, much more on a big hit. And so it was natural that the mechanical men wined, dined, and romanced me to get their wares waxed.

The scouting scheme went well for awhile, but after a few months of the new routine something occurred that led directly to my downfall as a scout for Edison Records.

On one of my semiweekly trips to New York, the mechanical man for Remick's—his name escapes me—was awaiting my visit with a new song he seemed really excited about. He summoned Remick's top team of songpluggers to his office to demonstrate the song for me. It was called "Carolina in the Morning," and the firm had paid a whopping royalty advance of $1,000 to the writers, Gus Kahn and Walter Donaldson. Moreover, Jolson was scheduled to introduce it in his new show at the Winter Garden, which, as I knew from actual experience, was a virtual guarantee of success for any new number.

"Carolina" sounded like a natural to me, and I would have liked it even without the feverish sales pitch and the promises of nationwide promotion. I took the professional copy home with me and spent an evening learning the words and music until I could demonstrate it with ease and facility.

34

At the next weekly session with Mr. Edison, I prefaced my demonstration of "Carolina in the Morning" with the nonchalant statement that I had found one of the big hits of the year. I began to sing and play it, but Edison stopped me cold after the first few bars. Occasionally, when he was not sure of what he was hearing, Edison would have me play the tune on the piano with one finger —just the single notes of the melody. He had a theory that people could easily be fooled when a tune was dressed up with an attractive arrangement. What he wanted was the bare bones of the naked, unadorned melody. He instantly recognized "Carolina in the Morning" as that kind of melodic fooler, and insisted that I play it with one finger, one note at a time, and slowly. He wanted the basic tune to sink in.

Did you ever try to play "Carolina in the Morning" with one finger? For a number that has stood the test of time to become one of the great song standards of this century, the one-finger version is one of the most unbelievably monotonous melodies ever composed. The same two notes over and over again. Run it over on the piano that way, or even in your mind—very slowly, forgetting the harmonies—and you will see what I mean.

I played the one-finger arrangement, *sans* all harmonies and without singing the lyrics, just as Edison wanted it. In that crude form, it seemed to take hours to get to the end of the chorus. Throughout the demonstration, I could see Edison squinting at me in disbelief. He strode to the window, looking out in reflective silence. Finally he spoke.

"You really think that will be the big hit of the year? I think it's just terrible!"

And with that he turned abruptly and walked out of the room without waiting for my reply.

At the end of the week I received a short note from the personnel manager, enclosing a check for two weeks' salary in lieu of notice. The note stated, very simply, "Your services are no longer required."

Thus ended my brief association with the greatest man I would ever meet in a lifetime. I was tempted many times afterwards to call his attention to the fact that "Carolina" had indeed turned out to be one of the smash hits of all time—but by that time Edison Records had gone down the drain, and I was far more absorbed in resuming my songwriting career.

Chapter Four

SONGWRITERS, SUPERSTARS, AND OTHER ECCENTRICS

Following my job in West Orange, I began going the rounds of Tin Pan Alley again, making up for lost time and renewing my former contacts. One of the first people I ran into was Bob Schafer, an energetic hustler, who described himself as a songwriter's agent. Bob offered to represent me, with no strings or obligations. I decided to give him a try.

The first place he took me to was a small cabaret uptown in Harlem called the Alamo.

"You've gotta meet me there tonight," he explained, "because there's a piano player up there I want you to meet. I signed him up because he's got a couple of terrific tunes that need lyrics."

At the Alamo, a dark, dingy basement joint, I was introduced to the pianist, a character who was known only as "Ragtime Jimmy." Jimmy served as accompanist for the half-baked acts that played the Alamo, and between shows supplied dance music with the rest of the band, which consisted only of a drummer named Jack Roth. It was not until I had collaborated on several songs with Ragtime Jimmy that I learned his full name, which was Jimmy Durante.

At the first meeting, Bob suggested that I form a songwriting team with Jimmy. Jimmy seemed quite flattered because the story of the lawsuit establishing my claim to "Grieving for You" had gotten around by this time, and Jimmy liked the idea of starting

36

his songwriting career with someone who had a song hit to his credit.

A bit unsure of what I was getting into, I asked Jimmy what type of music he wrote.

"Sen'imental mostly," was his reply. I felt better about that, because I was afraid the appellation "Ragtime Jimmy" meant that he specialized in composing rags and jazz, which were not exactly my cup of tea.

Jimmy played about a dozen melodies for me. I liked two of them, whereupon he scratched out lead sheets for me to take home. On the first one I tackled, I supplied a title which took up almost the entire title page when it was published. I called it: "I Didn't Start in to Love You Until You Stopped Loving Me." Despite the unwieldy title, Bob placed it with a small publisher for us, and six months later we received a royalty statement showing it had sold 31 copies—mostly to friends and relatives of Jimmy's and mine, I am sure.

The second song had a tune I was extremely fond of, a plaintive torch melody that Jimmy confided was a truly inspired masterpiece, the outpouring of an emotional binge. I wrote a strong lyric to it, which I titled "What'll I Do." Then Bob brought Jimmy and me up to see Jack Robbins, a dynamic young publisher who had recently started a new firm that was setting Tin Pan Alley afire.

Jimmy played and sang the number for Jack, looking for all the world like a frustrated Cyrano de Bergerac moaning about his lost love. Jack loved it and promised to make it a big hit for us— provided we would wait until the following year, because his program for the next twelve months was already mapped out. This made us hesitate, so Jack called in his bookkeeper and asked him to write us a check for a whopping advance. That decided us.

If you have gathered by now that "What'll I Do" became my second big song hit, you couldn't be more wrong. Jack Robbins found himself snowed under with songs and obligations to other writers, and when twelve months had passed, the manuscript still reposed in Jack's desk drawer. A few months later, Jack finally got around to it, and ordered copies printed.

Before it came off the press, Irving Berlin's *Music Box Revue of 1923* opened on Broadway with the only disappointing score Berlin had ever written—nothing in it that looked like a hit. Whereupon Irving quickly dashed off a typical Berlin ballad to give the show its much-needed hit song—a number called, of all things, "What'll I Do." His song, of course, is the "What'll I Do" you all

37

know, and ours never saw the light of day. It was just one of those unfortunate coincidences that every songwriter runs into every now and then. It happened to Irving himself, when he wrote and published a song called "When My Baby Smiles at Me," only to learn that Ted Lewis had just introduced, with tremendous success, a new Harry Von Tilzer song by the same title. And it happened again to me, on at least two other occasions. I have two songs called "Dancing in the Dark" and "Ramona," both of which were published in sheet music form a year or two before the great standards came out, with identical titles, by other writers. Unfortunately, you cannot copyright a song title.

Around this time another job came along, actually the first steady job I ever held with a music publishing firm. This time I wasn't looking for one, as by now some fairly good advances were coming along on new songs, enough to keep me going. But the job that was offered to me presented an opportunity to have a good "in" with a promising young Tin Pan Alley firm, and so I accepted it. It came about as follows:

I paid a visit to Mills Music on 45th Street to play a couple of new songs for them. During my conversation with Irving Mills, brother and partner of Jack Mills, who headed the thriving new company, Irving told me that one of their instrumental piano solos, Zez Confrey's "Kitten on the Keys," had suddenly hit the bestseller lists, more than a year after publication.

"But, you know," Irving told me, "it's a damned funny thing— the stores tell us that people are complaining because there are no words on the copies. Now, can you imagine anyone expecting to find a lyric on the sheet music of an instrumental that's as tough to play as 'Kitten'? They don't realize the tune just has too many notes to put a lyric to."

"Are you sure, Mr. Mills?" I ventured. "I'd love to have a crack at it."

Irving looked at me incredulously. "You would? Go on—I dare you!"

I am sure that in presenting this challenge, Irving thought that nothing could possibly come of it, that I would find it an insurmountable task.

I know that even at this late date there are very few song historians who are aware that there is a vocal edition of "Kitten on the Keys," an edition that enjoyed a huge sale when it came out, and that my name is listed on the cover as a co-writer with Zez Confrey. Actually, it did not turn out to be as backbreaking an assign-

38

ment as I had feared, although it is quite a mouthful to sing. For those who still do not believe this famous instrumental has lyrics, here they are:

> There's a catchy melody that's spreadin' all around the
>   country
> And they call it "Kitten on the Keys,"
> Ev'ryone's buying it, ev'ryone's trying its brand new
>   harmonies,
> You can close your eyes and just imagine there's a little
>   kitten running up and down the ivories,
> Anyone listenin' can't help a-whistlin' "Kitten on the
>   Keys."

> Raggedy melodies, beautiful harmonies
> Haunt you in each little strain
> Jazzy improvements of raggiest movements just rattle
>   around in your brain
> It isn't easy to sing it 'cause I know a fellow who tried
>   it one day—
> He found it a riddle, got stuck in the middle and stran-
>   gled to death so they say.

> It's best to take your time before you sing this rhyme,
> You better start to sing it this way:

> "Puff, puff, puff, puff" (*Breathe as if out of breath*)
> Crackerjack piano players practice up for hours just to
>   get its tricky technicalities,
> And when they master it, Oh! how they plaster it, all
>   over the keys.
> All you have to do is play it fifty-seven thousand times
> Before you get the knack of it with ease,
> Oh how they swing when you're playing the king of
>   ragtime symphonies.

When I showed up with the lyric a few days after accepting the challenge, it caused a minor sensation at Mills Music. Irving called in the entire staff, saying, "You won't believe this, but you've gotta hear it!"

The upshot was that Irving and Jack offered me a job, which I accepted. They needed what is termed in the music publishing business a band-and-orchestra man, a staff member whose function was to visit the dance bands in the New York area and induce them to feature the firm's songs. Every large publisher had one, but Mills, having been in business only a couple of years, was just getting around to it. These activities were to occupy my evening hours, and by day I was to write lyrics for more instrumentals the firm was getting out. I was to receive $40 per week as salary, plus royalties on the songs.

Most of the lyrics I wrote were for tunes written by a well known jazz group, the Memphis Five, headed by Phil Napoleon and Frank Signorelli, two musicians famous in jazz annals. The songs were all recorded by the group, and a couple of them, like "Great White Way Blues" and "Stop Your Kiddin'," were popular sellers in the record shops.

However, it was during my nocturnal assignments as band-and-orchestra man that some really interesting things occurred. I already knew a few of the name maestros like Whiteman and Lopez, but the job also enabled me to meet and become friends with many of the others—Ted Lewis, Ray Miller, Paul Specht, Ben Bernie, Emil Coleman, Jan Garber, Fred Waring, Leo Reisman, and other dance band luminaries of the early Twenties. All of them were to prove very helpful later in my songwriting career by recording many of my songs.

The most unusual encounter of all was meeting Duke Ellington, then a struggling young bandleader who had recently arrived from Washington, D.C. Duke had landed a job heading a combo at a downstairs basement joint just off Times Square, the Kentucky Club. He could give me very little help at that time, because he had yet to make his first record and he played to very small audiences in the little room. But I got into the habit of making it the last stop during my nightly rounds, because the Kentucky Club stayed open until dawn and became an early-morning rendezvous for show-business personalities after work. I always got a great kick out of Duke's jazz piano artistry and the vocals of his drummer, Sonny Greer.

One morning around 3 a.m., over a cup of coffee at a rear table with Duke, a sudden thought occurred to me. "Hey, Duke," I asked, "how is it you're not recording? You've got some great musicians in this little outfit, and you ought to be on records."

The immediate gleam in Duke's eyes told me I had hit home. "That's what I want to do more than anything in the world," he fairly shouted. "How do I get on records?"

"Well," I replied, "I was just thinking—my boss, Irving Mills, has just started a new record company. Just a small label, sort of a subsidiary of Mills Music. But I see no reason why he shouldn't record you. I think your band has a great new sound for records. Besides, Mills isn't getting any of the big name bands on his label. Why not?" I'll never forget Duke's hopeful look as I left him that morning. Sort of like a prayer.

The next day at the office I told Irving there was a great new band at the Kentucky Club he ought to listen to. Sign them for your label before someone beats you to it, I pleaded. "Let's drop down tonight," I continued. "It's right near the office."

Irving was an extremely busy young executive and couldn't make it that night. I reminded him on a few other occasions. After several weeks, he told me he had dropped into the club the night before. He liked the band but had not made up his mind yet. Crashing through with a black artist was a tough project in those days; almost all of the big record sellers were white bands.

After several visits Irving finally decided. He asked Duke to bring the band to the recording studios the following day to record a group of his own compositions.

The rest, of course, is history. Irving Mills became Duke's personal manager, signed him to a longterm contract as leader, composer, and arranger, and not only recorded him on the new Mills label but also farmed out the outfit, under various other names like the Washingtonians, the Harlem Footwarmers, and the Jungle Band, to various major record labels. Their instrumental jazz and blues recordings were an immediate click, and Irving was to eventually maneuver the band into New York's largest supper club, the Cotton Club, book them on lucrative tours all over the U.S. and Europe, and publish Duke's great standards like "Sophisticated Lady," "Mood Indigo" and the rest. The Ellington-Mills partnership was a long and fruitful association that spanned more than a decade. Irving would wind up spending most of his time managing Duke's career, leaving brother Jack to run Mills Music, and the Ellington song catalogue became one of the major sources of income for Mills Music. The association resulted in Duke becoming the most celebrated name in the jazz world, and both Irving and Duke became millionaires.

However, recollections are will-o-the-wisps. Today Irving has forgotten who first urged him to go down to the Kentucky Club and listen to the Ellington band. More than fifty years have elapsed, and I am certain that Irving, now in his late seventies, is being perfectly honest with me in saying that he does not remember the occasion. Irving and I are still good friends nevertheless, and I look him up whenever I visit the West Coast, where he now lives.

Be that as it may, the story is completely true, and Duke recalled the Kentucky Club episode on several occasions when I met him in later years. I had nothing to do with guiding his destinies, and even if I had not asked Irving Mills to record him, there isn't the slightest doubt that Ellington would still have become America's top jazz figure and composer. Nevertheless, it has always been a source of great satisfaction to me that I happened to be the springboard for the historic Ellington-Mills takeoff.

Of course, I should have followed through by remaining at Mills Music to write lyrics for some of Duke's great instrumentals, a collaboration which Duke himself suggested. It just wasn't meant to be, however, for the ink was hardly dry on the Ellington-Mills contract when fate intervened in the form of a tempting offer I received from another publisher.

Mark Stark and Ruby Cowan, two well known figures in the Alley, had recently quit lucrative executive jobs with Will Von Tilzer's firm to go into business on their own. They had already attracted two top songwriters, Edgar Leslie and Grant Clarke, plus a promising new composer named Harry Warren, whose first song with Stark and Cowan, "Rose of the Rio Grande," was already a smash. And now Mark and Ruby, intent on building a stable of prolific young songwriters, flattered me greatly by offering to add me to that distinguished company. I was offered a weekly drawing account against royalties which amounted to more than twice as much as Mills was paying me. I was, moreover, becoming weary of being typed as a writer of lyrics for instrumentals. I yearned to go back to writing both melodies and lyrics, so I jumped at the chance and regretfully bid goodbye to Mills Music and Duke Ellington.

My Stark and Cowan contract was for a long term of years, but I had the option of bowing out after the first six months in the event I was dissatisfied. Like most leading songwriters, I now had a term contract with a publisher, and it gave me the feeling that I had arrived. I was filled with enthusiasm, and determined to justify Stark and Cowan's confidence in me.

The very first song I turned in under my new deal became Stark and Cowan's second hit, a Spanish comedy novelty called "Wanita—Wanna Eat?". I wrote it in collaboration with another

42

44

Peter DeRose, of Deep Purple fame, was 20 when he collaborated with 17-year-old Sam

When Russ Columbo (second from right) had his big opening at the Waldorf's Starlight Roof in 1931, friend Sam gathered with bandleaders Buddy Rogers and Paul Whiteman to salute the new singing sensation

BEBE

NOVELTY FOX-TROT SONG

Introduced with Great Success by Eddie Cantor in the Ziegfeld Follies

Lyric By
SAM COSLOW
Author of "WANITA"
"GRIEVING FOR YOU" etc.
MUSIC BY
ABNER SILVER
Composer of "ANGEL CHILD"
"SAY IT WHILE DANCING" "CARRY ME BACK TO MY CAROLINA HOME" "WHEN WILL THE SUN SHINE FOR ME"

M. Witmark & Sons
New York

46

The Renaissance Man
of Tin Pan Alley
also played in some films.
Here he is with
June Clyde in an early
Warner Vitaphone short

A neighborly
get-together at Pickfair

Al Jolson   Ronald Colman   Douglas Fairbanks   Joseph M. Schenck   Samuel Goldwyn
    Mary Pickford   Gloria Swanson   Charles Chaplin   Eddie Cantor

47

New Victor Records
(ORTHOPHONIC RECORDING)

	Number	Size	List Price
My Angel (Theme Song of the Motion Picture Production "Street Angel") *Pipe Organ with Guitar and Vibraphone*	21630	10 in.	.75
Out of the Dawn (Theme Song of the Motion Picture Production "Warming Up") *with Male Trio, Marimba and Whistling* **Jesse Crawford**			

Some Day—Somewhere—Waltz (We'll Meet Again)
(Theme Song of the Motion Picture Production "The Red Dance") *with Vocal Refrain*

Neapolitan Nights—Waltz (Oh, Night of Splendor) (Theme
Song of the Motion Picture Production "Fazil") *with Vocal Refrain*

The Troubadours

} 21633   10 in.   .75

How should a waltz be played? We might answer, "Hear this record and find out," but instead, we'll tell you that "Some Day," has a dream of a "sax" solo, melody that will warm your heart, novel touches to keep you interested, and a vocal refrain that gets you. "Night of Splendor" comes second only because we couldn't put both numbers first!

What D'Ya Say?—Fox Trot (From George White's "Scandals")
with Vocal Refrain

Blue Shadows—Fox Trot (From Earl Carroll's "Vanities")
with Vocal Refrain Johnny Hamp's Kentucky Serenaders

} 21632   10 in.   .75

The Dance Fan, who is fond of lovely saxophone, trombone, and clarinet passages in good, snappy fox-trots, will find this record a "Seventh Heaven." Johnny Hamp has the combination for putting the right amount of whoopee into jazz . . . Hear this record and you'll agree.

I Can't Give You Anything But Love, Baby!
(From "Blackbirds of 1928")

I Must Have That Man (From "Blackbirds of 1928")

Grace Hayes

} 21571   10 in.   .75

Two of the reasons why "Blackbirds of 1928" is one of Broadway's biggest, brightest shows! Add the fact that Grace Hayes, in her first Victor record, sings them . . . with "it" in quantities . . . . and you just know this must be one record to hear and to have.   IT IS.

King for a Day
You're a Real Sweetheart   Sam Coslow

} 21631   10 in.   .75

You've heard "King for a Day"—and who hasn't? Well, now hear how really dramatic it *can* be, what with a melodious and expressive singing voice, together with a few lines of dramatic recitation with music. The other side of the record is in much the same style, and just as appealing. Better hear this record now!

RCA-Victor display sheet: the new records for October 5, 1928

New Victor Records—October 5, 1928   Victor Talking Mach. Co., Camden, N. J.—Form No. 704—RS/TV—Printed September, 1928, in U. S. A.

50

YOU WANT LOVIN'

(BUT I WANT LOVE)

by
SAM COSLOW
LARRY SPIER
AND
JACK OSTERMAN

UKULELE
ARRANGEMENT

As featured by
Rudy Vallee

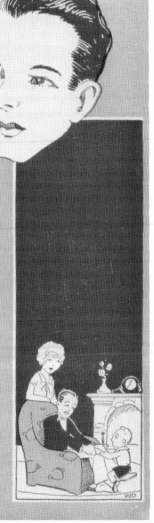

SPIER and COSLOW
745 SEVENTH AVENUE
NEW YORK

MADE
U.S.A.

51

SING YOU SINNERS

HONEY

WORDS AND MUSIC BY
W. FRANK HARLING
AND
SAM COSLOW

A Paramount Picture
STARRING
NANCY CARROLL
AND
STANLEY SMITH
FEATURING
LILLIAN ROTH
SKEETS GALLAGHER
AND
"LITTLE MITZI"

DANCES STAGED BY
DAVE BENNETT

In My Little Hope Chest
Sing You Sinners
I Don't Need Atmosphere
(to Fall In Love)
Let's Be Domestic
What Is this Power I Have?

MADE IN U. S. A.

FAMOUS MUSIC
CORPORATION
NEW YORK

52

Richard Whiting collaborated with Sam Coslow on the score of The Dance of Life, *the 1929 film musical that yielded* True Blue Lou

Benny Leonard was wearing the lightweight crown in August 1923 when Abner Silver "kayoed" him at his training camp. Sam Coslow stands ready to aid the wounded champ

At a 1915 ASCAP directors' meeting: Gustave A. ("They Call Me the Belle of New York") Kerker, Raymond ("Poor Butterfly") Hubbell, Victor Herbert (seated), Harry ("Irene") Tierney, Louis A. ("The Love Nest") Hirsch, Rudolph Friml, Robert Hood ("Chinese Lullaby") Bowers, Silvio ("Heart of My Heart") Hein, A. Baldwin ("Heaven Will Protect the Working Girl") Sloane, and 27-year-old Irving Berlin

The first ASCAP dinner at Luchow's on November 27, 1914. In numerical order: A. Seymour Brown, Albert Gumble, Channon Collinge (?), George Botsford, John Loeffler, Herman Paley, Benjamin Hapgood Burt, Jesse Winne, Gustave Schirmer, Robert Hood Bowers, Louis Hirsch, Julius Witmark, Henry Blossom, Ernest R. Ball, Stanley Murphy, James Weldon Johnson, George Maxwell, Victor Herbert, Nathan Burkan, Senator Frawley, Henry Marshall, Raymond Hubbell, Glen MacDonough, John Golden, Billy Jerome, Charles Klein, Silvio Hein, Isador Witmark, Tommy Gray (?), Hans Bartsch, George Hobart, Hugo Bryk, Ballard MacDonald, Bert Grant, Anatole Friedland, Jay Witmark, foreign publisher, unidentified guest, Walter L. Coghill, Jerome Kern, Meyer Cohen, Earl Carroll, F. B. Haviland, Jean Schwartz, Charles McCarron, Mose Gumble, Grant Clarke, Jean Havez, Louis Bernstein, Lee S. Roberts, vacant, Ted Snyder, Jimmy Monaco, Fred Belcher, Harry Collins, Henry Watterson, Daye Stamper, Gene Buck, E. Ray Goetz, Theodore More, Joe Goodwin, Edgar Smith, Gustave A. Kerker, Malvin M. Franklin, Max Stark, Joe Young, Edgar Leslie, George Meyers, Maurice Abrams, Sam Lewis, Harold Orlob, Charles K. Harris, Ray Walker, Louis Dreyfus young songwriter the firm had just placed under contract, Al Sherman. Al was to write many notable hits years later, including Eddie Cantor's famous depression song, "(Potatoes Are Cheaper, Tomatoes Are Cheaper) Now's the Time to Fall in Love." However, I always told Al that his greatest accomplishment was when he fathered two sons named Dick and Bob, who grew up to become Walt Disney's chief songwriters. They wrote the wonderful *Mary Poppins* score and many others for Disney.

I was acting on a strong hunch when I suggested to Al Sherman that we write "Wanita." The other Stark and Cowan writers were composing so-called commercial songs—mostly tearjerking ballads, because such songs were the biggest sellers of that era. At the same time, I knew that because of this many of the country's superstars were having trouble finding the sort of comedy material that had served them so well in the past. I knew that Al Jolson, Eddie Cantor, Eugene and Willie Howard and other Broadway stars were in great need of just such material.

My hunch was verified when all of the above stars, plus a great many others, featured "Wanita" as a show-stopping comedy song. It was done in four different Broadway musicals at the same time. Jolson's Columbia recording achieved great popularity, and the song itself sold more copies than any other comedy song of that year (1923) with the sole exception of the Billy Rose-Con Conrad hit, "Barney Google."

At the end of the six-month contractual period, I decided to exercise my right to walk out. I weighed it over calmly, and figured I could do far better free-lancing. Other publishers were hinting at large advances and number-one plugs, and I felt that Stark and Cowan now had too many writers on their staff for a new firm with limited output.

My decision proved correct, for my first song after leaving Stark and Cowan became a half-million-copy hit.

The song was "Bebe," and I dedicated it to the silent film star, Bebe Daniels. Lest you think this was a case of a fan with a crush on a beautiful movie queen, let me assure you it was nothing like that. It was just that girls' names were in vogue as song titles in those days, a fad that was touched off by the great success of the Davis-Robinson-Conrad hit, "Margie."

I wrote "Bebe" with Abner Silver, who made his headquarters at the publishing house of Witmark & Sons. Abner was not on the Witmark payroll, but he was "on the floor"—meaning that he would place songs with the firm and then spend his days at their professional offices demonstrating his numbers to various vaudeville acts who came up to hear new material. Abner was a hustling fool, and many of his songs became popular through his own promotional efforts.

Impressed with his great talents as a combination songwriter-songplugger, I visited him at Witmark's and suggested "Bebe" as a girl's name that had not yet been used in a song.

We wrote it as a rollicking foxtrot in a bright tempo, and Witmark accepted it without hesitation, knowing that Abner would land enough acts to create a demand for the song.

We needed a photo of Bebe Daniels for the cover, and I ran out to see her at Paramount's Eastern studio at Astoria, Long Island, where she was starring in a new movie. I told her I had just written a song for her, and an assistant director wheeled out the portable mood-music piano so I could play it for her. She seemed tremendously flattered and told me it was the catchiest melody she'd ever heard.

Abner was a revelation to me, and he gave me a real education in the fine art of songplugging. As soon as the first professional copies came off the press, he said to me, "You know Jolson well, don't you?"

I told him I did, but not all that well. However, Jolson had started off both of my previous hits, "Grieving for You" and "Wanita," and I thought I could get a sympathetic hearing. Abner's modus operandi was to get a big name to introduce a song first, which then made it easy to land many other acts. And Jolson, of course, was the greatest songmaker of his day, pursued by everyone in the music business.

We learned that Jolson was touring on the road with his show *Bambo* and was to play his home town, Washington, D.C., the following week. Abner and I took a train there on Monday morning, although I kept wondering all the way down whether Abner was leading me on a wild goose chase. Previously, I had always left it to the publisher's staff to submit songs to people like Jolson. It had never occurred to me that I could take the bull by the horns myself.

Arriving in the capital, we took a cab to the theater and told the stage doorman we had come to see Mr. Jolson. Al was rehearsing with the pit orchestra, but he came out promptly and greeted me with "Sammy boy! Have you got something good for me?"

We were in luck, for Al had been touring in *Bambo* for over a year and his songs were a bit tired by now. He wanted some fresh

58

new material, and on the road he was not besieged by songpluggers as he was in New York. With Abner at the piano, we demonstrated "Bebe." Al, obviously delighted, yelled, "Sammy, you've done it again!"

He asked us to hang around Washington for a few days with him, and Abner rehearsed him on the song afternoons, also scratching out a quick orchestration. Al broke the song in during one of the matinee performances later in the week, bouncing around the stage and snapping his fingers to the lively tempo. The impact on the audience was unmistakable. Before we left Washington that weekend, we knew we had a winner.

Through the years, I have heard Jolson's name bandied about by show people, for there have been many who did not like him and were critical of him. I have been told that he was self-centered and egotistical, unkind to fellow artists, all sorts of things. All I know is that I never could fault him from my own experience. Conceited—sure he was. But this was, by common consent, the greatest entertainer of the century, perhaps of all time. How could he not be aware of it? I have seen them all for the past fifty years, but never before or since have I ever seen anyone who had the electrifying impact on an audience that this man had. Unkind? Uncooperative? Most certainly I never saw that side of him, even if it existed. Although still a comparative newcomer, I always found him easy to see, receptive, ready and willing to give me a break, and wonderful company to be with. I often wondered whether the stories I heard about him were motivated by envy on the part of other performers.

About twelve years later in Hollywood, where Al had his own weekly radio network show for Shell Oil, he phoned to tell me he was devoting one of the programs to my songs, and asked me to appear on it with him. When he introduced me to the live audience, he took credit for discovering me and said he had introduced my first three hits, which of course was true. He then joined me in a medley of nine or ten of my best-known songs.

Back with me in New York again, Abner, indefatigable plugger that he was, was still unsatisfied, even with Jolson doing our song. "The next best bet on a song," he said, "is Eddie Cantor—and 'Bebe' was made to order for him. Let's go and see him."

Eddie was then co-starring with Fanny Brice in *The Ziegfeld Follies* on Broadway, and we caught him on his way into the theater. Abner sang the song for him in his dressing room, with no piano or any accompaniment whatsoever. The famous banjo eyes popped right out. One of Eddie's biggest hits had been "Margie," and he found he could do the same bouncy dance step, the one he was so famous for, to "Bebe." He learned the song, verse and chorus, in the next twenty minutes, and it went into the show about a week later. Eddie always announced the song with a gag line: "I will now sing the song of the seven B's." (The chorus started with "Bebe, Bebe, Bebe, be mine.")

Before many weeks had gone by, "Bebe" was among the top songs on the bestseller charts, and to say that it all happened through Abner's own tireless momentum would be no exaggeration.

I found that collecting the royalties, however, was a much less happy experience. When the first semiannual statement was due, Witmark was hit by financial difficulties and was on the verge of bankruptcy. Jay Witmark, one of the owners, asked me to run up to his office where he broke the news to a meeting of worried-looking songwriters. To save the firm from going under, he was asking all writers to whom royalties were due to accept a settlement of 25 cents on the dollar. My half share of the royalties came to about $18,000. I was asked to settle for $4,500. We were assured, in all good faith, that if the firm ever got back on its feet again, we would get the other three-fourths. But unless the songwriters all signed a waiver *now*, the firm would be in receivership. Abner and I checked around and learned that the other Witmark writers had agreed—Ernie Ball, Al Dubin, all of them except one black jazz composer who said, "I'll waive nothing except the American flag!" Abner and I reluctantly signed the waiver.

The P.S. to the above story is just as unhappy. Five years later, the house of Witmark was sold to Warner Brothers Pictures for something like three million dollars. I phoned Jay Witmark and reminded him of his promise. How about the $13,500 they still owed me, now that the Witmark brothers were back in the chips again? He mumbled something about business being business, and that he had my release in writing, and so forth, and he quickly hung up. I guess it takes all kinds. . . .

Contrasting with behavior like the above, there were those who proved to be loyal friends and boosters, very helpful at that stage of my songwriting career. Not only Jolson, but Eddie Cantor too, surprised me by falling into this category. Greatly impressed with the audience reaction he had received on "Wanita" and "Bebe," Eddie arranged for me to meet with him and his producer, Flo Ziegfeld, at the New Amsterdam Theater one day.

At the meeting, Eddie introduced me as an "up-and-coming songwriter" who could be relied upon to come up with the kind of song material he needed. He wanted Ziegfeld to work out an arrangement with me to create new Cantor material especially for the *Follies,* an arrangement under which Ziegfeld would buy the exclusive stage rights from me so that other comedians could not use the same songs as they had done with "Wanita."

We were seated in the back row of the theater, where Ziegfeld was holding auditions to pick a new dancing act. On the stage, a young chick in tights was feverishly doing an acrobatic routine, performing difficult handstands and splits, and literally standing on her head to get the job. I felt sorry for the girl, for Ziegfeld told her to keep dancing but paid absolutely no attention to her as he turned around to converse with Eddie and me about the song material. After Eddie told him what was on his mind, the first question he snapped at us was "What will it cost me? You know how much I'm already shelling out every week for writers, Eddie."

I soon gathered that Ziegfeld, despite the great lavishness of his productions, was not above driving a hard bargain on minor expenditures for the *Follies.* He looked the epitome of opulence—a fastidious dresser wearing an expensive tailored suit, a monogrammed silk shirt, and a ring with a stone that fairly blinded me. Two assistants were sitting next to him taking notes, flanked by a bookkeeper who kept handing him checks to sign throughout our conversation. On the stage was an extravagant set with spiral staircases and hangings that glittered with sequins. Yet here was the Great Ziegfeld trying to buy exclusive song material at bargain-basement prices and demanding to know how much of a cut he would receive on my publication royalties!

Actually, I was not in a bargaining mood and would have taken anything. I just wanted to write for Eddie to reciprocate his magnanimous gesture. And so I surprised Ziegfeld by telling him to name his own terms. When he heard that, his eyes immediately twinkled, and a broad smile lit up his face for the first time since I had arrived. He gave one of the assistants some notes on the arrangements to be made with me, the details of which I have long since forgotten except that they were nothing to write home about. Eddie gave me a grateful wink as Ziegfeld turned his attention back to the acrobatic dancer, telling her to leave her name and address although he hadn't watched a single part of her routine.

61

At the time, Eddie needed songs for only two spots in the show. But to give him as wide a choice as possible, I tailored about five or six to fit his exuberant stage personality. The two he selected were "I Want 'Em Wild, Weak, Warm and Willing (Or Else I Don't Want 'Em at All)," which was a bit risque for its time but gave Eddie a chance to bounce all over the stage with his familiar fast dance-step routine; also a successor to "Wanita," another Spanish satirical fandango called "Dumb Dora (You're the Only Baloney for Me)." The latter I wrote with Abner Silver, who had the idea for the song. Both proved highly successful as special stage material for Eddie, although they were hardly the type that sold copies. What was far more important to me was that I had broken the ice with an important Broadway show credit, something that would be useful to me on many future occasions. Plus the lifelong friendship of another top-ranking entertainment personality.

Writing special material for Cantor led to a number of inquiries from other performers who were also in urgent need of material. One that I vividly recall was Evelyn Nesbit, who was desperately trying to make a comeback in cabaret. Almost two decades earlier, Evelyn had been the central figure in the sensational Harry K. Thaw-Stanford White shooting affair. Thaw, who was Evelyn's husband, had shot and killed her lover, White, the most celebrated architect of his time, in a jealous rage. It was a well remembered Broadway scandal, and I had vaguely heard about the case from oldtimers. Those who have read Doctorow's bestselling novel, *Ragtime*, know some of the details, for Evelyn was one of the book's principal characters.

In the intervening years Evelyn, who had been a featured musical comedy showgirl before her marriage, had tried on several occasions to launch a vaudeville act. People came to see her out of curiosity, but she was only mildly received. Now she was trying a new approach, the night-club circuit. She had broken in an act in a couple of small out-of-town clubs, using popular song material which apparently was ill-suited to her. She was booked for a summer engagement in a leading Atlantic City nitery, due to open in a few weeks—but she had no act.

I received a call one day from an agent who was also the promoter and backer of Evelyn's act. Would I be interested in writing her a new act consisting of a half dozen or so song characterizations, running the gamut from comedy to highly dramatic story songs? I would receive ten percent of her salary, with $500 paid

62

in advance before I began writing. I gave the agent a definite "maybe." I would first have to hear her sing to find out whether I could handle this type of job.

An appointment was made for me to meet Evelyn at one of the publisher's offices the following day. When she arrived, I was not prepared for the slight shock I received. I had seen pictures of her —a ravishing brunette with a sexy, streamlined figure. The girl who came to meet me was in her middle forties, still with a hint of attractiveness, but rather wornout and tired looking. Her brownish-hued hair could have used the services of a good beauty operator, and the wrinkled suit she wore, like Evelyn, had seen better days. But she was still eager and ambitious, and she wanted to show me that she could handle a number, that she was worth writing material for.

She handed me a song copy, a torch ballad she had been doing, and I accompanied her as she sang it in a husky, low barroom contralto. Surprisingly, she did have a little talent. I had heard far worse in night clubs. She would need a lot of work—staging, coaching, and rehearsing—but she just might get by, I thought as I listened to her.

However, not being a longshot player, I finally decided to pass up the deal, telling Evelyn regretfully that I couldn't possibly write five or six special songs and work with her in the short time before she was to open in Atlantic City. The pathetic anxiety written all over her face made it impossible for me to be any more candid than that. But I helped her as much as I could, nonetheless. I suggested a number of songs I knew about that I thought would suit her, plus a couple of my own that were about to be published, and I phoned people I knew at the various publishing firms to take care of her. Her eyes were filled with gratitude and defeat at the same time. I left her, promising to look in at her rehearsals from time to time.

I don't know how her act was received in Atlantic City, for I never ran down there to see it. I felt it could be embarrassing if Evelyn flopped, and I preferred not to be there. I heard later that she played out a month's engagement, and then went on to do the same songs in another seaside resort. I never heard any more about her after that, so that may have been her final stab at a professional career.

Around this time the song publisher coming up fastest was the newly formed house of Irving Berlin, Inc., recently started when Berlin sold his interest in Waterson, Berlin, and Snyder to join

Chapter Five

RADIO—THE OVERNIGHT REVOLUTION IN SONGPLUGGING

At this stage of my career, a development occurred in the music business which radically altered the day-to-day operations of all Tin Pan Alley firms and left them confused and disorganized, and forced them to hastily restructure their songplugging activities—which were the lifeblood of the industry. This sudden development was the emergence of radio as the most powerful medium in popularizing new songs.

To get the full grasp of what this meant, I should give the reader a capsule summary of changing fashions over a century of hitmaking.

A music publisher can operate profitably and stay in business only by creating a demand for his products. The process of promoting his new songs is, as you have probably gathered, known as songplugging. In other words, the trick was to get his songs heard, over and over again, by the greatest number of people in the shortest space of time.

A hundred years ago, the best way of accomplishing this was through minstrel shows, for that was the form of musical entertainment that commanded the largest audiences. Some songplugging was also done in the concert field, mostly on so-called "art songs" featured by concert artists like Jenny Lind. But the most popular songs, from the 1820's until late in the century, were promoted via the minstrel shows. "Dixie" was popularized in that manner, as was practically every hit written by the great Stephen Foster.

Foster was, in fact, the first well known writer to engage in songplugging, a historical fact that only collectors of Fosteriana seem to be aware of. Foster made it his business to cultivate the leading minstrel performers of his time, and made sure that they introduced his new compositions. Occasionally, when short of money, he even went so far as to allow a minstrel star to add his name on the song copies. The original edition of what eventually became one of Foster's greatest standards, "Old Folks at Home," bears the name of E. P. Christy, the foremost minstrel performer of the middle nineteenth century, although Christy's name was deleted from later editions of the song. This deplorable practice, incidentally—cutting in a star for a share of the royalties as an inducement to perform the song—has persisted through the years.

Around the turn of the century, Lew Dockstader was the nation's top minstrel star, and he was a target for every enterprising publisher with a new song to plug. The familiar blackface portrayals in burnt cork by Al Jolson and Eddie Cantor in the first quarter of the present century were carryovers from the minstrel era, for throughout the nineteenth century the popular songs of the day were invariably sung by minstrel-show performers in burnt cork.

In the 1890's, minstrel shows were relegated to second place by the music halls, which soon became the favored outlet for songplugging. To land their "plugs," leading music publishers began to haunt these establishments, which were really glorified saloons seating upwards of a thousand people. The most celebrated music hall impresario and singing star of that period was Tony Pastor. His introduction of a new song at Pastor's Music Hall was the equivalent of a Jolson introduction in the Twenties or a Bing Crosby song debut in the Thirties. If Tony sang it, the song was made. The publishers also high-pressured the performers who appeared at Koster and Bial's Music Hall, as well as those run by Weber and Fields and others.

At that time, the hired songplugger had not yet appeared on the scene. It was the publisher or the songwriter himself who generally made the rounds to fast-talk his wares. Of these, the one generally credited by oldtimers as the first man to make a fine art out of songplugging was my old friend and mentor, Charles K. Harris, who is reputed to have invented the technique just after he wrote and published "After the Ball" in 1892. Harris told me

67

on many occasions of his experiences and successes in landing many of the country's topflight music hall and concert performers, making the rounds with song copies in his coat pocket. It paid off to the tune of a fortune, for over ten million copies of "After the Ball" were eventually sold worldwide, a record which still stands.

By the early years of this century, the music hall showed signs of dying out, and publishers, for the first time, began hiring songpluggers to frequent all establishments where songs could be heard. The first choices, naturally, were those places where the largest crowds gathered, for the publisher whose songs were heard by the most people achieved the quickest results. I was a baseball nut when I was a kid in public school, and I can recall many occasions when I played hookey to watch the Brooklyn Dodgers play in Ebbets Field or the New York Giants at the Polo Grounds. There I often heard the familiar hunchbacked songplugger, Jimmy Flynn, bellow the newest Feist song through a megaphone between innings. Sammy Levy, another legendary character in the Alley, performed the same task for Waterson, Berlin, and Snyder, although Sammy's voice, not being big enough for the ball parks, was generally heard in the resort cafes of Coney Island and at balls, benefits and even bar mitzvahs—wherever Sammy could get in.

At the same time, the musical comedy was coming into its own and was attracting large audiences. The shows composed by George M. Cohan and Victor Herbert were always filled with song hits in those years, and most publishers fretted and fumed because their numbers were shut out of these one-composer scores. The problem was finally solved when the musical comedy revue became a Broadway institution and the songpluggers found out that they could interpolate their new plug songs into these revues—because the revue stars preferred popular songs to the more conventional musical comedy scores. One of the earliest examples is the very first *Ziegfeld Follies*, which opened in 1907. Featured in that cast were some of the favorite songstresses of the day like Emma Carus, Grace LaRue, and Nora Bayes, who interpolated *Follies* numbers written by such early Tin Pan Alley giants as Gus Edwards and Will Cobb, Jerome and Schwartz, and Ray Goetz. J. J. Shubert's first annual edition of what became a revue perennial, *The Passing Show of 1912*, which starred Willie and Eugene Howard, contained an Irving Berlin song interpolation, "Ragtime Jockey Man."

Mentioning this early Berlin ragtime tune, incidentally, provides me with an opportunity to refute one of today's most widely held myths, namely that Scott Joplin was the man who exerted the greatest influence on ragtime. Scott did not, and Berlin did—as everyone will tell you who was around Tin Pan Alley during the first two decades of this century—the great ragtime years. I am not disparaging Joplin in making this statement, for his ragtime melodies, most of which came to light only in recent years, were compositions with all of the flavor of early ragtime. But the fact remains that he was virtually unknown in his own time, even though one of his compositions, "Maple Leaf Rag," was familiar to many pop pianists of his and later generations. I have yet to run into a music business oldtimer who ever knew his name during the ragtime era. I must therefore assert that his reputed influence on ragtime is grossly exaggerated. Berlin, beyond the question of a doubt, had the greatest influence of all, although I have heard Irving say that he didn't really know what ragtime was nor could he define it. Berlin's first ragtime song was "That Beautiful Rag," which he introduced himself in the Shubert revue *Up and Down Broadway* in 1910 when he was a featured member of the cast, appearing in a collegiate sweater and bearing a tennis racket. The following year he wrote the song which really *made* ragtime, his immortal "Alexander's Ragtime Band," introduced on Broadway by Al Jolson when Al was one of Lew Dockstader's Minstrels. This was soon followed by other Berlin ragtime smashes like "International Rag," "That Mysterious Rag," and "Everybody's Doing It"—all blockbusters of the day. Big ragtime hits were written by other composers too, like "Ragtime Cowboy Joe," "Raggin' the Scale," and others; but none were written by Scott Joplin. To repeat, it was chiefly Berlin's influence that was responsible for the great ragtime craze of the pre-World War I years, and no one should rob him of that credit, least of all an obscure composer whose work was not really brought to popularity until it was adapted by Marvin Hamlisch in the recent movie, *The Sting*.

The next plugging phenomenom held sway for a few years just prior to World War I. It was the illustrated song slide, which coincided with the early growth of the movie theater. Publishers would hire models and bit players to pose for slides of scenes illustrating the lyrics of their principal plug songs, especially those with a story that could be graphically illustrated. They would then send teams of pluggers (singer and pianist) to cover the larger movie houses, where the slides were usually sand-wiched in between the short one- and two-reel films of that time. Sets of these old slides are greatly prized today by antique dealers and collectors. During the day, the same plugging teams would appear behind the sheet music counters at leading Woolworth and Kresge stores, most of which then had gigantic sheet-music departments with pianos and small stages to accommodate the pluggers. In this case the pluggers doubled as salesmen, demon-, strating and selling thousands of copies of their firm's publica-tions and getting huge reorders from the stores. I used to haunt these counters when I was a kid, adoring the free entertainment. I recall seeing pluggers like Walter Donovan (who later wrote a big hit, "Abba Dabba Honeymoon") and Bob Miller, whom I got to know later when he headed the Song-Pluggers Union.

While all this was happening, vaudeville was slowly emerging as the greatest song exploitation development that had yet ap-peared, and it reigned supreme for many years. By the second decade of the century, vaudeville theaters were mushrooming. The large vaudeville chains of B. F. Keith, Marcus Loew, Gus Sun, B. F. Proctor, and Martin Beck's Orpheum Circuit soon blanketed the large cities of the nation. The publishers were now mostly entrenched in the original Tin Pan Alley on 28th Street, within hailing distance of some of New York's largest vaudeville houses. For the first time, a publisher could land an act knowing that the same act would feature his song over whatever circuit he was booked on, for an entire season. This enabled a song to satu-rate the whole country, city by city, eventually creating a nation-wide demand, something that had been most difficult previously. Vaudeville bills were changed weekly, and on the Monday open-ings, each plugger on a large publisher's staff was assigned to cover a different theater, interviewing that week's crop of singing acts backstage and pleading with them to drop up to the firm's office to hear the new songs. The highest paid pluggers were those with a large following of headline acts they were friendly with. With unlimited expense accounts provided by their bosses, these star pluggers would romance the most influential singers by tak-ing them to dinner and cabarets after work and getting them boxes at the World Series and choice seats at championship box-ing matches. "Anything for a plug" was their motto. Landing a song with an important Keith Circuit act—vaudeville's Big Time —meant that a demand for the new song might be created in forty or fifty key cities within the next twelve months, and so it was worth any price to get the song in. This led to one of the major abuses that plagued the music business in those years—the first payolas. Some acts were making a petty side racket of collecting $25 or $50 apiece every week from various second-tier publishers for featuring their songs. This eventually led to the formation of the MPPA (Music Publishers' Protective Association) which policed this racket and curbed it to a large extent, although it still reappears from time to time.

Vaudeville was still in its heyday when I entered the business, and it remained the principal medium used by publishers to popularize their songs until the early 1920's, when radio came along to disrupt everything. Suddenly, a song could be heard in a single rendition on a radio station by more people than were present in all the vaudeville houses combined! This staggering fact crept up on Tin Pan Alley before the Alley realized what was happening. Songplugging was revolutionized, practically overnight.

Publishers no longer found it necessary to cover all the vaudeville theaters. Instead, they sent their branch-office pluggers to make the rounds of the radio stations in New York, Chicago, Los Angeles and other cities. This did not require as much manpower; there were not many stations in those early days. So a large number of pluggers lost their jobs.

The first station to open was Westinghouse's KDKA in Pittsburgh. This was quickly followed by WEAF in New York, an affiliate of American Telephone, and WJZ in Newark, which soon moved to New York as the key station of the newly formed Radio Corporation of America (RCA).

Unsure of how the new medium would evolve, the publishers floundered as they tried to assess what types of songs would be right for the new medium and what promotional techniques to adopt. A temporary depression hit the business as vaudeville-oriented firms found their sales snowed under by the handful of more enterprising and daring houses that quickly decided to concentrate on radio plugs. Panic reigned among songpluggers as the impact of radio began to sink in and more pluggers were fired.

A new breed of professional manager emerged in the Alley. Typical was supersalesman Harry Link, the most successful promotion executive of the radio era, who guided the operations of Berlin's former company, still called Waterson, Berlin, and Snyder. The firm soon leaped to the forefront of the publishing industry as they concentrated on landing radio's most popular singers and dance bands and placed under exclusive contract

71

early radio superstars who broadcast their own compositions. The first of these to attract national attention was Little Jack Little, who accompanied himself on the piano as he crooned his numbers in a soft, intimate manner that was ideally suited to microphone amplification, announcing each number in an easy, chattery style that won him a tremendous following. Little Jack, a newcomer in the songwriting profession, quickly stole a march on other writers, coming up with hit after hit like his meteoric "Jealous," written in 1923.

I was attracted by the possibilities of radio when it was still in its infancy, and lost no time in contacting people I knew who had joined the music staff of WJZ. They phoned me one day to prepare a program of my compositions, asking me to show up at their broadcasting studio in Newark the following evening. It was in a small building on the outskirts of town, on the second floor above a streetcar barn, a crudely-contrived studio about as close to today's palatial NBC studios in Radio City, New York, as an antique model T Ford would be to a Lincoln Mark IV. There was a single sound engineer, in the same room I was broadcasting from, and only one other employee in the place, an announcer. Having no stagehands, the engineer and announcer wheeled out a small upright piano by themselves, and I was hastily introduced to the radio audience without the benefit of prepared notes or a script to read from. Completely ignorant of the mysteries of electrical sound transmission, I sat down at the piano and bellowed out my first song at the top of my voice, mindful that people were listening to me hundreds of miles away. The engineer waved his hands frantically after the first few bars of music, signalling that I should sing and play softly. Sponsors and commercials had not yet arrived on the scene, so I sang for a solid half hour without interruption. I was mentally visualizing a few friends in Brooklyn that I knew were listening in with their earphones and their crude, tiny crystal radio sets which were the only available receiving equipment at that early stage.

My second broadcast came about when Vincent Lopez, my former fellow-worker at the Charles K. Harris establishment, asked me to introduce a new song on his first orchestral broadcast. Vince was now New York's second most popular bandleader, ranking next to Whiteman, but in this instance he supplied his band at the minimum union scale, doing it strictly as a publicity stunt and bussing his boys out to WJZ because the idea of dance band "remotes"—broadcasts direct from the hotels and night

72

clubs where bands appeared—had not yet been thought of. As far as I know, this broadcast was the first time Lopez opened a program with his familiar "Hello everybody—Lopez speaking," which became his trademark, famous among radio listeners from coast to coast. A short time later, Lopez was to make radio history by becoming the country's first remote-control band, broadcasting nightly from the Pennsylvania Hotel.

A group of new singing stars was on the scene by now, the first to capitalize on the mushrooming new industry. They became household names overnight, and consequently were wooed and pursued by the plugging fraternity. Along with Little Jack Little, there was Whispering Jack Smith, whose voice was so soft it was barely audible until you heard it over a mike. He quickly catapulted "Cecilia" and "Gimme a Little Kiss, Will Ya, Huh?" to great popularity. And there were the two Happiness Boys, Billy Jones and Ernie Hare, whose nightly programs over WEAF on the new, burgeoning NBC network got many a new song hit off the ground. All three of these acts were quickly signed up by the leading record labels intent on cashing in on their large following.

Around this time radio stations were beginning to meet expenses by attracting the first sponsors—mainly local merchants, because the big national sponsors were not yet ready to plunge in. I was hired to write what was, to the best of my knowledge, the first commercial jingle ever done on the air. My father, still a textile salesman, did business with a clothing chain called Howard Stores, which had bought time on one of the smaller New York stations. Dad "sold" me to the Howard people, and suggested that I write a jingle to open and close their shows. I hesitate to name the title, for it was a naive little ditty based on a feeble pun. But for the sake of the historical record I will tell you that I called it: "How Would a Howard Suit Suit You?" So help me!

Around early 1924, I thought another innovation might be a song about radio itself. Using another play on words, I concocted a thing called "Radio Lady o' Mine" which I brought to Harry Link, for by that time I had become greatly attracted to Harry's radio-slanted activities at the Waterson firm. I still chuckle whenever I think of this song, for a reason that any songwriter will appreciate. Here's the story:

The song was published, and that seemed to be the end of it. "Jealous" and a couple of other radio hits had caught on for the Waterson firm, and my song got lost in the shuffle. It was never plugged at all. Six months later, remembering that Waterson's mechanical man had managed to land a recording for "Radio Lady," I asked Waterson's bookkeeper for a royalty statement. He handed me an envelope, which I didn't open until I had walked over to Lindy's restaurant across the street, where I was to join a friend for breakfast. My friend hadn't arrived yet, and I casually opened the envelope, expecting to find a pretty small check. I looked at it and almost choked on my orange juice. The check was for over eleven thousand dollars! Up to that time, I had seen only one or two royalty checks that size.

I figured it had to be a mistake, and for a moment I was torn between just depositing the check or going back to show the bookkeeper his "boo-boo." I looked hard at the statement—all it read was "mechanical royalties," without listing any recording companies. I went back to Waterson's after breakfast, and in the hall I ran into Walter Douglas, Waterson's general manager.

"Can this be right?" I asked him, showing him the check. His signature was on it.

"Sure it is," he replied. "Why do you ask—don't you think it's enough?"

"Enough? I thought you overpaid me by mistake. How come it's this much, Walter?"

Walter smiled. "Do you mean to say you didn't know? Your record was on back of 'The Prisoner's Song!' They've sold over two million so far, and there'll be more to come."

Believe it or not, I did not know about the backing. "The Prisoner's Song" was by far the biggest song hit of 1924, and my song had been released on the other side of one of its largest-selling recorded versions.

It was a rare stroke of luck, the kind that any writer with a large output is apt to run into occasionally. All single records, of course, consist of two songs back-to-back, and when a top-selling hit is released, some lucky writer or writers have a song on the B side which receives the same royalties as the hit.

It was my good fortune to fall into these unexpected bonanzas with a few later songs as well. The multimillion seller by Paul Whiteman's band of "Ramona" was backed up by a song of mine called "Lonely Melody" which, however, might have made it on its own because of the well known Bix Beiderbecke cornet solo featured on Whiteman's platter. Rudy Vallee's famous "Lonely Troubadour" was released by RCA-Victor in 1929 on the back of a halfhearted minor hit of mine called "You Want Lovin' But I

74

Want Love." And Bing Crosby recorded his smash "Atchison, Topeka and Santa Fe" on the back of my less successful "I'd Rather Be Me." The record also sold well over a million.

It was a bit later in that year, 1924, that the first transcontinental radio hookup took place, a milestone in the history of mass communication. An estimated 60 million listeners comprised the first audience. Table models and elaborate console sets were beginning to replace the crude crystal sets by this time.

At that time, I had a radio program of my own, singing and playing my compositions on WMCA, New York, every Wednesday at 6 p.m. for many weeks. Following this series, I became a regular on one of the most popular early network shows, Major Bowes's Capitol Theater Family, on which I was heard every Sunday night from Broadway's Capitol Theater. The leader of the theater's large orchestra, who provided me with many superb accompaniments, later became one of the country's most eminent symphony conductors. He was Eugene Ormandy, who led the Philadelphia Orchestra for many years. As for Major Edward Bowes, he was to continue in network radio for a lengthy period, later inaugurating his celebrated Amateur Hour. It was, in fact, on the Bowes Amateur Hour that a youthful contestant named Frank Sinatra first attracted public attention in the 1930's.

I spent most of the following year around the Waterson offices, cultivating Harry Link and working with some of their contract writers. I collaborated with Little Jack Little on several numbers including "What Are We Waiting For?" and "She's Still My Baby," which he featured on his broadcasts with the usual gratifying results. I also wrote a comedy novelty song with Harry himself and bandleader Freddie Rich titled "I'm Just Wild About Animal Crackers," which was featured by numerous name comedians. The bestselling song I gave the firm was "Hello, Swanee, Hello," which I got Jolson to interpolate in his show *Big Boy* and which was also a leading RCA-Victor record by George Olsen's Orchestra.

Chapter Six

REVUES, VAUDEVILLE, AND OTHER FORGOTTEN ARTS

Radio did not entirely kill vaudeville, although it did drive the first big nail into its coffin. It was not until the following decade that "talkies"—sound films—delivered the final punch from which vaudeville, the staggering invalid, never recovered.

At the professional offices of various publishers, where singing acts customarily rehearsed their new songs, I met many of the vaudeville headliners of the 1920's. One act I became friendly with was the Duncan Sisters, Rosetta and Vivian, who ranked as the highest-paid sister act to hit the circuit since the Dolly Sisters deserted vaudeville for musical comedy some years before. For the past year, my "Wanita" had been the mainstay of the Duncans' act, and as a result, they invited me to contribute several songs to their first starring vehicle on the musical comedy stage, *Topsy and Eva*. They had written most of the score themselves but needed a few comedy songs. They hoped I could come up with the "Wanita" type of buffoon humor that Rosetta in particular was so great at. Rosetta was a natural clown, one of the funniest comediennes of her time, and perfectly cast in the role of Topsy as a foil to the angelic-looking Little Eva, played by Vivian. I had the only interpolations in the show, including the words and music to a ridiculous ditty called "When It's Onion Time in Bermuda (I'll Breathe My Love to You)," which proved to be a rousing show-stopper for the girls in this musical version of *Uncle Tom's Cabin*.

On hearing the numbers I had written for the Duncans, one of my close friends, composer J. Fred Coots, thought the time had arrived for me to do a complete score for a Broadway show instead of merely interpolating songs. Fred had a hit then running on Broadway, Eddie Dowling's memorable *Sally, Irene and Mary,* and had been signed by the Shuberts to do the score for their forthcoming revue, *Artists and Models.* He told J. J. Shubert about some of the revue material I had written for Eddie Cantor and others, and J.J. asked Fred to bring me out to the Shubert country estate on the waterfront in Darien, Connecticut, for the weekend. J.J. had reserved that weekend to map out the entire revue, and to reach some decisions about casting, sketch material, and production numbers.

Fred drove me to Darien, and we spent most of the first day swimming in the Sound, having drinks on the expansive lawn, and dining in the large formal dining room on exotic culinary creations dreamed up by J.J.'s imported French cook. J.J. was a gifted raconteur, and he entertained the assembled production staff, both at lunch and dinner, with some side-splitting personal recollections—including more than a few racy ones. But very little was said about *Artists and Models.*

On Sunday, Shubert's most important composer, Sigmund Romberg, came out with Clifford Grey, a well known English writer who had done the lyrics for a couple of Jerome Kern musicals—and I began to wonder whether I had come out just for the ride. However, after dinner J.J. summoned the four writers to the library—Romberg, Grey, Coots, and me—and over snifters of nineteenth-century Napoleon brandy, he told us that he wanted all four of us to write the *Artists and Models* score. He thought it would take two writing teams to supply the thirty numbers he needed. I was to supply lyrics for Romberg's melodies, and Grey was to do the same for Coots, even though Fred had planned on collaborating with me.

Working with Romberg was an interesting, if hectic, experience. It was hectic because the man actually wrote scores for six Shubert musicals that season. He was composing at least three at the time he worked with me. In short, Romberg was a human music factory, for I estimated he must have written well over a hundred different songs that year, plus reams of incidental, ballet, and dance music for his productions. In case you doubt these incredible statistics, which I believe have never been equalled in the history of musical comedy, I have dug up the names of the Romberg musicals that opened on Broadway in that year of 1924:

1) *Annie Dear* starring Billie Burke (103 performances); 2) *Artists and Models* (261 performances); 3) *Innocent Eyes* starring Mistinguette (126 performances); 4) *Marjorie* (144 performances); 5) *The Passing Show* (106 performances); and, most surprising of all, 6), the name of which I will withhold until I relate the following short anecdote:

Romberg and I were working at his Central Park West apartment one afternoon when he suddenly glanced at his watch and said, "I almost forgot. Take a walk with me, just down the street. They're holding vocal auditions for one of my other shows. I have to be there. Then we'll come back here and finish." We walked briskly to the Shubert's Century Theater, several blocks away.

The other show, it turned out, was Romberg's immortal *Student Prince*, which was soon to go into rehearsal. Howard Marsh was picked for the title role at that particular audition, and I listened, a bit impatiently, as Rommy played the principal songs in the show for Marsh, never dreaming that "Deep in My Heart," "Golden Days," and "Serenade" would still be popular standards fifty years later.

His chore completed, Rommy and I walked back to the apartment to finish the revue number we were working on that day. I can't say that any one show was more important than another to him. Romberg considered the success of any show a completely unpredictable quantity. He was completely wrapped up in whatever he happened to be working on at the moment, and I am sure he devoted the same time and close attention to a revue number as to his operetta songs. I was in Romberg's party a few months later when *Student Prince* had its Broadway opening, and even though Rommy, all smiles, bowed profusely at the cries of "Composer! Composer!" that greeted the final curtain, I always had the feeling he himself was the most surprised person in the theater.

Artists and Models was noted for the unusual and innovative stage effects the Shuberts had imported at great expense from various French revues. But what stands out in my mind during the show's preparation was the appearance of the Shubert brothers, Lee and J.J., at the rehearsals in the Shubert Theater. J.J. was personally in charge at every rehearsal, but brother Lee, whose office was upstairs in the theater building, dropped in several times each day. Lee was a somber individual with a perpetual frown, invariably dressed in a black suit and an extra-high stiff collar that made him look uncomfortable. He looked more like an undertaker than a Broadway producer, I often thought. Although

78

equal partners in all of their productions, the brothers had had a violent argument some years before and hadn't spoken to each other since. But there were times when communication was essential, and on more than one occasion when I was seated next to J.J. while a number was being rehearsed on the stage, Lee would yell over to me from several rows away: "Tell my brother that was a lousy dance routine and should be cut out of the show"—or something similar. And brother Jake would invariably shout to me, although Lee was only a few yards away, "Tell Lee to stop worrying. He knows damn well I'll fix the number." And that's the way it was, right up to the opening night.

The show contained one song which was the subject of a rave in almost every newspaper review the day after the opening. The song was "Pull Your Strings," and I will take no credit at all for the accolades, because the reason the critics were so enthused had nothing to do with the words or the music, actually. In the staging of the number, a bunch of chorus girls ran out into the audience singing the song as they handed out strings to elderly males in the audience. The strings were attached to draped statues on the stage, and as members of the audience pulled their strings, the "statues" were revealed, each being an artist's model in the flesh, posing in something less than a G-string. It would probably be greeted with a yawn today, but it was quite daring for its time. A lilting love ballad called "Tomorrow's Another Day," the combined work of all four composers and lyricists, was scarcely mentioned by the critics, having been sung to great applause by a boy and girl who were fully clad.

Artists and Models was a continual sellout, both at the Shubert Theater and on the long road tour that followed, for over three years. A decade later Paramount made a film version starring Jack Benny, although very little was left in except the basic concept.

During the rehearsals, I had begun seeing a good deal of one of the girls in the show, Dorothy Addison, an attractive blonde dancer. I had just bought my first car, and when I learned that Dorothy lived with her family in Brooklyn, I got into the habit of dropping her off on my way home. She lived only ten minutes from me, and I soon found myself seeing her on Sundays also. Before I realized what was happening, we were engaged.

When the show was about to leave on its national tour, I realized there was one sure way to make her quit her dancing job, and so we were married. At twenty-one, I guess I was the youngest writer with a show on Broadway, and Dorothy was a couple of years younger. Just why in the world we wanted to be married at that young age, I never really knew, and I doubt if Dorothy did. Whatever it was—puppy love, chemistry, shmemistry, or whatever—certainly neither of us was ready for the responsibilities of marriage. Nevertheless, we bravely tried—for the next six years— to make it work. The fact that it didn't was my fault as much as Dorothy's. But more about that in the next chapter.

Vaudeville in the mid-Twenties, although more or less neglected by music publishers in favor of the larger appeal of radio, was nevertheless still in its heyday with the public in most large cities. As I mentioned earlier, I was a dedicated vaudeville fan since my childhood, and I was still cultivating headline acts that featured popular songs, even though Tin Pan Alley was no longer wooing them. In fact, as a result of this abandonment I found it much easier to induce many name acts to feature new songs for me.

Among these were the three most celebrated songstresses of vaudeville, Sophie Tucker, Belle Baker, and Nora Bayes. Sophie, already a veteran by that time, lived up to her billing, "The Last of the Red-Hot Mamas," making it easy to get her cooperation whenever I had a song that was slightly risque. You couldn't go too far with a lyric in those days, because every act was policed by vaudeville tycoon E. F. Albee himself, who had inherited the Keith Circuit, which comprised the largest vaudeville theaters east of Chicago. Albee was a straightlaced, churchgoing individual who insisted on all shows being suitable as family entertainment. Anything that smacked of double entendre was promptly reported to him and just as promptly deleted.

Belle Baker could tear your heart out with a ballad like no one before or since, but she was just as effective with a rhythm number. A few years later she was to score an outstanding success with my early swing hit, "Sing, You Sinners," while the dying art of vaudeville was heading down the homestretch.

Nora Bayes, whose real name was Dora Goldberg, headlined for many years with her husband, the dapper Jack Norworth, who never appeared without top hat and tails. But Nora insisted that the act be billed "Nora Bayes, assisted by Jack Norworth." One of my earliest thrills was hearing Nora sing my first hit, "Grieving for You," at the Palace Theater. Nora and Jack were also notable songwriters on their own, having turned out evergreens like "Shine On, Harvest Moon," among others. Later, when she and

80

Jack separated, she used two different songwriters (both good friends of mine) as her stage accompanists. The first was Seymour Simons, who composed her famous "Just Like a Gypsy," followed by Lou Alter, who wrote the brilliant, symphonic "Manhattan Serenade."

Other great vaudeville acts that still evoke vivid recollections for me were two teenage kids, Fred and Adele Astaire, a brother-and-sister dancing act that used to delight me when I played hookey from school to catch a matinee. Another superb dancing act, Tony and Sally DeMarco, ranked with the Astaires as one of the two best ballroom dancing acts I have ever seen. I used to enjoy Tony's spaghetti dinners. He was one hell of an Italian cook. Blossom Seeley, who divorced all-time great Giant pitcher Rube Marquard to marry her new vaudeville partner, Benny Fields (they introduced "Crooner's Lullabye" for me a few years later when it was cut out of one of my early Crosby films) . . . the Ponzillo Sisters, who harmonized popular ballads and broke up when sister Rosa became Rosa Ponselle, the Metropolitan Opera star . . . Pat Rooney Sr. doing his inimitable waltz clog to "The Daughter of Rosie O'Grady" . . . Eddie Foy and the Seven Little Foys (one of them, Bryan Foy, later was my director the first time I appeared before the movie cameras, in a one-reel musical short for Warner Brothers made in 1929 based on my songs). . . . Joe E. Brown when he first appeared, not as a comedian but as an acrobat. . . . George White as a hoofer in a dancing act, a few years before he began producing his annual *George White's Scandals* on Broadway. . . . Joe Frisco doing his famous Frisco dance to "Darktown Strutters' Ball" (I recall visiting him in his dressing room at the Palace and finding him knee-deep in *Racing Forms* and tout sheets) . . . the great Bill Robinson doing his dance up and down a short flight of steps on the stage . . . the delightful double act of Eddie Buzzell and Peggy Parker (Eddie was to become a successful director of MGM musicals, and Peggy married songwriter Abe Olman, who composed "Oh, Johnny") . . . and so many, many more that I have never forgotten.

The first dance band I ever saw in vaudeville was the five-piece Vincent Lopez outfit after they left the Pekin Restaurant in Times Square. It was through this vaudeville act that Vince first achieved recognition, and he soon expanded his band to twelve men. Another was the Paul Whiteman organization, a great success at the Palace. The vaudeville bandleader that outlasted all of them was Ted Lewis, who opened his act for many years by shouting: "Is everybody happy?" Ted's photo is on the cover of several of my songs that he used in his act, including "My Old Flame" and "True Blue Lou."

The acts that particularly delighted me as a kid were the big-name songwriter acts that toured the vaudeville circuits. These were the people who first inspired my dreams of one day becoming a member of that select fraternity myself. (Later in this chapter I will go into how I realized this childhood ambition when I did my own act at the Palace Theater, singing and playing my compositions.)

The supreme songwriter act of all of them was, of course, the Gus Edwards Song Revue, which Gus produced in a new annual edition for a dozen years or so. Gus, whose life story was later portrayed by Bing Crosby in his film *The Star Maker*, had written such all-time standards as "School Days," "In My Merry Oldsmobile," and "By the Light of the Silvery Moon." His act was one of the highest-paid and most lavish in vaudeville. Gus was handsome, debonair, and about as poised as any performer I have ever seen. I could scarcely wait for each annual edition to hear what his new songs were that year. What he was especially noted for was his uncanny knack of discovering new stars. No one in show business was ever responsible for unearthing more new talented kids than this man. Eddie Cantor started as a child performer in a Gus Edwards Revue. So did Ray Bolger, the Duncan Sisters, Groucho Marx, George Jessel, Eleanor Powell, Hildegarde, Eddie Buzzell, Bert Wheeler, and many more. Some of his proteges later became famous in other fields—Walter Winchell as a columnist, Sally Rand as a nude fan dancer, Jack Pearl in radio with Ben Bard, Ina Ray Hutton as a bandleader, Mervyn LeRoy, who became one of Hollywood's foremost director-producers (*The Wizard of Oz, Random Harvest,* etc.), film stars Ricardo Cortez, Mae Murray, and the Lane sisters, and Helen Menken as first lady of the Broadway dramatic stage.

Other songwriter acts I remember were "A Trip to Hitland" which featured ten composers at ten pianos on stage at the same time (Al Sherman, Bernie Grossman, Jack Stanley, Al Lewis and others); J. Fred Coots, who teamed up with Yankee star pitcher Waite Hoyt (who pitched for Erasmus Hall when I went there)— Freddy was amazed to discover that Hoyt had a fine singing voice when he played for him at a press party; Wolfie Gilbert and Anatole Friedland, who were songwriters, publishers, and producers of lavish tabloid musicals as well; Harry Carroll, Benny Davis,

82

the gloomy-looking George Meyer with his singing partner Artie Mehlinger; and the attractive Maude Lambert singing "When Irish Eyes are Smiling" and "Mother Machree" accompanied at the piano by her husband, the personable Ernest R. Ball, who composed these hits. And, of course, Irving Berlin, who occasionally did a one-week stint at the Palace—he refused to tour—singing in a soft, barely audible voice that nonetheless could be heard all over the large theater because you could hear a pin drop when Berlin walked onstage. He was generally accompanied by Arthur Johnston.

Having been a vaudeville addict for as long as I could remember, it was of course inevitable that I would be bitten by the vaudeville bug myself sooner or later. I hastily put together a routine of about a dozen of my songs—a few I felt that audiences would be familiar with plus some untried new ones—with some "snappy patter" in between, furnished by an aspiring gag writer I had met. I paid a visit to Fally Markus, a booker of smalltime vaudeville houses who customarily provided break-in dates for new acts. When I told Fally the titles of some of my songs, he booked me for a split week (three days) at the Academy Theater in Newburgh, about two hours from New York City. Though I had never appeared on any stage before, luckily the theater manager had heard me on radio and gave Fally the okay for the booking. To play it safe, I had decided to do the entire act glued to the piano bench. There I would be less nervous than on my feet and I eliminated the necessity of walking on and offstage. I was taking no chances. The curtain went up and there I was, seated at a baby grand. At the finish of the act, I was to sit there and bow while the curtain came down in front of me. It was easy, and a good safeguard for a novice like myself. However, when I had done my last song, the curtain failed to come down, and I just sat there and kept bowing and smiling, egg all over my face. The lone stagehand, whose task it was to lower the curtain, had gone outside for a breath of air and was standing outside the stage door unaware that he had missed his curtain cue. Not knowing what else to do, I sang another song—and still the stagehand was missing. I knew I had no choice, so I walked off briskly, pausing at the wings to take a final bow. Surprisingly, the audience seemed to approve. At any rate, I had leaped the first hurdle, and for the remainder of the engagement I walked on and offstage as if I had been doing it all my life.

The following week Fally booked me on another break-in date.

This one was a one-nighter—in a New Jersey suburb whose name I will refrain from mentioning because the one theater it boasted was just about the smallest of the smalltime anywhere. I think it had been erected around the time of the Civil War and had not been refurbished since. My dressing room was a backstage john, and the stage creaked as soon as I stepped onto it. Instead of a baby grand, I was given a rickety old upright piano that probably hadn't been tuned since World War I, and three or four of the keys were silent. About the only other thing I remember about the booking was that there was another male single act also making his vaudeville debut, a standup comedian with some really funny material. His name was Ken Murray, and he was starting out on a career that was to eventually make Ken a standard headline act in big-time vaudeville and revues. I remember comparing notes with him after the show and learning to my surprise that we both received the same salary for the one-nighter, twenty-five bucks.

Despite the drawbacks, I was again well received by the audience, and was particularly flattered when they applauded at the mere mention of some of the titles of my songs. They obviously knew them.

I had no idea for how long a period a new act was supposed to break in, and with the unbelievable conceit that comes of youth and inexperience, I felt that I was now ready for the big time. I called on one of the top-bracket vaudeville bookers, Harry Webber, at his office in the Palace Theater building—because I didn't know any better. Harry pointed out that while songwriter acts were then a hot item on the vaudeville circuits, none of the successful ones, except for Irving Berlin, were singles. In order to play the big-time vaudeville theaters, I must be part of a double act. He suggested that I keep in touch with him. Many performers drifted into his office, and he was bound to find a good vaudeville partner for me sooner or later.

Several months went by, and my vaudeville ambitions were beginning to cool. Then one day I received a phone call from Harry's partner and brother, Herman Webber. Would I drop by the office late that afternoon to meet a young lady that the Webbers handled? I said sure, hoping that my anxiety was not too obvious. The girl they introduced me to was a flamboyant, vivacious redhead named Flo Lewis, whom I had seen recently in a muscial comedy called *Twinkle Twinkle* in which she had won critical acclaim as a singing comedienne. Flo was now planning a vaudeville act, and she not only wanted someone to work with but needed some special comedy song material as well. In discussing the new venture at the Webber office, they had mentioned that I had written comedy material for Eddie Cantor and the Duncan Sisters. Whereupon Flo said, "Well, what are you waiting for? Get on that phone and get him right down here!"

The next few weeks were spent in feverish preparation for the new act. I wrote a batch of new comedy songs, all of which delighted Flo. We rehearsed and polished and repolished for many a long, arduous hour. Flo Lewis was a real pro and a perfectionist, and I learned a good deal from her about the importance of being letter perfect when you went out to face an audience. She directed my every move and gesture, down to the last detail. Finally we were ready to open—not in a smalltime break-in theater, but in the new deluxe Keith circuit house that had recently been built in New Rochelle, just outside of New York. The Webbers, who handled so many important acts that they could call their shots at the Keith booking offices, selected the New Rochelle theater because it was just off-limits for the New York City newspaper critics, yet close enough to be covered by all of the important Keith bookers who scouted new acts.

Our act was a solid hit right from the very first matinee, and this must be taken more as a tribute to a great performer, Flo Lewis, than as self-praise. Nevertheless, I carried off my end of the partnership confidently, in a manner that surprised even me. I came on stage first, driving a midget automobile that was almost a toy. Flo, dressed as a flapper of the period—tight plaid skirt with fanny sticking out, a ridiculous small feathered hat, and a pair of galoshes—came on from the opposite side, thumbing a ride. Our opening song was called "Hey, Mister, Gimme a Hitch" and Flo bounced all over the stage following the little car. We delivered our gag lines, in which I was the straight man while Flo got all the laughs. Then, while she changed into an evening gown, the curtain rose and revealed a grand piano, at which I sang and played a medley of my best-known songs. Flo reappeared, did a few songs to my piano accompaniment, and we finished with another duet in which I even did a little hoofing as I exited with Flo. I imagine I must have been pretty clumsy, but Flo was the kind of seasoned performer who could make anyone look good.

The following week we played at Schanberger's Keith house in Baltimore, where we headlined the bill. Then a week at Keith's Boston theater, considered one of the showcase houses of the circuit. After our first show, Harry Webber phoned us from New

85

York and told us that as a result of the out-of-town reports from house managers, we would play the Palace next week. The Palace! Frankly, it was hard to believe. The Palace, to a vaudeville performer, was the zenith, the goal which every act dreamed of reaching. When you got to the Palace, you had arrived—like a TV performer of today getting a network show in prime time. Here we were—booked into the Palace in our fourth week with a brand new act! Flo said it was unheard of, and we must spend all day Sunday polishing up the few remaining rough spots. Our first show at the Palace was the Monday matinee—remember?

The Palace, the world's most glamorous and renowned vaudeville theater, first opened in 1913 with Ed Wynn headlining a nine-act bill. For the first year or so, it suffered from scant attendance and was often referred to as "Albee's folly" because of its high unrecouped construction cost. Good seats were two dollars each, twice as much as other vaudeville theaters charged, and despite its advantageous location on the corner of Broadway and 47th, it was too new, too untested, to catch on immediately. The jinx was finally broken when Sarah Bernhardt, the First Lady of the Theater in every country on the globe, agreed to play the Palace in a one-act dramatic sketch in 1914. The Divine Sarah, as she was known, was then in her seventieth year, and she insisted on a salary of $500 per *show*, payable after every performance in *gold*. Apparently she trusted neither Albee's check nor U.S. currency (shades of De Gaulle!). This salary, incidentally, was not topped at the Palace until seventeen years later, when Eddie Cantor received $7,500 in 1931 for a week's engagement.

The thing I was most apprehensive about, once I knew we were to play the Palace, was the crowd of Broadway regulars who were always on hand the opening day. More than half the seats at the Monday matinee and evening performances were presold to a special subscription list, a majority of whom were show-business celebrities and professionals. If you were in or of the theater, you just had to be at the Palace on Monday, with no ifs, ands or buts. Aside from the leading newspaper critics, the capacity openings were crammed with Broadway producers, agents, music publishing executives, stars, songwriters, vaudeville circuit bookers, and the usual array of affluent firstnighters. Although I was not a season subscriber, I tried to catch the Monday shows as often as possible—frequently among the "standing room" customers because seats were unavailable. I saw many an act, having finally reached this pinnacle of vaudeville success, trying hard to over-

86

come the tension and excitement that gnawed inside them at the Monday shows. They were facing the toughest audience in the world, and they knew it. Some top stars like Al Jolson and George M. Cohan repeatedly turned down offers to play the Palace, chickening out at the prospect of facing an audience of their peers.

Among the regulars at the opening shows I recall seeing J. J. Shubert, Flo Ziegfeld, Charles Dillingham, Sime Silverman, several of the Warner Brothers, New York mayor Jimmy Walker, Sam Harris, E. F. Albee, George Jessel, Damon Runyon, Walter Winchell, Jack and Harry Cohn, Charles K. Harris, Buddy De Sylva, Harry Von Tilzer, Irving Berlin, Billy Rose, Gus Edwards, and Fanny Brice. Although critical when an act failed to meet their expectations, they were just as quick to burst into spontaneous applause when a new act met their approval.

Flo and I faced the harrowing ordeal of this awesome Broadway tradition for the first time on the 29th of August, 1926. We were dressed, made up, and ready to go on well ahead of curtain time, and stood in the wings waiting for our entrance music for fifteen or twenty minutes. My heart was palpitating, my hands were trembling, and I wondered if I would be able to hit the right keys on the piano. Flo giggled nervously as she looked at me and told me to relax, but I could see that beads of perspiration were shining through her makeup. She was scared out of her wits, even though we had done the act for several weeks by now and were familiar with the whole routine.

After what seemed like hours instead of minutes, the pit orchestra struck up the strains of "Bebe," our entrance music, and I drove the little car onstage. The audience tittered at the sight of the ridiculous vehicle, exactly as they had done in New Rochelle, Baltimore, and Boston. This reassured me, and I began to bolster my frayed nerves by telling myself that, after all, this audience was no different from the others we had faced—or was it? Flo, who had previously darted over to the opposite wing, now made her entrance. Her first few lines of dialogue brought immediate roars of laughter—much louder than the laughter at the other theaters, because the Palace had twice as many spectators. Instantly, our jitters vanished. We suddenly felt very much at home. As every stage performer knows, there is nothing that will steady the nerves and erase all tensions like the knowledge that an audience is in your corner, in the palm of your hands. Laughter and applause are the greatest of tranquilizers to those afflicted with stage fright. Once in our stride, the remainder of the act went smoothly, without a hitch, and we took our final bows to what seemed like deafening applause.

At the evening performance, I was a trifle nervous again when I saw Mae West, dressed to the teeth and glittering with blinding jewelry, sitting directly in front of me in the first row alongside her boyfriend, lawyer Jim Timoney. She was not more than five or six feet away. Mae kept staring at me from head to toe, up and down—especially down. It disconcerted me. However, after a few seconds, she gave me a reassuring wink, and I was no longer uncomfortable.

The week at the Palace led to bookings at many other Keith houses, and I enjoyed it all thoroughly. I remember one theater we played where Milton Berle, then a precocious eighteen-year-old billed as the Boy Wonder, appeared on the same bill, stopping the show at every performance. His ever present mother Sandra was invariably in the wings for a final look at his makeup and wardrobe just before he went on, quickly dashing to a front-row seat to watch every performance and laugh just as hard as if she were hearing his jokes for the first time.

On another bill we played, Houdini was the headline attraction. I recall that at one performance I was late getting made up because I was wandering around backstage like a yokel, completely intrigued with his array of magic paraphernalia, examining the box where he sawed a woman in half, and trying to figure out how he accomplished some of his legendary legerdemain. I suddenly realized that I was due on the stage myself in about ten minutes, so I rushed to my dressing room to apply my stage makeup. I had done only one side of my face when I suddenly heard our entrance music, and I sprinted downstairs in a panic. I tried to do the entire act with my left profile to the audience, hiding the side I had not made up. Flo laughed out loud when she saw me, insisting on turning me around so the audience could see the weird effect.

After several months on the Keith circuit, I was faced with a difficult situation. I had written a new song called "One Summer Night" with Larry Spier, who had quit his job as band and orchestra manager at Leo Feist's when he wrote a smash hit, "Memory Lane," in collaboration with Con Conrad and Bud De Sylva. Larry, one of the most enterprising and energetic music men I ever knew, wanted to capitalize on his new stature as the writer of a number-one song by acting as his own publisher on

"One Summer Night," and he asked me to join him in the venture. Even though I was appearing in vaudeville, I contributed by covering radio stations and music stores in the various cities I appeared in, to say nothing of featuring "One Summer Night" in the act. We invested a few hundred dollars apiece to print copies and orchestrations, and Larry opened a small office in the Roseland Building on Broadway. I was really impressed on my first visit there when I saw the lettering on the door that read "Spier and Coslow, Inc."

Larry hustled almost around the clock, getting all the dance bands he knew to use the song on their broadcasts—and Larry knew all of them intimately. Before we realized what was happening, the song had sold 100,000 copies and had been recorded on every major label. This was not exactly chickenfeed, for at the wholesale price of eighteen cents per copy it meant we had taken in $18,000 in the space of a few weeks, with record royalties and ASCAP performance fees from radio stations still to come. It represented almost all profit, because we had very little overhead —a secretary and a shipping clerk, and $100 a month for rent. We did all of the songplugging ourselves.

I could have gone on and played all through the hinterlands in vaudeville. We had been offered a tour of the Orpheum circuit out west. Or I could remain in Tin Pan Alley and concentrate on my new publishing firm, which had gotten off to such an auspicious start. In fairness to Flo, I discussed it with her, and she said she wouldn't mind at all if I chose to remain in New York, for she had received a flattering offer to co-star in a new show. I told Larry I would pass up the vaudeville tour and move into the office with him.

Our little office, the dimensions of which were about twelve by fifteen feet, soon became a beehive of activity. Attracted by the large number of radio plugs we were getting, other songwriters began offering new songs to us. Soon we were publishing songs by others in addition to our own. Important writers like Fred Coots, Alfred Bryan, and Con Conrad had songs published by Spier and Coslow, Inc.

We were starting to fall all over ourselves in the office, getting in each other's way. Larry's desk next to mine, plus an upright piano, a shipping counter and shelves full of sheet music, two executives and two employees, and frequent visits from songwriters, radio artists, arrangers, and others—the traffic was becoming nervewracking. We found larger quarters, soon expanding to half of a floor above the Brass Rail restaurant on 49th Street and 7th Avenue. On the floor above us, another new publisher-songwriter firm had just been launched, DeSylva, Brown, and Henderson, Inc.

Our activities included periodic visits to the leading record companies to show them our new songs. Following one of these visits, Larry returned to our office one afternoon with Nat Shilkret, RCA-Victor's recording manager, and Gene Austin, their bestselling artist. In addition to their recording activities, Nat and Gene also wrote songs. They had just revised and dressed up an obscure old spiritual which they wanted to record, but Nat felt that something was wrong with the lyric. At the RCA studios, they had played it for Larry and asked his opinion. Larry suggested that I might straighten out whatever was wrong with the lyric. Now they were in our office.

It was one of those songs that hit me right in the pit of my stomach as soon as they got to the first four bars of the chorus. I knew they were offering us a hit as soon as Gene sang:
"Look down—look down—that lonesome road"
Before they went on with it, I looked at Larry and said something like "Wow!" or whatever variation we used back in 1927.

They were right, however, about the need of a little doctoring up. The song seemed too long, and it ended rather awkwardly. The lyric had a couple of faulty rhymes, and the promise in the striking opening phrase lacked a punchy follow-through.

Nat quickly dashed off a lead sheet and left it with me. I locked myself in one of our tiny piano rooms and spent the rest of the afternoon doing the necessary surgery. Nat and Gene came back the next day and proclaimed the operation a success.

"Lonesome Road" helped greatly to establish Spier and Coslow, Inc. as a new firm to be reckoned with. The springboard, of course, was Gene's great recording, Victor 21098, released shortly after his famous "My Blue Heaven." I have never doubted for a moment that as good as our song was, we rode on the coattails of Gene's all-time bestselling "Blue Heaven" record. It was a lucky shot.

"Lonesome Road" has grown in popularity over the years, and is still selling. As the publisher of the song, I was mainly concerned with getting out as fine a product as I possibly could, so I never added my name as a co-author or cut in on the writers' royalties, although I could have legitimately asked their permission to do so.

90

Our next hit, which we published several months later, was a song I had placed with Waterson, Berlin and Snyder the year before. Waterson had shelved the song—a great boner on their part, because after they released the song back to me, Spier and Coslow, Inc. really hit the jackpot with it. The song, "Was It a Dream?", was a melody I had composed, with the title and most of the lyric supplied by one of Waterson's lyricists, Addy Britt. The song had only a chorus and no verse, so Larry Spier became a co-writer by virtue of adding a verse, thus preserving our team identity.

It was one of those rare numbers than ran into absolutely no resistance anywhere. Everyone seemed to love it. Many of the leading ballad singers on radio and in vaudeville quickly added it to their repertoires, and it was the most requested waltz of that year with dance bands. Fred Waring's Pennsylvanians were among the first to record it, soon followed by the historic Dorsey Brothers record, when Tommy and Jimmy Dorsey were still together with their first band, in 1928. It was, in fact, only the sixth record turned out by this celebrated aggregation of great musicians, and their first smash hit. There have been, during my career, probably some 1,200 or so recorded versions of all of my compositions; but if you were to ask me which is my favorite, I guess this one would have to be it. It was one of the longest dance arrangements ever recorded, spanning both sides of a 10-inch platter, Part I and Part II, and a sheer delight to listen to.

While the song was climbing up on the bestseller charts, we received an irresistible offer to turn over the publishing rights to T. B. Harms, the publishers for Gershwin, Kern, Rodgers and Hart, Youmans, and Cole Porter. The offer was personally telephoned to me by Max Dreyfuss, one of the two Dreyfuss brothers who owned the Harms firm, considered the "class" publisher of the industry. Naturally, the offer flattered us. We closed a deal with Dreyfuss under which we received what I understood was the largest advance ever paid up to that time on a single song, $25,000—against royalties and a substantial share of the profits. Between our own firm and Harms, over a million copies of "Was It a Dream?" were eventually sold, and it turned out to be the biggest hit of my pre-Hollywood days.

By late 1928, vaudeville was a not-so-spry old gentleman who was still getting around, but obviously on his last legs. By that time we were concentrating chiefly on two other songplugging media: transcontinental network radio, which had now matured into a powerful force, and secondly, a potent new type of plug that was attracting the attention of all music publishers—the rapidly growing list of deluxe movie palaces in the larger cities, where shows were seen by three or four thousand people, four or five times a day. That added up to about 150,000 patrons a week per theater, a shattering body blow to vaudeville houses. At first, the stars were popular organists like Jesse and Helen Crawford at the Paramount Theater in New York, Milton Charles at the Chicago Theater, and Milt Slosser at the Missouri Theater in St. Louis, among others. They would feature a new song preceding the movie, with dynamic audience impact because the lyrics were being flashed on the screen while they played, as bouncing balls and other devices leaped from one word to the next. The next major development, led by the enterprising movie theater chains owned by Paramount, Warner Brothers, and MGM-Loew's, was the introduction of lavish stage shows, with a large band on the rear of the stage instead of in the pit. It was revolutionary, a new twist in entertainment for the masses, and it caught on quickly. The competition was overwhelming for the struggling, outdated vaudeville houses—the combination of a new first-run star-studded movie, plus three or four name acts (who were paid far more than they ever received in vaudeville), accompanied by a large house band. Vaudeville fought hard against this challenge for another year or two, then finally gave up the ghost. The only holdout was the Palace, which somehow managed to continue its all-vaudeville policy until July 1932, the last of a dying breed. It expired in dignity, Harry Richman and Lillian Roth headlining the closing bill. The Palace was then converted into a first-run movie theater.

But I am jumping ahead of my story, and will flash back to the late Twenties again. Spier and Coslow, still expanding, found it necessary to rent added office space, taking on a dozen staff employees in various departments: pluggers, office and stockroom help, salesmen, and local representatives in Chicago, Los Angeles, Boston, and Pittsburgh. With a staff fully qualified to take the load of detail off our hands, Larry and I now concentrated on cultivating the most important plugs ourselves, particularly the personality leaders who emceed the extravagant stage shows in the movie palaces. At first, the king of them all was the legendary Paul Ash, whose domain was the colossal new Oriental Theater in downtown Chicago. Rudy Vallee came on the theater scene a bit

92

later, at the Brooklyn Paramount, eventually surprassing Paul Ash's fan following. Ash and Vallee attracted the first mobs of screaming, swooning, hysterical females that would start lining up at daybreak and wait for hours to buy tickets to hear their idols. They were the forerunners (and in many cases the mothers and grandmothers) of the latter-day mobs who exhibited the same hysteria over Crosby, Columbo, Sinatra, Elvis and the Beatles.

Paul Ash was one of our choicest plugs, and every time he used one of our publications it immediately caught on in the populous Chicago area, selling thousands of copies. He featured "Was It a Dream?" in at least four or five different stage shows, to my knowledge.

Rudy Vallee was one of the most cooperative stars of the lot. A keen judge of a song, he was hard to please. But once you gave him one he liked, he went out of his way to give it a great sendoff, dressing it up with the best arrangement he could command, going all-out to plug it, and occasionally recording our number for RCA-Victor as well. I have heard many stories about Rudy being aloof, hard to get to, unobliging. These legends are simply not true, at least in my experience. When Larry and I were starting out, in the infancy of our publishing venture, and Vallee was the hero of the debutante set at the Heigh-Ho Club in New York, we found him sympathetic and receptive at all times. Never once do I recall him being standoffish or too busy to see us. He always greeted us with the same affable charm, sly humor, and democratic camaraderie. I once heard Frank Sinatra address a Songwriters' Hall of Fame dinner with the following opening line: "If it weren't for you guys, I'd still be selling shirts." And I know that Vallee always felt the same way, appreciative of any and all whose talents provided him with song material he could use.

Larry and I soon adopted the practice of running out to see stage bandleaders out of town. Dick Powell, for example, was a local sensation at the Stanley Theater in Pittsburgh, and so were Ed Lowry in St. Louis, Teddy Joyce in Boston, and Maurice Spitalny in Cleveland. Not to mention Maurice's brother Phil, who was soon to become the first male leader of a name all-girl orchestra that toured the country's large movie theaters. How many of you remember Evelyn and her Magic Violin? (Evelyn later married Phil.) These and similar stage-band superstars were our supreme plugs as the 1920's drew to a close, plugs that made many a song take off for our young publishing firm.

But there was still another music phenomenon that had recently appeared on the horizon. Al Jolson had starred in a film called *The Jazz Singer* for Warner Brothers, a silent film that contained several sound sequences featuring Al's singing voice. Audiences from coast to coast were electrified as they saw and *heard* Jolson sing "Mammy" and "Toot, Toot, Tootsie" in the film. Now Jolson's second starring film, *The Singing Fool*, was released, a film that catapulted DeSylva, Brown and Henderson's "Sonny Boy" to the top of the bestseller lists. Vaguely, I began to sense that a new era in entertainment history was beginning to dawn.

Chapter Seven

TIN PAN ALLEY GOES HOLLYWOOD

I will never forget that bright spring morning in 1929 when Larry Spier burst into my office and said, "Stop whatever you're doing. Morris Press wants to see us right away!"

"Who? Who's Morris Press?"

"One of the Paramount executives at the home office in the Paramount Theater Building. He just phoned us. Let's go!"

We hurried across Times Square and were at the Paramount offices in five minutes. Morris, a warm, amiable, enthusiastic individual, came right to the point. "Warner Brothers," he told us, "are trying to grab up all the music publishers in sight. They have just bought Harms, Witmark, Remick, and a few others. MGM is on the verge of closing for Feist and Robbins. We've had our eye on you two guys and we like what we see. Now that talkies are here to stay, all the film studios are feverishly preparing big musicals. Al Jolson proved they're a gold mine. We need prolific songwriters, a catalog of songs to pick from, and music promotional executives."

An hour later, we left the Paramount offices—not walking but literally floating on a cloud. A quick deal had been made, and a letter of intent signed by a Paramount V.P. was in my pocket!

The deal we had agreed on called for Paramount to purchase 80 percent of Spier and Coslow, Inc., change the name to Famous Music Company (after Famous Players-Lasky Paramount, the parent corporation), with a straight five-year employment contract for both of us. Larry was to be general manager of Famous Music in New York, which was to be expanded into a major publisher with larger offices and added staff, while I was to go right out to the Hollywood studios to write scores for important musical films.

The price we arrived at was not high by current standards—$150,000 for the 80 percent ownership. But even $75,000—my share—was more money than I had ever seen in my life, and I still owned ten percent of what was to be built up to a top publishing house—plus a five-year contract with no options, and a handsome weekly drawing account against royalties.

It was not a bad deal considering that we had been in the publishing business for less than two years, had a catalog of only a few dozen publications, and were still a couple of young fellows in our twenties, with the whole world ahead of us. Moreover, I had seen the handwriting on the wall and knew that publishers without movie connections were doomed. It was the wave of the future and overnight the music publishing industry had been revolutionized. It was now possible, for the first time, to give a new song the superconcentrated exploitation of being plugged in thousands of deluxe movie palaces from coast to coast —simultaneously! The possibilities, to a music man, were staggering. Which explains why Larry and I found the offer just too irresistible to pass up.

A few weeks later the formal contracts were signed, and I was on the Santa Fe "Chief" on my way to Hollywood, one of the first three Broadway songwriters to be exported to the West Coast under longterm contracts. The other two were Dick Whiting (composer of "Japanese Sandman," "Till We Meet Again," "Ain't We Got Fun," etc.), and lyricist Leo Robin (who had recently collaborated with Vincent Youmans on the smash Broadway musical, *Hit the Deck*. Naturally, I was flattered to be in such distinguished company. Our little trio was the vanguard of a horde of songsmiths who deserted Tin Pan Alley for the canyons of Hollywood over the next few years.

It was a time of feverish activity for the movie industry. The advent of sound called for some lightning changes, such as soundproofing all the shooting stages. Studios raided the radio networks to bring in dozens of sound engineers, a new breed of technician never seen before in Hollywood. Contract players in every studio were ordered to attend voice and elocution classes

96

from which many with unrecordable speaking voices soon headed for oblivion. It was a new challenge for the industry, fraught with confusion, uncertainty, and experimentation.

In my first week on the lot, Whiting, Robin and I were assigned to write a score for Paramount's gigantic all-talking, all-singing musical, a film version of the Broadway stage hit *Burlesque*. The studio had renamed it *Dance of Life*. The script was already completed and we had to work fast to come up with nine new songs for Nancy Carroll, Hal Skelly, and others in the cast. Offices for the new music department were still under construction, so we had to knock out the nine songs in various and sundry places like hotel rooms, apartments, and a few odd corners of the studio where rehearsal pianos were placed.

Shortly before the first scheduled shooting day of *Dance of Life*, we arrived at the studio to find that the newly rebuilt sound stage had mysteriously burned down during the night. With a large cast and scores of dancers and singers now on the payroll, studio executives were horrified. Resourceful studio manager Sam Jaffe came up with a brainstorm. Why not change the shooting schedule to all-night shooting, from midnight to seven a.m., when airplanes, traffic and other noises were at a minimum? The idea was adopted, shooting commenced, and we, like the cast and crew, soon found ourselves in a frenzied, topsy-turvy world, working all night and sleeping all day.

It was an exciting time for all concerned. The studio was learning how to make sound musicals, mostly through trial and error. We three writers conferred and consulted with Nat Finston, Paramount's newly imported music head (formerly the music head for all of the Paramount Theater orchestras), and a score of other new arrivals—conductors, arrangers, choreographers, and sound men —who were all learning the hard way. On the first song we shot, a production number called "The Flippity Flop" requiring a large chorus line and a vocal group, we ruined dozens of "takes" before we discovered that it was far easier to record the soundtrack beforehand and later shoot the scene silent with the singers mouthing the lyrics to a playback of the soundtrack. This enabled the directors, Eddie Sutherland and John Cromwell, to move around the stage without worrying about shifting microphones and cables all over the place. We were all stabbing in the dark, but new techniques were discovered almost every day during shooting. There was a continuous interchange of information, thanks to the camaraderie of Hollywood musicians and sound men. Any recording innovation discovered in one studio spread like wild-fire to all of the others. Nevertheless, the first musicals were still crude affairs technically, and it took two or three years before most of the kinks were ironed out.

Dance of Life resulted in one fairly sizable song hit, "True Blue Lou," which Dick, Leo and I wrote for Hal Skelly. It got up to as high as number three on the bestseller list and was released on all major record labels. Tony Bennett revived it on Columbia Records 34 years later.

My hunch had proved correct: an important musical film could establish a big song hit practically overnight. By means of the film, the song was pounded into the ears and brains of millions of people—literally captive audiences. With radio, you could keep on talking, reading, playing cards, or doing any number of things that might take your attention away from the music. But in a movie house, you had no choice but to listen—and we made damn sure that it was reprised vocally a few times in the film, and scored orchestrally at the hint of any love scene. It was far and away the most effective form of songplugging the public had ever been exposed to, and the Hollywood music crowd capitalized on it to the hilt. Formerly, it had taken a publisher several months or more to make a song hit via the older, more conventional song-plugging. Now, songs were suddenly hitting the Top Ten in sheet music sales even while the films were still in their early first-run weeks around the country. Instant hits—the songwriter's Utopia!

It was the heyday of writers and publishers who were lucky enough to have movie outlets. In my first few years at Paramount I turned out dozens of songs which were swiftly catapulted to hitdom, including "Sing, You Sinners," "Thanks," "Down the Old Ox Road," "Cocktails for Two," "Just One More Chance," "Moon Song," "This Little Piggie Went to Market," "Learn to Croon," "My Old Flame," "A Little White Gardenia," "In the Middle of a Kiss," "The Day You Came Along," and numerous others. I'll get around to most of these in later pages.

Following the completion of *Dance of Life*, the new building to house Paramount's music department was finished, having been erected in something like sixty days by Paramount's light-ning-fast carpenters and construction workers, who were accus-tomed to building lavish sets in a hurry. Besides the individual staff offices, it contained a mammoth recording studio and a large music library. Our offices were a row of soundproof cells, each containing a desk and a small upright piano. Except for the soundproofing, the general effect was reminiscent of the publishers' offices in Tin Pan Alley. Dick and Leo shared the cell next to mine; the other cells were unoccupied at first. But by that time, Paramount had scheduled so many new musicals for the next season's release that the other cells were soon taken over by a steady stream of newcomers, more Broadway importations. There were new arrivals almost every week. Dick Rodgers and Larry Hart, Ralph Rainger, Rudolph Friml, Grant Clarke, and Newell Chase were among the first "inmates" to join us, soon followed by foreign imports like Oscar Straus from Vienna and Clifford Grey from London.

Later on, we were joined by Frank Loesser, Hoagy Carmichael, Mack Gordon and Harry Revel, Jerome Kern, Kurt Weill, Burton Lane, and Abel Baer. It seemed as though Paramount was trying to gobble up everyone who had ever written a hit song. But this was the heyday of the Hollywood musical, the early Thirties, and the studio was turning out more than sixty new features a year, most of them with musical sequences.

Within that two-story building, I soon found myself surrounded by what must have been the greatest collection of popular music giants ever assembled under one roof. Yet I couldn't help feeling that it was somehow like a huge assembly line of talent, manufacturing song after song from ten to five daily. They were throwing scripts at us so fast that some of us found ourselves working on four to five movies at a time.

Nevertheless, we were a friendly crew, all quick to cooperate with one another, with very little prima-donna rivalry in evidence. Larry Hart, who with Dick Rodgers occupied the cell on my right, found it all too frantic to work during daylight hours, and spent much of his time dropping into my cubicle for an afternoon chat, mostly about the "good old days" back on Broadway, which he sorely missed. Remember his line in "The Lady Is a Tramp"—"hates California, it's cold and it's damp"? Sometimes, when I was working against time, Larry would offer to help on my lines—for free. He would say, "What are you trying to come up with there? Can I hear it?" I would read my pencil-scribbled lyrics to him, and on more than one occasion he would pace up and down, digging for a good punchline for me, just as if he were collaborating on the song. I used a few of his suggestions, happy to get them. Many writers would have asked for a cut on the royalties, but not Larry. That's the kind of a guy he was. He loved his craft, and he felt a fraternal kinship to everyone else who worked in it.

One of the questions I am asked most frequently is: "What was Hollywood like in those days?" It was, as I have indicated, a time of transition—without a doubt the major revolution to hit the film industry since it began at the turn of the century. The metamorphosis from silents to talkies was violent and swift. Suddenly, silent movies were unwanted and unattended. "Garbo talks!" "Gloria Swanson sings!" Those were the catchphrases that were pulling the patrons into America's deluxe movie houses, which had quickly been wired for sound. Twenty thousand other theaters, the second- and third-run houses, were to be equipped within the next twelve months.

New soundstages were going up like weeds all over town. New faces were seen in Hollywood's restaurants, night clubs, and drawing rooms—the faces of famous Broadway stars, directors, playwrights. And more songwriters. And older heads were rolling!

Big silent-screen stars, caught in the holocaust, were feeling shaky and insecure. Many survived the big changeover, finding the new medium very much up their alley. Mary Pickford and Douglas Fairbanks Sr., for example, had starred in Broadway plays and knew how to project vocally. Garbo talked—huskily and magnificently. Janet Gaynor, Charlie Farrell, Joan Crawford, Claudette Colbert, Adolphe Menjou, Buddy Rogers, Wallace Beery, Norma Shearer and William Powell took to it like ducks to water.

But the two top drawing cards of the day suffered a different fate. Clara Bow, the sex symbol of the Twenties who epitomized flappers, the Jazz Age, and the Charleston, managed to get by quite nicely in spite of her Brooklynese accent. When her dazzling career was cut short a few years later, it was not due to the talkies but to a series of unfortunate nervous breakdowns. But the speaking voice of the number-one male star of the day, John Gilbert, was a shock to his public. It was thin, weak, and high-pitched. Foreign accents killed off a few like Vilma Banky, Nita Naldi, Pola Negri and Nils Asther. Other silent idols like Billie Dove, Monte Blue, Rod LaRocque, Jack Pickford, and Valentino's favorite leading lady, Agnes Ayres, never quite adjusted to the mike and soon vanished from the scene.

In their place came seasoned, sure-tongued stars of the Broadway stage. There was my good friend Edward G. Robinson, one of the mildest, sweetest men it was ever my privilege to know—who became Hollywood's top tough guy in roles like *Little Caesar.* A Broadway hoofer named James Cagney was also converted into a screen bad guy, as was Humphrey Bogart. Famous stage leading ladies like Ruth Chatterton, Ann Harding and Miriam Hopkins made new careers on the Coast. Renowned stars of musical comedy like Eddie Cantor, Mae West, Vivienne Segel, Hal Skelly, Jeanette MacDonald, Fred Astaire and the Marx Brothers now appeared before millions instead of thousands. Hollywood even recruited stars like Maurice Chevalier, Jack Buchanan, and Carl Brisson from across the Atlantic.

Top silent-screen directors, too, were wondering about the sudden influx of Broadway stage directors like George Abbott, Robert Milton, John Cromwell and George Cukor. Most of the top-bracket silent directors, however, leaped the hurdle beautifully. Movie scenario writers, on the other hand, were nervous, even panicky. How could they possibly compete, with their outmoded "John exits, turning back once to frown at Mary" type of silent scenario, against the illustrious New York playwrights who had been writing dialogue for years?

The exodus left Broadway deserted. I remember, on one of my trips East in the early Thirties, how bleak and barren it seemed in my old hangouts like Lindy's, Sardi's, and my favorite speakeasy, Twenty-One. The former customers were now congregating in the new Vine Street Brown Derby, Henry's, and the Hollywood Montmartre.

The film capital, in those days, was nothing at all like the big, overcongested metropolis of today. Hollywood Boulevard resembled the main street of a small town, except for the brand new edifice known as Grauman's Chinese Theater. In contrast to today's high-rise buildings, the tallest one I saw then was ten stories high. Once you got off the Boulevard, the palm-lined streets were quiet and serene, neat little rows of bungalows such as you would see in any middle-class suburb. Sunset Boulevard, as it left Hollywood to enter Beverly Hills, had a bridle path down the middle, where on Sunday mornings I would see oldtime star Hobart Bosworth and others riding horseback.

The nightlife was glittering, gay, and star-studded. The most glamorous room I ever saw was the celebrated Cocoanut Grove in the Los Angeles Ambassador Hotel, where the stars loved to dine

101

and dance. A tourist could get a thrill there any night in the week —if he could get a reservation—because the place was always jammed with the Who's Who of the film colony. The first time I had dinner at the Grove, I recall seeing at nearby tables Joan Crawford, Al Jolson, Loretta Young, Clara Bow holding hands with Harry Richman, Nancy Carroll, Tom Mix (without his horse), and a new twosome, Fanny Brice and Billy Rose—all in the same evening. The stars danced there to Gus Arnheim and his Orchestra, and in late 1930 Gus hired the three Rhythm Boys as his band vocalists. The names of the three were Bing Crosby, Harry Barris, and Al Rinker.

The Grove's chief rival at that time was the Blossom Room in the Hollywood Roosevelt, a hotel owned by movie magnate Joe Schenck, who lived and gave lavish parties in the hotel's over-sized penthouse which occupied the entire top floor. I guess you would say the town's number-three spot at that time was the Cotton Club, which was really not in town but in Culver City, a fifteen-minute drive from Beverly Hills. The tourists used to flock to the Cotton Club mostly out of curiosity, because the M.C. of the floor show was the once-famous and now infamous Roscoe "Fatty" Arbuckle, fighting desperately to make a comeback after the Virginia Rappe scandal which had rocked the town and wrecked his career. Sunday night was the big night at the Cotton Club because the rest of the floor show had a night off, and Roscoe would call on celebrities and friends in the audience to come up and do a number or at least take a bow. Roscoe spotted me at a ringside table one Sunday, after having met me at director James Cruze's swimming party earlier that day, and nothing would suffice except that I come out on the floor and play and sing a medley of my songs.

Having watched Roscoe struggle for laughs which never came, I was glad to help him out with the medley. It became a bit annoying only when Roscoe got into the habit of phoning me Sunday after Sunday to please come down and do another medley —gratis, as always. I obliged a few times and then begged off, mainly because after hearing me sing my head off, Roscoe never even extended the courtesy of having the management pick up the check for my party.

Although the niteries were popular, Hollywood folk got together mostly in their homes. Prohibition was still in effect, and in the clubs you couldn't buy anything stronger than a bottle of pop. At the homes of the stars, it was a different story. Bootleg

102

liquor flowed freely and the locals could raise hell and do damn well as they pleased.

However, if I thought I would see some of the wild Hollywood parties I'd heard so much about, I was due for disappointment. The ones I attended were pretty tame affairs. Lots of drinking, noise, and dancing the Black Bottom, but never once did I see an orgy or a drug binge, or hear a starlet scream that she's just been raped in the garden—dammit. Actually, the film folk usually left early because if they were shooting they were bound to have a 6 a.m. makeup call and had to get a few hours of shuteye to avoid looking like the wrath of God before the camera. By midnight, anyone left at a party was either not working, a nonpro, or paralyzed drunk.

One of the first parties I was invited to ended in tragedy. It was at the Maple Drive home of an old friend I had known in New York, Lew Cody, well known silent star and husband of Mabel Normand. It was Lew's birthday and Mabel, sad to state, was at the Monrovia Sanitarium suffering from T.B., so Lew was having just a small stag dinner party for some of his male cronies. Buster Keaton, Jack Pickford, and Buster Collier shared a table for four with me in the playroom. Seated near us were cowboy star Hoot Gibson, artist John Decker, and W.C. Fields. And a few other faces that I recognized.

All evening Lew kept asking me to play a song he had heard me do in New York, and which seemed to give him a big charge. The song, titled "The Show Is Over," was one I had written with Con Conrad and Al Dubin. It had not yet been published. It was a real tearjerker, and Lew, who was slightly in his cups, kept requesting another chorus every half hour on the half hour. Myself, I was getting damn sick of it, but I wouldn't turn down or offend my host.

I was at the piano doing the song for about the seventh time when the phone rang. Someone said, "It's for you, Lew. The Monrovia Sanitarium calling." I stopped playing.

Lew grinned. "That's Mabel calling to wish me a happy birthday," he said. He picked up the phone. A moment later he slumped over, his face buried in his arms. Someone poured out a big slug of straight Scotch. Lew gulped it down. He hadn't said a word, nor shed a tear. But the grief was written all over his face, and we knew what the phone message was.

Mabel Normand was still a fairly young woman when she died, but she had been a Hollywood legend for years. To the public,

103

she was a household name. She had co-starred with Charlie Chaplin and figured prominently in the notorious William D. Taylor murder case in the early Twenties. Her long-standing romance with Keystone comedy director Mack Sennett had been followed with bated breath in the fan magazines. Even as late as the 1970's, a new Jerry Herman musical comedy about their romance, called *Mack and Mabel*, was to hit the Broadway stage.

Lew and Mabel's married life had been brief when she was stricken with tuberculosis. It was obvious that her sudden passing was a shock that Lew would not get over easily. Just an hour before, I had heard him happily telling his friends that he was hoping he could bring Mabel home in a matter of weeks.

I never could find a spot for Lew's favorite song in a Hollywood film, and a few years later I gave it to a London music publisher, Irwin Dash, while I was on a trip over there. It made the top of the British Hit Parade. But ever since the tragic incident at Lew Cody's birthday party, I have never been able to play "The Show Is Over" without getting the shudders.

At the studio, things were still hectic. It was decided that there were too many new scripts in the works for the studio to maintain the luxury of having three songwriters working in collaboration. Whiting and Robin were paired off, and I was given a solo assignment to write a couple of numbers for Maurice Chevalier in *Paramount on Parade*, a lavish musical revue in which almost every star on the lot would participate, with Maurice to get top billing.

I did two songs for Maurice, one of which wound up on the cutting-room floor. The other one, "Sweeping the Clouds Away," emerged as the only number in the movie to make the bestseller charts, although twelve different songwriting teams had written songs for the various stars. When I first played "Clouds" for Ernst Lubitsch, who was to direct the Chevalier sequences, he adlibbed the whole production number right on the spot. "I can see Maurice as a chimney sweep on the rooftops of Paris, singing the song as he sweeps. Then ve bring out a hundred beautiful girls to dance mit him on the roof. Ve put the Eiffel Tower in the background and ve make it a big number." Ernst's German accent was a bit difficult for me to follow, and I had never seen a chimney sweep, so I didn't really get the concept. But he was so carried away, and had such a reputation as an imaginative director, that I figured he knew what he was talking about. He did.

Next on my agenda was a thing called *Honey*, another Nancy

Carroll musical. W. Franke Harling collaborated with me on some of the songs. Just a few days before the start of shooting, the studio had still not found a leading man for Nancy. The part called for a good-looking young fellow in his early twenties who could really sing. A dozen unknowns were tested and discarded. Finally we were up against the wire. The casting director was tearing out his hair. When we played the score for Ben Schulberg, Paramount production head, he said, "Say, you guys ought to know a fellow who can sing and play this part. Any suggestions?"

Sure, I had a suggestion. But I didn't say what it was. I asked Ben if I could do a little checking first, and report back to him in a day or two. "Work fast," said Ben. "We're desperate."

That night I drove to Loew's State Theater in downtown L.A., where Paul Whiteman and his band were headlining the stage show. The Three Rhythm Boys were still Paul's band vocalists. This was just before they joined the Gus Arnheim band at the Cocoanut Grove.

The hunch I had, the one I was not ready to divulge to Schulberg, was that one of the trio, Bing Crosby, was right for the part. I knew Bing well from his New York night club days with Paul. What I wanted to check on was a rumor I'd heard that Bing was ready to leave the band.

I found Bing backstage, and at first I felt him out cautiously. I was not really sure the rumor was accurate. What I had heard was that Bing was somewhat burned up at Whiteman for breaking his promise to give him a solo number in Whiteman's starring film, *The King of Jazz*. All that Bing had in the picture was a brief appearance as one of the Rhythm Boys.

I was right. Bing was ready to leave the band for a real part in a movie. He was confident he could get by with it. Acting didn't seem like such a tough chore.

"All right," I said, "I'll try to get them to come down here and catch your show. How much should I say you want?"

Bing hesitated for a moment. Then he mumbled something about "Two hundred a week. That's what Paul pays me. I wouldn't want to take a cut. And it would have to be a term deal. After all, I have a steady job with this outfit." Bing spurted it all out rather apologetically. I could see he was afraid he was asking for too much.

I said I didn't think two hundred would be any problem, if I could only sell the studio on him.

"What about Harry and Al?" Harry and Al were the other two Rhythm Boys.

"They could fit right in, too," I replied. "The script has a few band sequences and we'll need some band vocals."

Next evening, on my suggestion, Schulberg sent down a couple of Paramount talent scouts to Loew's State to catch Bing. For about 24 hours, he was under consideration. But the following day they auditioned a young actor named Stanley Smith. He couldn't sing very well, but somehow he got the part—don't ask me how. It was a big letdown for me, since I had a couple of real Crosby songs in the score. Stanley turned out to be a pretty fair actor, and he photographed well. But he certainly couldn't handle those songs.

This story had an ironic twist for Paramount. Stanley never did set the world afire, and the studio eventually dropped him. But a year or so later, they put Bing under a longterm contract, for in the meantime he had become one of the country's radio idols. But they were obliged to pay him not the $200 a week they could have had him for, but $50,000 a picture, with options that eventually ran his salary up to hundreds of thousands. But, as Sidney Skolsky always said, don't get me wrong—I love Hollywood.

Honey was almost through shooting when something occurred that told me we were in trouble again. The director, Wesley Ruggles, asked me to lunch with him one day. "I've just run a rough cut of 90 percent of the picture," said Wes. "The numbers sound fine, but one very important element is missing. We must have a big, rousing, hot production number for the final reel. Without it, we're just building up to a big letdown."

We adjourned to a projection room, and Wes ran the rough cut of the picture. He was correct. For the most part, a bright, pleasant little musical, then suddenly—nothing. I knew I had to come up with something dynamic to save *Honey*.

I usually work well under pressure, but this time I didn't. I stayed awake for a couple of nights in a row digging for a red-hot production idea. It just wouldn't come. What made it tough was that Ruggles wanted something that would not only excite the eardrums but would be visual as well—a production number that the cameraman could have a ball with.

Deciding I might fare better if I got away and relaxed for a couple of days, I joined some friends for a drive to Tijuana, Mexico, that weekend. On the way back to L.A., we passed a large tent on the outskirts of one of the small towns north of San Diego. As we approached the tent, we heard a swell of noise, handclapping, and music. It was a Sunday evening revival meeting, something I had never seen. "Let's go in and see what it's like," I suggested.

106

I don't know whether it was all that uplifting, but it was certainly great entertainment. About a thousand people, obviously carried away by religious zeal, were chanting in a steady rhythm, clapping their hands and stomping their feet. Some of the more fanatic ones were rolling on the floor as if in an epileptic seizure. A few inspired souls staggered up to the platform to be "saved."

Before we left the tent, I knew I had the germ of the idea I wanted. Driving home, my friends thought I had been infected with a sudden dose of religious frenzy. I just kept staring out at the road and snapping my fingers loudly. What they didn't know was that I had hit on a logical title for the missing production number, and was mentally trying out various rhyme schemes that would fit it.

The title I was so enthused about was "Sing, You Sinners." Although I arrived home quite late, I phoned Franke Harling, woke him out of a sound sleep, and asked him to meet me at the studio at nine a.m.

As is the case with most inspired ideas, it took very little time to write the song. It made a rousing production number and was choreographed, rehearsed, and shot within a few days. It was performed in the film by Lillian Roth (in her prealcoholic period), child star Mitzi Green, and a vocal chorus.

"Sing, You Sinners" not only turned out to be the hit song of the score but my biggest movie hit to date. Far more important, however, is the fact that "Sinners" was actually one of the first smash swing numbers of the great Swing Era of the 1930's. It was featured by some of the great swing bands of the day, and right up to the present time remains one of my top standards. Over the years, it has been recorded innumerable times, but my favorite recording is still the very first one, the extremely rare Duke Ellington version that came out on the now obscure Hit of the Week label. As late as the 1960's, Sammy Davis Jr. and Tony Bennett were opening their night club acts with "Sinners."

Following *Honey*, the studio gave me an assignment I rebelled against, but on the insistence of a star I greatly admired, I filled it. Paramount was about to film the great Friml operetta, *Vagabond King*, and Dennis King was to star in it. While the film script was in preparation, some giant brain in the studio—I never did find out whom—sold the company on the idea of changing the title to *If I Were King*, despite the fact that the original title was worth millions of dollars at the box office as an internationally famous stage success.

One of the strange quirks of that era was that every picture had to have a title song. Studio publicity heads were convinced that if a movie had a song by the same title, that title would be mentioned on the air thousands of times every day, whenever the song was played or sung on a radio station.

These countless free plugs, they reasoned, were worth a fortune at the box office. Accordingly, orders from the New York home office were issued: every film must have a title song. Finston divided them up among all the songwriters on the lot. Some of them were ridiculous, like "Death Takes a Holiday." But someone at the studio wrote it nevertheless—with great reluctance, I am sure. At another studio, a new film was called *Woman Disputed*. It actually contained a song called "Woman Disputed, I Love You"—believe it or not.

And so it was that I was asked to write "If I Were King" as a title song to be interpolated into Rudolph Friml's immortal score. I objected on the grounds that it was a sacrilege and a dastardly thing to do to Friml. But Friml had left for Europe and Dennis King felt he needed a new love song to sing to Jeanette MacDonald in the film. Dennis, one of the most persuasive and pleasant cajolers I ever knew, finally talked me into it. In collaboration with Leo Robin and Newell Chase, I did write "If I Were King." Leo's lyric was exactly what Dennis craved, and with it he sang his heart out to Jeanette MacDonald.

Before the film was completed, studio executives, in a sudden burst of sanity, changed the movie's title back to *Vagabond King*. But Dennis King's big love song, "If I Were King," stood up so well that it remained in; and, as all Late Late Show fans know in this day and age, it is still in the picture.

But for Paramount, there was an aftermath that the studio heads didn't relish. Everyone had forgotten that Friml had a clause in his contract to the effect that there were to be *no interpolations* in *Vagabond King*. When Friml saw the picture, he hit the ceiling. Next day, Friml's attorney phoned Paramount and threatened to sue. The picture was already in release, and my song was so interwoven with the story that it couldn't very well be cut out. Paramount finally stalled off the lawsuit by paying Friml an extra $50,000—a hell of a lot more than I ever made on the song. By a strange twist of fate, Rudolph Friml received more money on my song, "If I Were King," than for any of the other *Vagabond King* songs.

I've said very little thus far about my personal life in Holly-

108

wood, and the reader may well wonder by this time whether I had any. The answer of course is that I did, although it was cut to a minimum. In those early sound days, I found myself spending at least twelve hours a day writing lyrics and music, working with the performers, screenwriters, directors and producers, attending rehearsals, recordings and shootings of the musical numbers, sitting in on script conferences, and doing hundreds of other things that kept coming up. Often I worked at home far into the night on a lyric or a tune, especially when I was on three or four films at the same time. Exhausted, I would show up at the studio around 11 a.m. for more of the same.

Nevertheless, I did manage, somehow or other, to squeeze in a personal life of sorts, doing the necessary socializing at which so many studio decisions are actually made, keeping up with a group of friends, and doing my homework as well with a small family of my own.

But at this point in my narrative, both my social life and my professional life were interrupted by a great personal tragedy that literally knocked the pins from under me, and rendered me powerless to do any creative work for the next few months.

To flash back for a moment to my departure for Hollywood, I had left my wife Dorothy in New York with our small son so that she could dispose of our 73rd Street apartment and arrange to ship out our furniture while I found a place to live on the Coast. This all took a couple of months, after which they joined me in an exquisite little domicile I had found on the shores of Toluca Lake, a body of water about twenty feet wide, halfway between Hollywood and Burbank. Our nextdoor neighbor was Charlie Farrell. Across the road lived Richard and Jobyna Arlen, and Belle Bennett, the silent-film star of *Stella Dallas* fame. The Bob Hope and Bing Crosby estates had not yet been built. They would eventually be on the next block or two.

Frankly, Dorothy and I were not as compatible as we might have been. On the other hand, I was completely wrapped up in my five-year-old son Barton, for whom I felt a love that amounted to an obsession. He was my constant companion every morning before I drove to work, and all weekend.

I received a phone call at the studio one afternoon from Belle Bennett, who told me to rush home immediately. She had just seen Barton hit by a car that ran out of control while he was riding his tricycle on our front lawn. By the time I arrived home, he had been taken to a nearby emergency hospital. He died there, in my arms, an hour later. Dorothy was out shopping and didn't find out about it until it was all over.

The event shattered me. It was the saddest shock of my entire life. Even at this late date, I find it impossible to relive or retell the whole terrible nightmare and the subsequent depression it plunged me into. Suffice to say that grief kept me away from the studio and my writing activities for the next three months or so.

At the time of the tragedy, Dorothy was pregnant again, and the shock almost made her lose our second child. Luckily, however, a normal birth occurred three months later and a new son, Larry, arrived. To a large extent he helped fill the void.

It was now early 1931, and I was back at the studio again. I was delighted to find that a good friend of mine had been brought out from New York by Paramount to join the music staff. It was a pleasure to greet Arthur Johnston, who had just left Irving Berlin after many years as Irving's personal arranger, pianist, and all-around music assistant.

I asked Nat Finston if I could have Arthur exclusively assigned to me and to the musicals I was working on. To my surprise, the request was granted. It was a great break for me, and made my work a good deal easier. I recalled that Irving Berlin, for all his miraculous composing talent, was a one-finger composer. Arthur, the man he hummed his tunes to, did all the rest. He would fill in the rich, gorgeous harmonies, put the piano arrangement on paper, demonstrate the songs whenever necessary, and teach them to the artists in Berlin's shows.

Although I play with all ten fingers, I used to secretly envy the help Berlin received from Arthur. I often wished I could afford someone like him. And here he was—Arthur handling all the musical details for me, with *Paramount* footing the bill!

I was on a couple of unexciting assignments at the time—something called *Dance Palace,* and a couple of songs for young Jackie Cooper in his first starring vehicle, *Skippy.* Neither script looked like there would be a spot for the kind of song hit I wanted to sink my teeth into. Mostly situation numbers and special material, that sort of thing. Actually, I always found it fun writing such material. But after my long absence from the studio, I felt that what I needed most was a smash hit.

I was lunching in the studio commissary with Arthur one day. "Besides all these movie tunes, do you ever squeeze in just a plain, ordinary pop song? Something that's not in a picture?" he asked.

110

"Well, frankly, I hadn't thought about it lately. There's always so much to do around here. Why do you ask?"

"No special reason," Arthur replied, almost apologetically, "except that I thought of a hell of a song title last night."

Arthur was a bit cagey, and refused to disclose the title until we could get to the piano in my office. I knew that he wanted very badly to write songs in addition to his arranging and coaching chores, and I saw no reason why I shouldn't encourage him.

Back at my office, he blurted out the title—"Just One More Chance." I liked the sound of it instantly. He also had a musical phrase to fit the title, just the first four notes. He didn't seem to know where to go from there, and the next phrase popped into my brain like a flash. I hummed it to him, and he tried it on the piano. With only the first eight bars of the chorus, I instinctively knew we had a winner.

"I could finish this with you like rolling off a log," I said. "But what do we do with a song and no picture—just hold it and put it in the trunk? The radio bands aren't playing *anything* these days except movie songs."

But Arthur, way ahead of me, had an answer to that one. "What do you think of Bing Crosby?" he queried.

"I know him pretty well. Bing will go places."

"So what's wrong with getting a hit Crosby record instead of a movie? This number sounds like it was made to order for him."

I saw the point. Since I had last seen Bing, he and the other two Rhythm Boys had left the Whiteman band and were now with Gus Arnheim's Orchestra at the Cocoanut Grove. It was an open secret that the Grove was jammed every night, chiefly because Bing's solos with the band had caught on with the movie crowd. Arnheim was featuring him on the nightly Grove broadcasts over the NBC Pacific Coast network. And, for a clincher, Brunswick had just signed Bing to do his first solo recordings.

We finished "Just One More Chance" before the afternoon was over, tailoring the song especially for Crosby's croony ballad style. The finished product sounded very satisfying, even exciting. We felt we had come up with some kind of a hit. To make sure we weren't kidding ourselves, we called in Eddie Janis, Famous Music's West Coast manager, who had an office at the studio. Eddie listened as I sang and Arthur played. Soon he was practically drooling. "How fast can I get it?" was his excited response.

We got a similar reaction when we played it for Bing. Arthur rehearsed him on it, and Bing introduced it a few nights later on

111

Arnheim's 10-to-12 radio broadcast. We were at the Grove ourselves to hear the song's debut that night, and heard the crowd of Hollywoodites on the dance floor demanding encore after encore. Bing had stopped the show with the new song.

Night after night on the Grove broadcasts, "Chance" was Bing's feature solo. To say the results were startling would be an understatement. Calls at the music stores were coming in so fast that Famous Music dug up a Los Angeles printer who almost broke his printing press rushing out copies overnight. Jack Kapp, who headed Brunswick Records, flew out to the company's Hollywood plant and made his employees work around the clock preparing a Crosby recording session in a big hurry.

Precisely two weeks after the premiere broadcast, "Chance" was the number-one song on the West Coast. Famous Music then went all out on a promotion campaign, and within a month it was the top seller nationally. Never before, and never since, has a song of mine been established as a smash hit so quickly.

Jack Kapp must have used sleight of hand or something, because records were in the shops a week or so after the sheet music. "Just One More Chance"—Brunswick catalog number 6120— was the second of the historic Crosby Brunswicks, the series which is today among the most coveted of all items by record collectors. Almost all of Bing's previous records had been as a band vocalist, with Whiteman or Arnheim getting top billing. Now Bing got solo billing, and his "Chance" record took off just as the sheet music had done.

Among the celebrities in the crowd at the Grove the night of the first broadcast was producer-director Mack Sennett, who loved Bing's voice. Mack asked Bing to stop at his table for a drink, and offered him the princely sum of $750 to play the lead in a one-reel musical short to be titled *Just One More Chance*. It would feature the song, one of a series of song-title shorts. To Bing, who had just married Fox starlet Dixie Lee, $750 for a few days' work seemed like a fortune. He accepted Sennett's offer eagerly.

Looking back at it all, it is striking how a single song, as it soared to the top of the charts, also helped to send soaring the careers of Bing Crosby and Jack Kapp, Jack's struggling Brunswick firm, and the infant Famous Music Company. It also launched a new series for Mack Sennett, who was working hard to make a comeback. And, of course, it enhanced the stature of Arthur Johnston and myself as songwriters.

Shortly afterward the three Rhythm Boys, in a dispute over money with the Grove management, walked out on their contract.

They had doubled and tripled the Grove's nightly business, even with the country in the throes of a depression, and they felt they deserved a raise. But the hotel management, very shortsightedly, insisted that Bing, Al, and Harry live up to their original contract. In walking out, the boys found themselves in big trouble with the musicians' union, who blacklisted them locally. This was the end of the Rhythm Boys as a combo.

Being shut out of West Coast engagements, Bing, with his brother Everett and their wives, decided to give New York a try.

Everett quit his job as a truck salesman, convinced that he could fare better as Bing's manager, on a commission of ten percent of Bing's earnings. Everett felt that he could get Bing a solo radio network deal on the strength of Bing's West Coast radio popularity and the success of his first Brunswick recordings. Bing himself was not so sure, but realized he had no choice except to give it a try. By mail, Everett got a promise from CBS to give Bing an audition—if it was held in New York.

A week later, the New York audition took place. Bing dug up his old pal, guitarist Eddie Lang, to accompany him. Bing was apprehensive, but Eddie, the greatest jazz guitarist around despite being unable to read a note of music, gave him the self-assurance he needed.

There was an amazing coincidence connected with the audition that Bing didn't know about at the time. A week before, CBS president William Paley had been on shipboard, on his way home from Europe. Next to his deck chair, a small boy with a record player kept playing the one record he owned, over and over. The record was Crosby's "Just One More Chance." Paley asked the kid to show him the platter, and he jotted down the name of the singer. He would have the talent department of CBS look him up one of these days. It was a different kind of sound, and it got under Paley's skin.

Back in New York, Paley listened to an aircheck recording of Bing's audition. "That's the guy I was going to have you find for me," he fairly screamed. "He can stand a big CBS buildup. Sign him!"

Everett was sent for, and Bing was signed to a CBS contract at $600 a week, with more to come if they were able to land a sponsor.

A huge publicity buildup was launched, and a premiere date announced for a nightly series of fifteen-minute programs at prime time, 7 o'clock in the evening, on the coast-to-coast CBS network. No one before had ever received such a royal opportunity on radio. And yet, believe it or not, Bing blew it. So fraught with anxiety was he on the announced premiere date that he rehearsed all afternoon, singing for four solid hours. By 6 p.m. he had lost his voice. He was barely able to manage a croaking whisper. A throat specialist, hastily called in, diagnosed it as a severe case of laryngitis and sent Bing home to bed. At 7 o'clock a whole nation of curious radio listeners who had followed the publicity campaign tuned in, only to hear an announcer regretfully say that the Crosby debut had to be postponed.

It happened again, on two subsequent premieres. Bing had still not recovered his voice, and was beginning to wonder if it would ever return. Each time, the same announcement came over the airwaves: "The Bing Crosby program is postponed. Consult your local newspaper for the new opening date."

Finally, on the fourth try, Bing made it. Still shaky and not completely recovered, he held on to Eddie Lang for dear life, facing the microphone and backed by Freddie Rich's allstar CBS house orchestra. His brow shining with beads of perspiration, Bing felt his voice crack on one or two notes as he began humming a few bars of his new signature theme, "Where the Blue of the Night." The opening song on this history-making Crosby network debut was "Just One More Chance." By the time Bing was past the second bar, he knew his vocal chords were back on the track. This was confirmed by a smile and a wink from Eddie Lang as Bing, now brimming with confidence, let out full blast.

Two or three radio columnists printed some snide cracks about how fitting it was for Crosby to plead for "Just One More Chance" in his opening song after all those postponements. But the show was nevertheless an immediate success. Hundreds of telegrams poured in from all over the country during the first week. The "sustaining" program—which in radio parlance means sponsorless—was broadcast for only a brief time before a national sponsor, Cremo Cigars, bought the show for the entire season. The show, still done nightly, was lengthened from fifteen minutes to a half hour, and by midseason Crosby had developed such a national following that he threatened to usurp the throne of the current radio superstar, Rudy Vallee.

It was natural that a number of other pop singers began to copy Crosby's crooning style. Most were quickly dismissed as bad imitators by the radio critics. One of the few who made it was the late and great Russ Columbo. By a quirk of fate, I was involved in the start of that career too. And in a most hilarious way, I thought.

114

Russ was one of the first people I had met when I arrived in Hollywood. He was then a "mood music" violinist, a holdover from the silent film days. Mood musicians are an extinct breed today, but in those days they were indispensable on every shooting set. With no sound yet being recorded, they played whatever music was necessary to provide inspiration for the scene. If Mary Pickford had a weeping scene, for example, a pianist and violinist were right behind the camera playing the saddest music they could think of. In a love scene, they would help the lovers emote with a chorus of "Kiss Me Again." And so forth. There were still a few of them around when sound first arrived, since many of the stars' closeups were still being shot silent. Columbo worked as a team with pianist Solly Biano (later head casting director for Warner Brothers), and during my early days at Paramount they were still mooding it up for Clara Bow and Evelyn Brent, who always demanded their presence on the set.

But by late 1930, most of the mood musicians were out of work, victims of technological progress. Russ found work with several dance bands, doubling as violinist and vocalist. For a brief time, he worked with the Arnheim band at the Grove, one of the musicians backing Bing Crosby's solos. Russ himself had a very soft, barely audible singing voice that you couldn't hear ten feet away. But on a mike something magical happened. Amplified, the same faint voice suddenly had quality, feeling, and a remarkably smooth way of phrasing the lyrics. Russ soon put aside his fiddle —he never was much of a threat to Heifetz or Kreisler—and concentrated on his vocalizing, changing jobs frequently.

He was an incredibly handsome young man, with features that reminded you of Valentino. So I was not surprised when I found him on a Paramount set one day playing a small part that called for Russ to sing a song or two. After the first day's rushes were screened, the studio executives decided he photographed like a million dollars and ordered his part built up to a more important role. But no singing! Russ just mouthed the lyrics, while a singer who hasn't been heard from since dubbed the actual songs. Russ, of course, went on to become the second great new singing star of the early Thirties, outranked only by Crosby. Which I suppose proves something about the judgment of Hollywood's powers that be.

When Bing began clicking on network radio from New York, Russ changed his style. From a straight whispering baritone he became a Crosby-style crooner, adopting many of Bing's vocal

115

tricks; the same slurring and sliding up to a note, the whole works. The Crosby style was in and had created a big vogue, and Russ was now singing it for local consumption on independent radio stations around Los Angeles. He was by far the best of all the Crosby imitators, and he soon built up a strong local following.

It was around this time that famed composer Con Conrad entered the Columbo orbit. Con was one of my closest friends, first in New York and now in Hollywood. He seldom made a move without phoning to tell me about it. Having composed some pretty successful love songs like "Memory Lane" and "Lonesome and Sorry," Con now decided he must provide a romantic theme song for Russ Columbo, who by now was being talked about in music circles. Night after night Russ would come on local radio "cold"—without a theme song to his name. Con, having in mind what Crosby had done with "Just One More Chance," insisted that I must be the one to write a Columbo theme song with him. He would have it no other way. Regretfully, I told him I had to pass. Paramount had just farmed me out to a local stage producer named Franklyn Warner to write fifteen songs for a musical revue named *Temptations of 1931*, due to go into rehearsal in a month.

For me, it was a most unfortunate bit of timing, for *Temptations* never got off the ground. Because of the depression, Frank Warner's backer went broke and had to bow out. But Con and Columbo kept up their search. A girl named Gladys DuBois, who earned her livelihood as a movie extra, ran into Con at a party and showed him a lyric she had written. It was her first attempt, and she called it "You Call It Madness, But I Call It Love." Con set a tune to it, and it became the Russ Columbo radio theme. The sheet music came out with Russ's name as a co-author. I honestly don't know whether he actually had a hand in the writing or whether Con had merely cut him in. Whatever the case may be, the song was destined to become one of the great all-time standards.

Impressed with the way Con had come up with the much needed radio theme, Russ soon entered into a business arrangement with him. Con was to be his manager, receiving 25 percent of his earnings and footing all the bills for publicity expenses, travel, wardrobe, and whatever else was necessary.

About this time, Larry Spier phoned me from New York to say that he had persuaded Paramount to revise our contracts and give

116

us both a nice salary raise. The Paramount attorneys wanted me to meet with them in New York the following week to work out the details.

When I told Con I had booked a compartment on the Super-chief for New York, a sudden brainstorm hit him. "We'll all go—you, Russ and I," he fairly shouted. "The time has come for me to do what Everett Crosby did for Bing. I'm going to sell Russ to the *other* network—NBC!"

We were a happy threesome on the Superchief—I with antici-pations of an important new studio deal, and the Columbo-Con-rad duo full of enthusiastic plans. I had no part in their setup, except that Russ had been plugging a lot of my songs on his Los Angeles radio shows and I knew he would continue doing so if he landed a network spot.

Russ shared Con's tiny apartment in New York, and I checked into the St. Moritz Hotel around the corner on 59th Street. Con, who was a human dynamo if I ever saw one, lost no time in hiring not one but three press agents for Columbo, all working at the same time. The plan was to publicize him as the hottest new radio crooner to emerge from the Coast since Crosby, get his name in the leading columns every day—Winchell, Ed Sullivan, and the rest—and just play it cool until NBC was attracted by the buildup and sent for them. Every record company was looking for another Crosby, and Con had no trouble convincing RCA-Victor that he had the solution. Columbo records were waxed and rushed out in a hurry.

All kinds of publicity stunts were planted. Con arranged for Russ to get the key to the city, dedicate the newest skyscraper, and present the cup to the winner of the Belmont Stakes. I met the two of them in Lindy's one midnight, and I could see at a glance that something was amiss. It was written all over their faces. Russ had become the best-known *unemployed* celebrity in New York, his name in the papers seven days a week. But NBC hadn't called yet. What they needed was some kind of a blockbusting publicity stunt that would set the whole town talking about Russ Columbo, not the trivial fiddle-faddle that had been printed about him.

I could see they were both dejected, and tried to change the subject. "Guess who's staying at my hotel," I volunteered. "I saw her in the elevator twice today."

"Who?"

"Greta Garbo—that's who. She's right on my floor, three doors

117

down the hall. She came slinking out of her room in an old beatup raincoat this morning, and we rode down fifteen stories to the ground floor before I realized it was Garbo."

The flash in Con's eyes told me he was percolating. I could almost see the wheels going around inside his skull. Suddenly he snapped his fingers, vigorously.

"Hot damn!" he shouted. "You just sparked a hell of an idea, Sam."

Oldtimers and show business historians, if you asked them today, would swear up and down that the hottest romance of the early 1930's was the Garbo-Columbo affair. It captured more front-page space than any other showbiz event of its time. They would be correct on the latter count, but on the former one— sheer, unadulterated fiction. Here you have it right from the horse's mouth. I was in on the whole stunt from its inception, and I can now reveal, for the first time, that the entire mad affair was a figment of Con Conrad's delirious imagination. What actually happened was the following:

Con got one of his three flacks to plant an item in several well read columns to the effect that the *real* reason Russ had come to New York was because he couldn't bear to be three thousand miles away from Greta. One columnist hinted that Russ and Greta had been having an undercover romance in Hollywood, meeting on the sly so the studio heads wouldn't get wind of it.

Garbo at that time was without question the world's foremost box-office attraction. Anything and everything she did was news —important news to millions of fans. In the natural sequence of events, therefore, the various Manhattan city editors were bound to pick up the small item from the gossip columns and look into it —just in case. No newspaper wanted to miss out on what might be a big story about the great Garbo.

G.G., of course, was as elusive as ever. Her phobia about reporters and interviews was well known, and she would go to almost any lengths to avoid publicity. But one enterprising reporter for the tabloid *New York Graphic*, unable to reach her on the phone, camped outside the hotel entrance until she emerged from a taxicab late one night. Garbo had already been forewarned, having been cautioned by MGM's publicity men that reporters were on her trail.

The MGM boys had no idea whether she and Russ really were an "item," and didn't even bother to ask, knowing that she always shunned all questions about her personal life like the plague.

118

The *Graphic* man stopped Greta and asked her point-blank if she and Columbo were romantically involved. Greta stopped short, looked him right in the eye, and said, "I have *absolutely nothing* to say! Please go away!" She brushed him aside quickly, and fairly ran to the elevator.

The reporter phoned Russ bright and early the next morning. "I saw Miss Garbo last night and she refused to discuss the subject of a romance with you. How about you, Mr. Columbo?"

Russ, coached by the ever present Conrad, pretended to be furious. "What the hell kind of a cad do you think I am?" he burst out. "If the lady told you she has nothing to say, what makes you think you'll get anything out of me? Did it ever occur to you that people have a right to privacy?" Then he hung up quickly.

That did it. It was still speculative, not yet a front-page story. But the newspaper writers figured that if it were untrue, Garbo would have denied it immediately instead of refusing to discuss it. Feature writers on several papers played up the item, pro and con. Winchell's broadcast said the romance was for real.

A few days later, Con went to a Park Avenue florist and sprang for the largest and most spectacular basket of roses in the shop. Even in those deflated days, the basket set Con back some $150, plus an extra five to have it delivered to the St. Moritz Hotel at once. Con had previously run over to the St. Moritz and estimated the width of the elevator door. At the florist shop, he made sure the spread of the roses was just a little too wide to get inside the elevator. To one of the largest stems he tied a large card that read, in Russ's own handwriting: "To Greta—I'm sorry they are bothering you. Hope this makes up for it. Russ."

Con's press agent had already tipped off the city editors that there might be a break in the story that afternoon, right in the St. Moritz lobby. The reporters were there when the flowers arrived. With no way to squeeze the basket inside the elevator, the roses were parked in the center of the lobby—long enough for a few flash bulbs to pop, including a closeup of the card from Russ. Other newspaper men and photographers, alerted to the story, kept popping in all afternoon.

This time it did make the tabloid front pages. The reporters bit like a bunch of hungry swordfish. Garbo meanwhile left town, insisting to the last that she had "absolutely nothing to say about it—no comment whatsoever. Just leave me alone, please!"

Russ, whose beautiful features were now familiar to newspaper and magazine readers, was finally signed to an NBC radio deal

119

and booked for starring engagements in leading hotel niteries. Meanwhile, "You Call It Madness" climbed high on all the record charts. He was definitely on his way. In no time he had become Crosby's chief rival. There was even a stretch where he was booked into the Brooklyn Paramount Theater in opposition to Bing, who was headlining at the New York Paramount across the river. Paramount's press agents went on a publicity spree with that one, calling it the "Battle of the Baritones." Capacity audiences jammed both theaters. Eventually, Russ fronted his own band, successfully toured the country, and wound up back in Hollywood, starring in musical films. When the Garbo tale was long forgotten, Russ kept sailing along on his own talents—a smooth, silky voice that never failed to thrill the nation's female half even though it still sounded somewhat like Bing's, plus unforgettable charm, good looks, and impeccable taste in every performance.

I revealed the whole story of the phony Garbo romance to only one person, Jerry Wald, who was then breaking into the newspaper game with a radio column in the *Graphic*, but I first made him swear on his life that he would not print the story. Jerry kept his word, but a year later he wrote a three-page outline about the Garbo-Columbo stunt and sold it to Warner Brothers as the basis for a Dick Powell musical. Jerry insisted that the Warner deal include a clause to bring him to Hollywood to collaborate with the writers of the screenplay and to act as "technical advisor." By the time the film was previewed, Jerry had talked Jack Warner into a deal to produce his own musicals for the studio, a career in which his rise proved to be as rapid as it was aggressive.

But despite the whole epic publicity stunt, and despite the Dick Powell musical and the legend that has persisted to this day, I can assure you that right up to the time of his tragic and untimely death three years later, at the age of 26*, Russ never did get to meet Garbo—not even once. In fact, to my knowledge the only

*Russ Columbo was accidentally killed on September 2, 1934, at the home of a friend. The friend, about to light a cigarette, struck a match on an antique pistol that he was using on his desk as a paperweight. The pistol, which no one knew was loaded, went off and the bullet ricocheted off the desk and into Columbo's head.

Just prior to the accident, Russ had suggested to Universal Pictures that they borrow my services from Paramount to write the score of a new Columbo musical Universal was planning to make. (Con Conrad was tied up, writing songs for Fred Astaire and Ginger Rogers in *Gay Divorcee*.) I had just attended several meetings at Universal to discuss the loan-out arrangements, and I have often wondered how our two careers might have evolved if the tragedy had not occurred.

serious romance Russ ever had in his short life was with another legendary star, Carole Lombard. There was no make-believe about that one. Russ himself confided to me that it was love, not madness. I knew that Carole felt the same way on that sad day in September 1934, for I was then working on songs for her forthcoming Paramount film *Hands Across the Table* and speaking to her frequently—more about Russ than about the film.

And now, to get back to my original reason for the New York trip. I found that the Paramount home-office attorneys had prepared a completely new contract for me. Up to then, I was getting a weekly drawing account and salary which was supposed to be fixed for five years, a straight contract with no interim raises. Now they were changing it to provide for a raise of $250 every year for another five years. But there was one big hitch. Larry and I each still owned ten percent of the music publishing firm we had sold, and Paramount now wanted that. I didn't know what to do. Larry, too, was in a quandary.

I had recently taken on an agent in Hollywood, Arthur Landau. I felt that he should have gone to New York to represent me, but Landau was preoccupied with managing Jean Harlow at that time and couldn't take the time off. I phoned him when I got back to the hotel, telling him about the new twist that had come up. Paramount wanted my remaining ten percent in return for a new contract with annual salary hikes. Landau advised me to hold out for a lump sum of money in addition to the new contract. "Look," he pointed out, "you've given them four smash song hits in less than eighteen months at the studio. They need you more than you need them. If they turn you down, I can get you a better deal at any studio in town."

I didn't believe him, so I settled for the new contract plus a small fraction of the lump sum Landau had advised me to hold out for. The Paramount people told me it was the best they could do: things were really tough all over the country, and studio budgets were being cut drastically.

It wasn't long before Larry Spier and I both realized that selling our remaining shares was a bad piece of business judgment. Today, Famous Music is one of the country's music-publishing giants. I'd love to own that ten percent interest right now.

I returned to the West Coast right after Russ Columbo's Waldorf opening and was assigned to a new musical that was planned as a starring vehicle for Lily Damita, fresh out of a two-year run as the star of the J. Fred Coots-Benny Davis Broadway musical *Sons of Guns*. The film was titled *This Is the Night*. For some strange reason, almost everything about it has vanished from my mind. The one thing I do remember is that a fellow named Cary Grant had just done a pretty good screen test and was making his Hollywood debut in the film.

Somewhere around that period—I appear to have a mental block about the date or the month it happened—I seemed to sense that something was wrong at the studio. Shooting starts were being postponed. Scripts were scrapped. Deals that had been heavily publicized were being cancelled left and right. Players' options were being dropped instead of taken up. People around the lot were suddenly looking grim.

It was a rough period in the Great Depression, and it was finally catching up with Hollywood, which had escaped it up to then. Paramount, like most other studios, was merely being defensive, cutting down on every possible expense. The film industry was financed by Wall Street, and Wall Street was in a heck of a lot of trouble during those years. The message the studio received was to cut everything to the bone.

I wasn't worried myself. I had a contract that still had a long while to go. What bothered me was that several new pictures I was assigned to were suddenly shelved. For the first time, I found myself sitting around with time on my hands.

Idleness is something I have never been able to accept. The few times in my life it has been forced on me have been periods when I would rack my brain to dream up a project I could become absorbed in. This unexpected lull came at a time that tried the souls of all creative people. The depression had now reached such depths that it was all but impossible to get new projects off the ground. I had a couple of musical show ideas that Broadway producers had been intrigued with, but now I found that enthusiasm was hard to arouse. People were not buying tickets, and show backers were jumping out of Wall Street skyscrapers.

Moreover, despite the security of a weekly paycheck, there were signs of the times in Hollywood that I found scary. Banks began to fail all over town. Mortgages were being foreclosed at the drop of a payment. I shuddered a bit at my first sight of a breadline. It was all very depressing. I began to wonder whether the studios would eventually close their doors as other businesses were doing. The gloom around town was thicker than the Los Angeles smog.

In the midst of it all, I received a phone call one day from my friend Charles Vanda, a press agent who, like so many of his colleagues, was out of work. But I knew he was too resourceful not to be able to outthink the situation.

Charlie had learned that Hollywood's leading hotel, the Hollywood Roosevelt, was looking for a dance band. He wanted to drop over to my office to discuss it. Ready for any opportunity to keep busy, I told him to come by.

Becoming a bandleader had never crossed my mind, but Charlie soon convinced me that it was a logical field for any composer. He knew the management of the hotel, and phoned them from my office. Scarcely believing what I was hearing, I heard him elaborate profusely on my capabilities while he rattled off a list of my song hits and the vocal recordings I had made. "When can I bring him over?" I heard him say. "Would this afternoon be too soon?"

Next thing I knew we were driving to the Roosevelt. In a few minutes were seated in the manager's office.

I did very little talking. Charlie had all the sales arguments at his fingertips. So persuasive was he that before long the manager was apologizing to Charlie because all the hotel could afford to pay for a band was $1,750 a week.

"You know business has been way off in the room," he explained. "We'd be happy just to break even. But anything over $1,750 would put the room in the red."

We finally settled for $1,750 plus half of any cover charges above $15,000 a week, with the deal hinging on whether I could obtain a leave of absence from my Paramount contract.

I rushed back to the studio, arranged for the leave, and spent the rest of the day and evening lining up musicians. Quite a few of the better studio musicians were very much available in those lean days. I was able to hire ten outstanding men, two of whom were also arrangers, at the local scale, which in that deflated year was around $85 a week.

We rehearsed furiously for about ten days. I learned the words to a few dozen of the songs then currently popular. We finally opened at the Blossom Room in the Hollywood Roosevelt, following Ben Bernie and his Orchestra. Arthur Johnston had given me a lightning course in conducting, and I fell into it much more easily than I thought I would.

My opening at the Blossom Room was a glamour-studded night that is still as fresh in my memory as if it were the night before last. Charlie Vanda, who was now handling the publicity for both me and the hotel, had arranged for a barrage of kleig lights outside the hotel, a radio announcer from KNX to catch the celebrities coming in, and all the usual trimmings. Very nervous and unsure of myself, I took up the baton for the first dance. A minute later was amazed to see, dancing before my eyes, a number of well photographed faces like Jean Harlow, Joan Crawford, and Norma Shearer. Many of my friends from New York showed up. I noticed Eddie Cantor with his wife Ida and several of their daughters walking over to a ringside table during that first dance. And it seemed as if the whole Paramount crowd drifted in en masse during the rest of the evening. Promptly at 10 o'clock, we began the first of my regular nightly programs over KNX. I opened the broadcast with "Just One More Chance," still on the bestseller list after all these weeks.

There was something of a letdown after opening night. It dawned on me that the Blossom Room did a sellout business only on the premiere nights. The manager was right when he said business was off.

Nevertheless, the room did manage to break even, and I stayed on the job week after week. One summer afternoon I was rehearsing the band. During a short break, I joined some of the musicians who had found a good place to sun themselves, a broad terrace just off the third floor of the hotel. I looked around and noted a lot of good space going to waste, except for a few stray sunbathers. Something clicked in my head. I rushed down to tell the manager I'd like to try opening the third floor terrace as a roof garden at night, moving the band up from the Blossom Room. It was a warm summer, and the airconditioning in the Blossom Room was primitive and inadequate, as most hotel airconditioners were in 1931. Outdoors, however, the California nights were pleasant and balmy. You could always depend on the weather at that time of year. The rainy season would not start for months.

Just before we switched over to the Roosevelt Roof, my drummer quit to join a traveling band for more money. I auditioned some new ones. The one who got the job was a young man with an elfish grin named Spike Jones. He arrived with not only the customary gear that drummers use, but also a whole trailerful of paraphernalia including a full octave of automobile horns, washbasins, anvils, fire alarms, sirens, and you name it. Spike had just come in from the sticks, looking for his first professional job.

The Roof Garden did the trick for me and the hotel. Lean grosses were a thing of the past. The place caught on to such an extent that every night was a sellout. We were topping the

Cocoanut Grove's business. Hollywood stars were tipping Joe Mann, the affable maitre de, twenty-five and fifty dollars just to get a table. For the first time, the hotel was going beyond the $15,000 weekly cover-charge total, where my override began. I received $3,500 in salary-plus-percentage after my second week on the Roof. Other establishments began noticing the successful business on the Roof. Soon a new roof garden opened atop the Montmartre Restaurant down the street on Hollywood Boulevard, featuring Hal Grayson and his band.

By the end of the summer, the hotel was paying me a goodly sum every week in cover-charge percentages. Then the management asked me to take a cut before going downstairs again to the Blossom Room. MCA was offering to put in other bands who were willing to work for a flat salary of $1,500 or less.

I chose not to take the cut, not only because I resented it after packing the place night after night in the depths of the depression, but also because the Paramount people were asking me how soon my leave of absence would be over. They hadn't intended for it to be an indefinite leave, they told me, just for a few weeks or so. They even hinted that I was abusing their generosity.

Two weeks later—enough time to give notice to my musicians —my brief career as a bandleader ended, and I was back in my office at Paramount.

When I learned why the studio had wanted me to end my lucrative leave, I was fit to be tied. There was still not a single important musical on the Paramount schedule for the second half of 1931. Musicals had reached the saturation point by mid-1931— the old story of giving the public too much of a good thing. Moreover, musicals were just too expensive to make in that period. They were to be revived with a bang a year later, but of course I had no way of knowing that. At any rate, the only tune flickers on Paramount's schedule were several for the Latin-American market, entirely in Spanish. South American countries and Mexico were still demanding them. So I spent the rest of the year on low-budget Latin films like *Honeymoon Hate* composing tangos, rhumbas and boleros which never saw the light of day north of the Rio Grande. Most of Paramount's stable of songwriters were off the payroll except for Rodgers and Hart, who had contracted to do a new Chevalier script which was postponed to the following year. Dick Whiting was farmed out to score the Broadway musical *Take a Chance*. Leo Robin and Ralph Rainger were on temporary leave. So I drew the unappealing Latin assign-

125

ments. I also did a couple of numbers for a Western epic called *Stampede*. All in all, a boring autumn.

To add to my irritations, things were not going well domestically. The incompatibility between Dorothy and me had widened during the summer, while I was spending six nights a week away from home at the Roosevelt Roof. Finally she packed up and left for the artists' colony in Key West, Florida, taking our son Larry with her. Dorothy had a flair for painting, and I knew she wanted to pursue an artistic career. We were divorced within a few months of her departure.

My first 1932 film was not really a studio assignment but a songwriting contest. Director Josef von Sternberg, on leave from Paramount to direct *The Blue Angel* for UFA in Berlin, had discovered a sexy-looking actress named Marlene Dietrich in a German stage musical and had starred her, with great success, in that memorable film. In 1930, von Sternberg brought Marlene back with him to Hollywood. He convinced studio heads Jesse Lasky and Ben Schulberg that Marlene could be Paramount's answer to Garbo.

A massive publicity campaign was launched. Dietrich was touted as "the woman that all women want to see." I vividly recall her arrival in Hollywood, amid great fanfare. Her first appearance in the Paramount dining room created something of a sensation. Even established stars like Claudette Colbert, Carole Lombard, and Nancy Carroll were craning their necks for a glimpse of the new arrival.

Von Sternberg introduced Marlene to American audiences as Gary Cooper's leading lady in *Morocco*. So great was her impact that the studio next decided to give her solo-star billing in a lavish musical, remembering that she had first attracted attention on the Berlin stage in revues.

The studio invited me and a number of prominent free-lance songwriters to a studio projection room one day for a screening of *The Blue Angel*, especially to see the classic sequence where Marlene sang "Falling in Love Again" astride the back of a chair.

We were all impressed, but none of us cared much about the proposal to write songs for La Dietrich on "spec," with the star and her director, von Sternberg, selecting the best ones. All of us were writers of established hits. We were supposed to be beyond that sort of thing. However, a few of us had songs "in the trunk," either unpublished or discarded from other films. These we submitted.

126

Several days later, the songwriters who had submitted leftover songs met with Marlene and her director in a rehearsal room in the music building. They played their songs. I felt like a novice on an audition for a job, but I thought I did have a pretty good song that might otherwise go to waste. We went in one at a time. I was last. Dietrich was sitting up straight in a high-backed armchair, looking for all the world like her characterization of Catherine the Great. I couldn't help but wonder if she was beginning to believe her publicity. Joe introduced me, and she stuck out her hand as if I were supposed to kiss it or something. I didn't; I just shook it.

The song I played was one I had written to a lyric of Leo Robin's called "You Little So and So." I knew that it would fit beautifully into a sequence in this first Dietrich musical. It was to be called *Blonde Venus*, and I had already read the shooting script. Before I was halfway through the chorus, I could see that Dietrich was obviously delighted. Suddenly she lost her aloofness. Her eyes lit up, and she began humming along with me.

"That's the only one I've heard that I like," was her verdict, and I knew that Leo and I had won the contest. Not only that, but she asked the studio to assign us to write most of her other numbers for the score. Among the other *Blonde Venus* songs we turned out was Dietrich's celebrated "Hot Voodoo," a rhythmic production number which was later revived by Paramount in the 1975 film *Day of the Locust*, adapted from the Nathaniel West novel about Hollywood in the Thirties.

I supervised the recording and shooting of the *Blonde Venus* songs myself, and found Dietrich a joy to work with. She was a good trouper, cooperative, and nothing at all like the secretive, Garbo-like woman of mystery the Paramount press agents and fan magazine writers were selling to the public. I guess one reason I felt such rapport with her was that I had read in a publicity release that she was born on the same day and the same year as I. Was it written in the stars that I was destined to compose her first American score? Maybe so—except that I don't believe in astrology.

The next film luminary I worked for was his highness, the great Cecil B. DeMille. It was only one song, and nothing to write home about; but the story of this assignment reveals something about Hollywood bureaucracy.

DeMille, one of the founders of Paramount, had just returned to the studio after an eight-year absence. He had not yet met the music executives, but I had run into him casually at parties. I saw him in the commissary one day, and he asked me to drop in to his office on the lot the following morning. I arrived on time, and after searching inspections by a number of receptionists, secretaries, and assistants, each in turn, I was ushered into the private office of the renowned producer-director.

DeMille was then in the midst of preparing for one of his super-epics on biblical subjects, this one *The Sign of the Cross*.

"It's not a musical," he explained, "but I was wondering how you'd feel about writing one song for a big festival sequence."

Somewhat dubiously, I said I wouldn't mind. What kind of a song did he have in mind?

I have never fogotten the exact answer he gave me, and so I will quote it verbatim:

"What I need here is a sort of early Roman blues—the kind they used to play around the time of Christ."

For a moment, I thought he was putting me on. So I laughed, just to go along with the gag. But I soon realized he was serious as he described the number as he visualized it.

I took part of the script home with me and spent one whole evening staring at it in perplexity. DeMille was by far the most important producer I had ever worked with. I didn't want to fluff this assignment. But an early Roman blues circa the time of Christ? How in the world was I going to tackle that one?

Almost desperate, I found a poem by Keats that seemed to fit the mood of the scene. I set a quasi-religious, mournful blues melody to it. If this wasn't what he wanted, I was prepared to bow out.

I sent DeMille a message that the song was finished, but got no reply for something like two months. I knew that he had thousands of details to occupy his mind in a blockbuster production like *The Sign of the Cross*, and I secretly hoped that maybe by this time the sequence and the song had been cut out of the script. No such luck. Eventually I received a phone message that Mr. DeMille would be in my office to hear the song "on the first of next month, immediately after lunch."

On the appointed day, someone phoned me as soon as I arrived at my office and said, "Mr. DeMille will be in your office at exactly one-thirty p.m."

Around noon, another phone caller informed me: "This is Mr. DeMille's secretary. He is just leaving for lunch, and will go directly to your office when he finishes—around one-thirty."

At one o'clock, I was back from my own lunch. The phone rang again. "Mr. DeMille will soon be through lunching, and will go right to your office."

By this time, the message had really sunk in. By God, I knew that the Great Man would honor me with his presence precisely at one-thirty p.m.

It was now 1:25. Again, the ring of the phone. "Mr. DeMille is just leaving the restaurant." This time it was an entirely new voice, and I interposed: "I know, I know—he'll be right over. Right?"

"Right."

I placed an armchair next to the piano, emptied a few ashtrays, and tried to look as nonchalant as possible—although I was now keyed up to the point of nervous prostration.

About ten minutes later, my door opened. It was Mitch Leisen, then DeMille's artistic assistant, in the days before his own brilliant directorial career. Mitch walked in and sat down, with one brief announcement which I still find difficult to believe: *"Mr. DeMille is approaching!"*

Maybe next there should have been fanfare of trumpets and sirens. But all that happened a moment later was that DeMille entered, attired in the usual puttees and surrounded by a whole battalion of assistants, script girls, and stooges. He looked at his watch and said, "I have exactly eight minutes to get back to the set. Can I hear the song, please?"

The best theatrical climax to this story would of course have been for DeMille to turn it down after the elaborate buildup. But to my surprise, he liked it. He was particularly stuck by the lyric. I was much too flustered to tell him it was a poem by John Keats, although at a later date I did inform him of this.

After the song was shot and recorded, I attended a screening of the sequence in DeMille's projection room and was not a bit surprised to find that only a snatch of it was left in, heard dimly in the background during an important closeup scene dominated by dialogue. You had to have pretty good ears to catch it. I attended the gala premiere of *The Sign of the Cross* later that year at the L.A. Paramount. It was a studio must. To my great astonishment, up on the screen, in giant letters, was my name among the major credits before the film began. It read (and still does):

"LYRICS BY SAM COSLOW"

To you, John Keats—wherever you are, up there among the immortals—my humble apologies!

DeMille asked for me on only two other occasions. The first

was when he asked me to write a pirate song for *The Buccaneer,* a song that was again reduced to a mere quickie behind dialogue. The last occasion was very brief, but just as unbelievable as the "early Roman blues." C.B. phoned me at home one evening, explaining that he was working late at the studio editing a film that was soon to be sent over to the music department for background scoring. I can't remember which film it was, but I'll never forget his words:

"Sam, in your opinion who would be the best classical scorer in the music department to compose a ten-minute background sequence on the order of Beethoven's Seventh Symphony?"

"Gosh, I don't really know. Why don't you *use* Beethoven's Seventh, C.B.?"

"No, I don't want anything that's ever been heard before. This picture must have all original music. Every bar."

"It's a mighty tall order, a symphony like Beethoven's Seventh. How much time would our man have to write it?"

"I must have it by Tuesday."

"Tuesday! Good grief, C.B., it took Beethoven *four years* to compose the Seventh!"

"Yes, I know, but they've cut down on my budget and I'm on a split-second schedule."

I referred C.B. to music head Nat Finston, and I know he got his Beethoven-type ten-minute symphony. I have never heard it so I cannot comment on its quality.

Now, I do not mean to imply by the above anecdotes that De-Mille was an idiot. He certainly was anything but that. He was, in fact, a genius, an exacting perfectionist to the last detail, as efficient as he was artistically talented. The only way he could issue orders was to phrase them in everyday language that could be easily understood. Watching him direct a big mob sequence from high up on a camera crane, with five hundred things going on at once below him, each individual segment commanded by a different deputy, you knew that this man had to work with a meticulously organized staff, trained to operate with clockwork precision.

Spring 1932 was a critical period. The depression was now accelerating so severely that theaters were unable to pay their film rentals, and for a while Paramount was threatened with bankruptcy. However, by summer it became apparent that the public was starved for musicals after the long hiatus. Rodgers and Hart

130

had finally completed their Maurice Chevalier score for *Love Me Tonight.* The film had been rushed into release and was doing capacity business. Warner Brothers was beginning to prepare the scripts for the first elaborate Busby Berkeley films, which were to set the standard for plush musicals in the early 1930's. With unemployment now around 25 percent, musicals were escapist entertainment by which jobless people could forget their troubles for a few hours for the small sum of 25 or 50 cents a seat, which was all the traffic could bear in those depressed times.

As a result of this mass flight from everyday problems, the movie industry was one of the first to recover financially. In mid-1932 studio budgets were expanded in a courageous display of optimism.

By this time, Paramount executives had become aware that "Just One More Chance" was an outstanding international success. Producers on the lot began asking for Arthur Johnston and me for their songwriting team. Arthur received a new contract to write songs exclusively, in place of his coaching-arranging deal, and we were asked to work as a team henceforth. I had a few misgivings about this. I had enjoyed the freedom of choosing collaborators to suit my fancy, or writing both words and music alone, as the mood hit me. I had never worked as part of a steady team, and wondered if I would find the new arrangement too confining and inflexible for my working style. However, I knew that both Arthur and I could write either lyrics or music as the need might arise, and we could supply production ideas as well. I began to reflect that perhaps two heads might be better than one. Should one of us have a dry spell, chances were that the other would be in good form. So I agreed, after a bit of soul-searching.

The first musical we were assigned to was a starring vehicle for Kate Smith. The foremost female radio songstress of the day, she was practically without serious competition. The film was to be called *Hello, Everybody,* Kate's familiar greeting to open her radio shows. The studio, at great expense, had hired Fanny Hurst to write the original story.

It was an easy assignment for us. Kate was strictly a pop singer, preferring the type of song that we were most at home with. We turned out a score of eight numbers in short order, like rolling off a log. But getting Kate's approval turned out to be a bit trying.

Kate had rented a Beverly Hills mansion, and Arthur and I were invited there one evening to play the score. Kate was there with her manager, Ted Collins, and both were eager to hear the new songs. The demonstration took hours. After each number Kate just looked at Ted, who would say "Let's hear it again." We soon gathered that Ted made the decisions for Kate: the selection of songs, her scenes in the script, and just about everything else. Each number was played about a dozen times and thoroughly discussed from every angle before Ted nodded approval.

As the evening wore on, I could see Arthur getting restless. Seated at the concert grand piano which graced the living room, he looked nervous. I saw him throwing furtive glances toward the adjoining room, which looked like a small, cozy den. I should explain here that Arthur was what might be best described as a "nipper"—not really an alcoholic, but a thirsty soul who liked to have a glass of something or other within arm's reach throughout the evening. Earlier on that warm, sultry night, we had driven out to Jack's-on-the-Beach for a seafood dinner, so by now Arthur was thirstier than usual.

By the time all of the songs were played, replayed, and discussed, I looked at Arthur and his tongue was practically hanging out. It was by now close to midnight. Kate, obviously a teetotaler and a respecter of the Prohibition laws, had not offered so much as a Coke or a glass of water, let alone what Arthur craved. We had saved our best number, "Moon Song," for last. When Ted nodded approval, Kate stood up with a broad smile and announced, "I'm going to the kitchen for a few minutes. I'll be back with some *refreshments.*"

Arthur beamed, looking like a death-cell inmate who had just been reprieved from the gas chamber. He winked at me and played another chorus, replete with flourishes and arpeggios.

Kate soon returned, bearing a large tray that held an assortment of little cakes or something, which we gathered she had made herself. They looked perfectly luscious and I ate a dozen or so. But Arthur, who now appeared on the verge of collapse, begged off with some excuse about being on a diet. He was miserable.

The outstanding hit of the picture was, of course, "Moon Song," which since then has become so linked with Kate Smith as to be almost a mark of identification surpassed only by her famous theme, "When the Moon Comes Over the Mountain," and of course "God Bless America." Apparently the only bad decisions Collins made were his approval of a shooting script and title, for the film itself bombed. Judging from the reported grosses, a more appropriate title would have been *Hello, Nobody.*

132

Somehow, the public did not spark to the idea of Kate starring in a romantic love story and languishing after cowboy star Randolph Scott. The *New York Herald-Tribune* in its review stated: "Untouched by humor or even the suggestion of lightness, the picture's principal attraction is the songs." Lou Diamond, one of the home-office executives from New York, told me afterward that "Moon Song" had saved the day for the film: Famous Music's profit on just that one song represented far more money to the parent corporation, Paramount, than it lost on the film. Kate, although she never made another movie except for a spot in *This Is the Army* ten years later during World War II, resumed her role as the queen of the medium that had made her a star, radio. Today, 44 years after *Hello, Everybody,* Kate still turns up in big TV specials.

Following "Moon Song," our second number-one song in a row as a team, the studio began throwing musical scripts at us from all directions. However, there was one script they hadn't sent us, and we wanted that one more than all the rest.

Paramount had just used Bing Crosby as one of a big cast of radio stars in *The Big Broadcast,* a revue type of film about the radio industry. Actually, it was a new and experimental kind of musical, with the studio mostly interested in finding out which of the nation's radio favorites were also potential film stars. Of the long list of airwave names that had spots in the film, only two acts, Bing Crosby and Burns and Allen, received the sort of acclaim that meant Hollywood stardom. Paramount signed both acts to star in future musicals.

Following the release of *Big Broadcast,* Bing was back in New York still selling smokes, this time as the star of the weekly Chesterfield hour. He was also turning out hit after hit on Brunswick Records, starring in deluxe night-club engagements, and headlining in stage shows at the country's largest movie palaces—all at the same time. His four-a-day appearances at our company's large Paramount Theaters in Times Square and in Brooklyn stretched out to 28 consecutive weeks, smashing every box-office record at those houses. From all these activities, the money was pouring into the Crosby coffers. Brother Everett was soon forced to hire consultants to find places to invest Bing's burgeoning wealth. Orange-juice packagers, office buildings, racetracks, and show-business enterprises were to be among the vehicles used for investment. The man who only a year before was struggling to

133

provide a bare living for his new wife and himself was now well on the way toward amassing what eventually became one of the two largest individual fortunes in show business, the other being that of his future co-star, Bob Hope. I don't think Bing ever knew how much money was rolling in each week, or how fast it was all pyramiding. Everett, now augmented by two more Crosby brothers, was relieving Bing of all the business details, leaving Bing to concentrate on his singing and his golf. The fact that many of these investments were accumulated at the bargain-basement prices of the early Thirties, when anyone with some cash could acquire practically anything he wanted for peanuts, didn't hurt much either.

Arthur and I had learned that the studio was preparing, as Crosby's first solo starring vehicle, a lavish filmization of *College Humor*, adapted from the popular novel *Bachelor of Arts* by Dean Pales, a book we had read and knew to be sprinkled with logical spots for numbers. That was the script we wanted. Crosby had by now become a real powerhouse as a songmaker. The combined impact of his radio appearances, the eagerly awaited monthly recordings on Brunswick's release list, and now the big musical films planned for him, were enough to catapult any good song to the top of the charts. We were well aware that the *College Humor* score was a prize that every songsmith in the land coveted. I say this without fear of contradiction, for aside from the five Crosby films I worked on, other Crosby scores were later written by such immortals as Irving Berlin, Cole Porter and Rodgers and Hart.

As much as we wanted to do *College Humor*, at Paramount you just didn't ask for an assignment, any more than a doctor goes after a wealthy patient. The accepted thing to do was to just sit there and wait for it. Sometimes you got the one you wanted. Other times the dice came up with someone else's number. So we did just that—sat there and waited, making a pretense of reading the other scripts that had been sent to us. Sat there and just hoped that the studio heads would see the obvious justice and good sense of giving the plum to the team that had turned out Bing's biggest-selling song hit. Day after day, we sat around waiting for news. The suspense was something awful.

The anxiety ended one morning at Oblath's Diner across the street from the studio. I was having breakfast and reading Louella Parsons' column in the *Los Angeles Examiner*. Right there in her column was the item we were waiting for. Louella revealed that she had learned through the grapevine that Paramount was assigning the score of Bing's first starrer to the writers of his popular hit, "Just One More Chance."

Arthur and I went to the Grove that night and opened a bottle of champagne. We were so elated that we forgot to be sore at the studio for telling Louella before us. In fact, that night we weren't mad at anybody.

College Humor, as we expected, was a juicy, gratifying assignment. The picture, directed by Wesley Ruggles, established Bing as a film superstar and was one of the top grossers of 1933. Three of our *College Humor* songs achieved hit status: "Learn to Croon," "Down the Old Ox Road," and "Moonstruck"—all remembered to this day as early Crosby standards.

"Learn to Croon," in fact, contained a vocal trick for Bing which he capitalized on forever after. The middle section of the chorus goes:

> You murmur "Boo boo boo, boo boo"
> —And when you do,
> She'll murmur "Boo boo boo, boo boo"
> And whisper love words to you.

The "Boo boo boo" sound has been the familiar Crosby trademark throughout the years.

"Down the Old Ox Road" was a sneaky bit of lyrical quasi-pornography which somehow got by the censors. I'll never know why. Especially in those Victorian movie days, when the Motion Picture Producers Association rules did not even permit a word like "damn" to be used. In the script, it was brought out that when a college boy seduced a girl into sexual fulfillment, he was taking her "down the old ox road." Girls who had been down the ox road were the ones most likely to succeed with college lads, as we were reminded throughout the story. The short chorus of the song really left nothing to the imagination if you knew the code words, which apparently the MPPA censors didn't. I was almost sure it would be deleted from the final cut of the film when I wrote:

> Down the old ox road,
> Though you'll never find out where it is by looking in
> maps,

With a little investigation you'll discover perhaps
That this old tradition's not a place, but just a
   proposition
On the old ox road, the old ox road.

The lyric got by that way, and has never been changed.

Shortly after the film was completed, I attended a gala house-warming party at the palatial new home Bing had just built at Toluca Lake. The party also served for the christening ceremony of Bing and Dixie's first son, Gary. It was during this party that Everett Crosby told me that Arthur and I were also to do the second Crosby starrer, *Too Much Harmony*. Once again, we were the last to find out!

The second script was already nearing completion, an original screen play by Joe Mankiewicz (who went on from there to become one of Hollywood's top-ranking writer-director-producers). Bing had very little time off between the two films. As for us, although we had only a few weeks to write the score, we nevertheless came up with four more numbers that were high up on all the charts, and earned even more royalties than the three *College Humor* hits had done. The score contained "Thanks," "The Day You Came Along," "I Guess It Had to Be That Way," all featured by Bing, and a fourth standard, "Black Moonlight," which was sung not by Bing but by Kitty Kelly, who we all knew got the number because she was the girlfriend of the producer, Bill Le Baron. Kitty did a creditable job with it, although many people still think of "Black Moonlight" as a Crosby number, doubtless because of his great recording. It was revived in the Fifties by Perry Como, who came up with a brilliant recording.

Too Much Harmony, which was directed by Eddie Sutherland, landed Bing Crosby solidly in the Top Ten box-office attractions of 1933 in the national poll of theater operators. Bing was up there with film veterans like Will Rogers, Wallace Beery, and Greta Garbo. Paramount, in their full-page ads for *Too Much Harmony* in the *Hollywood Reporter* and other trade papers, proclaimed to the nation's movie theaters: "Flash! This is the *third* picture this year for which Sam Coslow and Arthur Johnston have contributed America's top song hit."

Meanwhile, back in my personal life, with a couple of songs in the hit category, I decided it might be a good time to get married again. I was never cut out for the singles game, and soon I started

136

seeing a good deal of a young actress named Esther Muir, who had just divorced Busby Berkeley and was ready to be caught on the rebound. On a sudden impulse, we drove across the border one Sunday and were married in Mexicali by a Mexican judge.

We leased Garbo's former home on Angelo Drive in Beverly Hills, and every day during the twelve months of our lease a busload of tourists stopped in front of the house precisely at 5 p.m., walked up to our front lawn, and took dozens of snapshots with great enthusiasm. The house was still listed as the Garbo home at the office of the sightseeing bus. When I told the bus driver she hadn't lived there for several years, he turned to the tourists and said, "See what I mean? She's still denying it!"

Actually, the previous occupant of the house had been the Mexican firecracker, Lupe Velez, during her hectic affair with Gary Cooper. The owner of the house, when he first showed us through it, pointed with pride to some kingsized dents in the master bedroom walls and told us, "That's where Lupe threw some heavy vases at Gary during their fights. It's a lucky thing he ducked."

I was busier than ever during this period. Besides working on important studio musicals and embarking on a new married life, I was also doing a great deal of moonlighting. Previously, after my stint at the Roosevelt Hotel, Nat Finston had arranged for me to record "Isn't It Romantic," the Rodgers and Hart-Chevalier hit, on RCA-Victor records with the full Paramount studio orchestra in back of me. It became a rare item—a twelve-inch vocal recording on 78, one of the few made in that size.

The record attracted some attention and led to a resumption of my RCA recording contract, which I had dropped in midstream when I embarked for Hollywood four years before. RCA by now had a West Coast recording studio, and I did a number of recordings for them. All my recent songs had already been done by other RCA artists, so I recorded songs written by other writers. I made the RCA vocal records of Irving Berlin's "Say It Isn't So" and "How Deep Is the Ocean," Rodgers and Hart's "Give Her a Kiss," and other big sellers of that era.

Don Lee, who owned radio station KHJ, the West Coast key station of the Mutual Network (where Crosby had done his first sustaining programs), heard a disc jockey play my records on his station and asked me to do some guest appearances on his Sunday night coast-to-coast program, California Melodies with Raymond Paige and his Orchestra. This led to my own program on the

137

Mutual Network, a weekly show sponsored by Philip Morris cigarettes. With Paramount's permission, I did the show for over a year, billed as "The Voice of Romance." It was on my show that Johnny, the midget bellboy of Philip Morris cigarettes, was first introduced, opening each show with the familiar "Call for Philip Morris!"

A year later, it was decided to move the show to New York, and I was invited to go there with it. I had a mental tussle that kept me awake several nights trying to make the decision. Crosby and Columbo were on top of the world, and romantic singers were in vogue as never before. Should I try to go that route? On the other hand, I was on a winning streak as a Hollywood songwriter. Each of my last three film scores had top song hits. I had another important musical soon to come up at Paramount, Earl Carroll's *Murder at the Vanities*, so I finally decided not to interrupt the continuity of my writing career. It was going too well to risk breaking it off, even for the royal opportunity of network radio stardom. I have wondered many times how my career would have turned out had I made the other decision.

Before I break off the narrative of my aborted crooning career, I must flash back to one story which had a most ironic—perhaps I should say pathetic—twist.

The in social club of the Hollywood elite at that time was the celebrated Mayfair Club, which gathered once a month at the Beverly Wilshire Hotel for a formal dinner dance. Only the Who's Who of the town were in the exclusive membership, and the film folk, unobserved by curious outsiders, really let down their hair.

Dave Hillman, who was handling publicity for the Los Angeles Biltmore Hotel, decided it was time the Mayfair had a little competition. With the help of Baron Long, owner of the Biltmore, he announced a new club for the film colony called the Saturday Nighters, with a dinner dance to be held every week in the famed Blue Room of the Biltmore. Dave asked me to round up the former members of the dance band I had used at the Roosevelt Roof, and to front them at all the Saturday Nighter affairs.

I was able to nail down most of the boys, including Spike Jones, now established locally but many years short of forming his own group. An imposing list of local celebrities consented to serve as the Board of Governors, in full agreement that the town sorely needed a second exclusive club. The full board consisted of Jesse Lasky Jr., Billy Wilkerson (owner of the *Hollywood Re-*

porter), Don Lee, Rodney Pantages, Bebe Daniels and Ben Lyon, Ruth Roland and Ben Bard, Harry Ruby and Bert Kalmar, Al Kaufman (a Paramount V.P.), plus Dave Hillman and myself.

The word was spread around, the Blue Room was redecorated, and handsome engraved invitations that looked like Whistler etchings were sent to every celebrity and socialite within fifty miles of Hollywood. The invitation automatically made the recipient a life member of the Saturday Nighters. I had two weeks to whip the band into shape again. We rehearsed every day in the Blue Room.

By a week before the opening, enough reservations had poured in to assure us of a capacity attendance, and we were forced to turn down all further requests for tables. The event was to be broadcast over the Don Lee Pacific Coast network for four solid hours commencing at 9 p.m. Saturday.

About five days before the premiere date, the first disturbing event occurred. There were runs on major banks in several key cities, and newly inaugurated President Roosevelt closed all of the country's banks to prevent a national financial disaster. The following day, representatives of the leading studios, at their wits' end, met in an emergency session and decreed that everyone on a studio payroll, from stars down to errand boys, would receive uncashable paychecks for fifty percent of their salaries for the duration of the bank holiday.

A large number of cancellations were phoned in, but the club sponsors were still determined to go ahead. The final blow that made the whole affair a catastrophe occurred in midweek. It came not from FDR or the studio moguls, but from higher up. It was an act of God. The severest earthquake that ever hit Southern California took place that day and the next—not one, but a series of six large tremors that scared the daylights out of everyone in town. I was driving on Wilshire Boulevard when the first one struck—a tremor so powerful it shook the steering wheel out of my hands. I thought my car was going to sink into a hole in the ground.

The next day the tremors were still taking place, and people were afraid to go outdoors. We called a hasty meeting that night with a few of the Board of Governors, trying to figure out what to do. Hillman had checked with the Cocoanut Grove and learned that there were less than 25 customers in the place. We knew we were fighting impossible odds, and decided that any opening the following night was bound to be a disaster. So we postponed it

139

until the panicky conditions subsided. But the following week, Hollywood was plunged into the depths of despair. The hotel, which was the Club's principal backer, withdrew its support. That made the postponement permanent. I doubt if any other nonevent in the history of entertainment, before or since, ever met with such a rapid-fire succession of calamities.

Fortunately, events at Paramount soon more than made up for the debacle. Within a few weeks, the financial emergency had subsided. The banks reopened, and the studios were going full blast again. The country was starting to pull out of the depression, hopeful that the new man in the White House had shown strong enough leadership to turn the tide. The studio doubled the budget on *Murder at the Vanities* to make it Paramount's major musical effort for the coming 1934 season. It was to be the film version of the successful musical that had run most of the previous year at Earl Carroll's theater in New York. Carroll was signed to come out as associate producer. Heading the cast were Kitty Carlisle, Jack Oakie, Victor McLaglen, Gail Patrick, and a new star Paramount had imported from Europe, Carl Brisson, who was being groomed as successor to Maurice Chevalier (who had decided to return to France instead of renewing his contract). At the last minute, Duke Ellington and his Orchestra, fresh from European triumphs, were added to the picture at the insistence of Arthur and myself.

When Carl Brisson arrived in Hollywood, his first concern was to find out who was going to write his songs. Bill LeBaron, who was producing the picture with Earl Carroll's assistance, assured him that Arthur and I could handle the job to his satisfaction. But Carl wanted to make sure. So the following day he dropped over to our office and introduced himself. He brought with him an entourage that included his doting wife Cleo and his son Freddy (who later married Rosalind Russell and became a leading producer of stage and film musicals). Freddy was then a teenager fresh out of Eton, and looked the part with his English schoolboy attire. Right behind them were their maid Juliet and Carl's uniformed chauffeur Jerry. (Carl, with his guttural Scandinavian accent, always called him "Cherry.") Jerry was carrying a small record player covered in gleaming white leather.

Introducing himself, Carl practically gave us a capsule biography. He had starred in a revival of *The Merry Widow* in a two-year run on the London stage, had been knighted by the King of

140

Denmark, and had been middleweight boxing champion of Europe. He was also a European recording artist, and currently had a top seller on the London record charts. In fact, that was the main reason he had dropped over. He had brought the record to play for us, to make sure Arthur and I could capture his style and write the kinds of songs that suited him. I could see he was not at all sure of this. He turned to the chauffeur and commanded, "All right, Cherry, the record, please."

Jerry put the record on the turntable and we heard a pleasant, sexy voice singing our recent Crosby hit, "Thanks." Carl kept watching our reactions, looking uncertain and concerned. Not sure whether or not it was a gag, Arthur and I, pokerfaced, waited until the end. I then asked if I could see the record, and noted that it merely said:

THANKS
(From the Film "TOO MUCH HARMONY")
Sung By
CARL BRISSON

As is frequently the case with foreign recordings, the writers' names were missing.

Arthur broke the silence that followed. "Mr. Brisson, I'm happy to hear that this record is a big seller, because it so happens that Sam and I *wrote* that song."

The tension ended instantly. Carl broke into his familiar infectious grin, and Cleo, Freddy, Jerry and Juliet beamed right along with him. Carl apologized profusely, saying he must be a bloody fool not to have known who composed his greatest record hit. Now he could go into his first American starring film feeling confident that he would get some great songs. The next thing was "Cherry—the snaps," and Jerry pulled a flask of aakvavit out of a small handbag, with a half dozen silver cups. We drank to the success of the forthcoming new score, and were the best of friends from then on.

Brisson's confidence was not misplaced. The principal song we wrote for him in *Murder at the Vanities* was destined to become the biggest seller of our entire careers—"Cocktails for Two." Which, as you shall see, is a story in itself.

I do not often get a song idea from a news event, but "Cocktails for Two" is one of the exceptions. On the day that Prohibition was repealed, it suddenly occurred to me that drinking songs had

141

not been heard for many years—not since the country went dry back in 1920. (I had forgotten for the moment the old "Stein Song," which Rudy Vallee had revived so successfully in 1930.) One reason was that one of the networks had a prohibition on drinking songs during most of that period. Hence there was little point in writing one, since it could not have been properly exploited. Now that was all over. We could drink again and sing about it as well. I brought this out right at the beginning of the verse:

> Oh what delight to be
> Given the right to be
> Happy and carefree again,
> No longer slinking,
> Respectably drinking
> Like civilized ladies and men.

I pointed out to Arthur that we had a chance to beat everyone to the punch and be the first out with a drinking song. Repeal had made *legal* drinking a topic of the day. People could hardly wait to legally order a cocktail for the first time in fifteen years. It therefore followed that the first new drinking song would be a timely conversation piece that would give radio performers and disc jockeys something to gab about. Although the film had not yet started shooting, it was the policy of Famous Music to begin radio exploitation on their plug songs several months ahead of the film's release date, because a musical that already had a song hit sold more tickets.

We finished the song in a couple of afternoons, and decided to try it out on Carl Brisson first. We went to his suite in the Beverly Wilshire and played it for him. He loved it, and felt sure we had given him a smash.

We were next obligated to play it for Earl Carroll, who was supposed to pass on all of the musical sequences and production ideas for *Murder at the Vanities*. Carroll had come to the Coast as something of a legend in the field of musicals. His annual editions of *Earl Carroll's Vanities* on Broadway had been box-office successes for many years, and Earl was hellbent on replacing Ziegfeld as Broadway's number-one impresario of lavish revues featuring beautiful showgirls. We barely knew him, and it was with some trepidation that we phoned to inform him that we were

142

ready to play the song we had written for Brisson's main production number.

Carroll came to our office to hear it, and if I said he was a cold cookie, I would be understating it. We were full of enthusiasm as we sang and played what we felt was one of our finest creations. Carroll was expressionless, his face like a mask. When we finished the demonstration, there was no reaction whatsoever. Arthur and I looked at each other in dismay.

Carroll reflected awhile before he spoke. Finally he came out with it. "That's not it. I wish I could have gotten with you fellows before you wrote the song and briefed you on what sort of a hit song a musical of this kind needs."

"What kind of song did you have in mind, Mr. Carroll?" I was trying to conceal the great letdown I was experiencing.

"Well, when I did this show on the stage, the big number we featured was a thing called 'Sweet Madness.' Something like that, lively and catchy, to add pace to the show."

I was too tactful to tell Carroll that the publisher of "Sweet Madness" told me he had broken his back trying to plug the song and that despite going well in the show, it had fizzled out as a copy seller. To tell Carroll that we felt sure "Cocktails for Two" could surpass it in popularity seemed like the height of arrogance. The meeting ended with a handshake as Earl said, "Better luck next time, boys."

Sometime in the next day or two, Carl Brisson dropped over and said, "Where's my song? Can I have a lead sheet and lyric so I can rehearse it?"

"Sorry, Carl, the song is out." And we told him about Carroll turning it down.

Carl, thoroughly incensed at losing a number he had great confidence in, would not hear of such a thing. He insisted on going over Carroll's head, right to the top brass. Minutes later, he came back to our office, bringing Bill LeBaron with him. Bill asked us to play the song. After hearing it, he said, "I think Carroll's out of his mind. The song stays in. You go ahead and learn it, Carl. Let me handle it."

Carroll stayed away when we shot the song. I heard later that he was in his office, sulking. Carl, in a memorable duet with Kitty Carlisle, performed it as part of an extravagant production number. The rest is history. It was an immediate click in every corner of the globe.

143

But the best part of the story is the P.S.

I will cut to sometime later, at the opening of a new Earl Carroll revue in his elaborate Carroll Theater Restaurant which had recently been erected on Sunset Boulevard in Hollywood. At the final curtain, the show received a tremendous ovation. Earl stepped out on the stage to acknowledge it. He began with the conventional thank you, you've been a marvelous audience, I find this very gratifying, etc. He then pointed out three or four stars who were in the audience, directing the spotlight on them and asking them to take a bow. As the audience applauded again, he spotted me seated directly in front of him, where he couldn't very well have missed me. He waved his hand to stop the applause, smiling broadly. "It gives me great pleasure," he began, "to introduce to you the man who wrote *the biggest song hit I have ever had in one of my productions*—Sam Coslow, one of the two writers of 'Cocktails for Two.' Stand up and take a bow, Sam!"

To flash back to the shooting of *Murder at the Vanities*, we encountered no further problems in getting the rest of the score okayed. LeBaron told us to play the completed numbers for him first. Of the other eight songs we had in the film, we were probably way ahead of the time with one called "Marijuana" which was dug up and rediscovered some forty years later by Bette Midler. Bette credits the song as the first to attract attention to her. She featured it again in a new record album in 1976. "Live and Love Tonight" was a ballad we thought might go places, but it was snowed under by the great popularity of "Cocktails for Two." However, the film had another song, "Ebony Rhapsody," which was Duke Ellington's feature production number. Ellington also recorded it in his characteristic style, and the record has been an Ellington evergreen for many years. Duke very rarely recorded songs he hadn't composed himself, and I always felt honored that he made an exception of six of my songs: "Ebony Rhapsody," "Cocktails for Two," "My Old Flame," "Live and Love Tonight," "I Met My Waterloo" and "Sing, You Sinners."

An interesting sidelight concerns the trip Duke and his orchestra made to England just before this film. There he played at many private parties for the Prince of Wales, who later became Edward VIII, and still later the Duke of Windsor. The Prince got a big kick out of sitting in with the band and playing drums, and he and Duke became great friends. He called Duke "Sonny" and

144

Duke called His Royal Highness "The Whale"—an unusual liberty to take with the heir to the throne of Britain, but the Prince loved it. (If you saw Cole Porter's show, *Jubilee*, you may recall the big laugh received by Mary Boland as the Queen when she told the Prince to "stop running around with Duke Ellington.") After Duke's trip overseas, the Prince of Wales remained an enthusiastic Ellington fan, requesting Ellington tunes every time he was within earshot of a dance band. He had a collection of Ellington records, probably one of the largest in existence. Shortly after the release of *Murder at the Vanities* I received a letter written on the stationery of the Equerry to H.R.H. the Prince of Wales stating that His Royal Highness would be very pleased to have a copy of the sheet music of "Ebony Rhapsody," which was not yet available in London. Arthur and I autographed a copy and mailed it to the Prince.

I cannot leave the subject of the *Vanities* score without mentioning that the question I am most frequently asked is how I felt about Spike Jones's famous recording of "Cocktails for Two." Spike, after my own band broke up, went on to play drums on some of Hollywood's top network shows. In the early Forties he became the leader of the country's best-known comedy band, one of the bestselling bands ever recorded on RCA-Victor. For some strange reason that I have never fathomed, Spike decided it would be a good idea to take a graceful, continental-style melody like "Cocktails" and record it as a noisy, slapstick, grotesque novelty. He never told me he was doing it, and the record was a shock to me. I hated it, and thought it was in the worst possible taste, desecrating what I felt was one of my most beautiful songs. To make matters worse, every time I tuned in on a disc jockey show at that time I heard the God-damned thing. It kept me boiling. Under the U.S. copyright laws, anyone can alter the arrangement of a song as he sees fit, and record it without getting permission from author or publisher, as long as royalties are paid. Spike used everything from automobile horns to exploding firecrackers on his record, and there was nothing I could do about it.

The blow was somewhat softened over the next few years when I received royalties for the sale of two million records of Spike's version, swelling the combined sales of the various recorded versions to around five milion records worldwide. Yet somehow, I think I still would have preferred Spike not to have made that record.

Murder at the Vanities turned out to be an auspicious start to one of my best years in Hollywood. In that same year, 1934, I was to do the Mae West musical, *Belle of the Nineties,* for which Arthur and I provided a few more songs that have since become standards, like "My Old Flame"; one song for *Eight Girls in a Boat* that topped the charts, "This Little Piggie Went to Market"; and a solo assignment writing the words and music for Carl Brisson's second movie. The latter included "A Little White Gardenia," which was to become Carl's theme song.

Chapter Eight

HOLLYWOOD'S
GOLDEN AGE

The middle 1930's were palmy days in Hollywood. By that time the film factories were in high gear. Every studio scheduled fifty or sixty features a year. Everyone was working. The rest of the country was still in the first stages of recovery from the depression, but Hollywood was already booming. Paychecks there were astronomical compared to other regions, and with prices still unbelievably low, film workers were having a ball. Dinner at the Derby was still a buck and a half.

The night life was glittering, saturated with a magic that has never since been recaptured. The Trocadero opened on Sunset Strip and became the film colony's favorite night spot. If you were lucky enough to get in, you found yourself rubbing elbows with dozens of stars in the crowded room. You danced to Phil Ohman's Orchestra and were captivated by the songs of his new vocalist, a bright-eyed young girl named Mary Martin. Mary didn't stay with the band very long. Too many film executives were eyeing her from the ringside tables, and she soon received offers to appear in musicals.

Around the corner and up the hill was the very posh Colony, a private membership club for film folk exclusively. It was private because they had gambling upstairs, and was actually a holdover from Prohibition days: peephole in the front door, the whole works. Like everyone else we knew in the film set, Esther and I were charter members—not because we wanted to gamble, but because the Colony had the best steaks in town. The owners were the Wertheimer brothers, who had run socialite gambling establishments in Detroit. They had two partners named Goldie (I never knew if that was his first or last name) and Farmer Paige, who was reportedly the gambling czar of Hollywood, with hush-hush political connections. I doubt whether he knew very much about agriculture.

They also had a branch in the middle of the desert, a sort of number-two Colony which was equally as popular. The film crowd had just discovered Palm Springs, a couple of hours from Hollywood. It became the in place for weekend trips, taking the play away from Agua Caliente on the Mexican border. But they couldn't gamble in Palm Springs as they could in Caliente, so the Wertheimers built a small gambling palace twenty miles away in the desert. You drove up to it, and after being carefully scrutinized by a couple of western-style doormen with two-gun holsters, you suddenly found yourself in a room that looked like the creme de la creme inner jetset salon in Monte Carlo, elaborately decorated with costly chandeliers, Remington and Russell paintings, and rugs a foot thick.

I remember once, when a dinner was to be given by Paramount in honor of boss Adolph Zukor's birthday, the studio had scheduled a surprise trio appearance by Jack Benny, George Burns, and Bert Wheeler, all of whom were then working on the lot. The three comedians wanted to do just one song together to entertain the guests at the affair. Jack asked me to write it. I whipped up a number which started with a verse that asked the question "Who has all the money in Hollywood?" The chorus supplied the answer, starting this way:

> Wertheimer, Goldie, and Paige,
> The money-making wonders of the age.

At the dinner, I accompanied the trio at the piano. When they got to the first line of the chorus, the laughter was so deafening that the trio had to stop for a minute or two before they could go on with the song. Half the guests at the party had lost thousands of dollars at the two Colony Clubs! Benny and Burns, who went everywhere together, never performed the song for the public but sang it many times at house parties. Every once in a while I'd get a call from Jack or George to meet them at some party or other to

148

play the song for them. George will sing the lyric for you even today, if you ask him.

A couple of years later a reform wave hit Southern California, and the Colony Clubs closed up shop. Goldie and Paige, I heard, transferred operations to Las Vegas and were among the pioneers who put the resort town on the map. But Lew Wertheimer hung around Hollywood, trying to figure out what to do with himself. Hollywood film magnate Joseph Schenck, who had recently put together the gigantic Twentieth Century-Fox merger and built a new studio in West Los Angeles, was Lew's closest friend. Joe attempted to solve his problem by hiring him as a producer at the studio.

I ran into Lew while lunching at the Fox commissary one day. We discussed his new job over a cup of coffee. He was completely bewildered. "I feel like a lost soul around here," he confided. "I sit at a big desk all day, and the story department keeps sending me scripts to read. But I can't tell if they're good or bad. I don't really know what the heck I'm supposed to do. After all, I haven't read very much before—always been too busy, working all night and sleeping all day. And I feel guilty as hell. They gave me a contract and a four-figure salary, but nobody tells me what to do."

I don't know if Lew ever found out how to produce pictures. He occupied the office and drew the four-figure salary for some time, as I recall. Perhaps Darryl Zanuck gave him the axe when he came in later to head the studio—or perhaps he didn't. Lew was such a likable guy and so much fun to be with that I don't suppose anyone really cared. Life in Hollywood was so pleasant and easygoing in those days.

At Paramount in that period a frequent topic of conversation was the meteoric rise of Mae West. After her secondary role in a George Raft film, the studio moguls suddenly realized they had a new star on their hands. They pulled out all the stops to promote her in *She Done Him Wrong* and *I'm No Angel*. The producers' hopes were more than fulfilled. By the time *Belle of the Nineties* was announced, Mae had skyrocketed. She was now one of the five top-grossing stars in the film industry. Her rise came at a propitious time for the studio. Their previous sex symbol, Clara Bow, had lost her luster at the box office. Mae filled the gap like a million dollars, or perhaps I should say millions of dollars. Her old contract was torn up, replaced by a new one at $300,000 per film plus an additional $100,000 for writing her own screen plays. She was the highest-paid film star of the middle 1930's.

Mae could belt out a blues or a honkytonk song with the best of them, and a musical like *Belle of the Nineties* was a plum assignment that Arthur and I were eager to get. We asked for it and got it. Having had three hit musicals the previous year, we could call our shots.

Mae was a joy to work with, at least for us. Studio officials had a few problems with her. Paramount production chief Ernst Lubitsch was annoyed with the overpowering roles she wrote for herself. Lubitsch maintained that no one else in the cast had a chance. But he never could budge Mae. Actually, she was right. No one else knew the Mae West formula that made the box-office cash registers ring as well as Mae herself. If her great movie vogue was based on a tour de force, Mae was too smart to tamper with success.

She worked like a warhorse. I happen to know that for months before shooting, she would be up half the night writing her scripts. She made her apartment at the Ravenswood her office. We would run up there to play our songs and rehearse her, sometimes in the midst of costume fittings or conferences with directors, producers, or agents.

In person, she bore a remarkable resemblance to the characters she tailored for her screen plays. Flashes of sharp wit came rapid-fire like a machine-gun when she talked to you, and her talk was often subtly off-color. Sometimes, if we laughed hard enough, she would say, "Was it really that funny?" and hastily jot down the remark for use in her script. She was also a great prankster, forever putting people on. I will never forget my wife's astonishment on Christmas Day, 1934, shortly after the release of *Belle of the Nineties*. Mae's chauffeur drove up with a gigantic gift-wrapped package to our Beverly Hills home. We took off the wrapping and found a large oil painting of Mae—stark, staring nude. We learned later that she was so taken with the artist's rendition that she paid him to dash off a half dozen more, and they became her Christmas gifts to Leo McCarey, who directed the film, Bill LeBaron, her producer, myself, and a few others.

The only respect in which the real Mae and the screen Mae differed was in her private life, which she never discussed. Once when Arthur and I were working with her at her apartment, I casually asked her about the rumor that her bedroom ceiling was all mirror, never dreaming for a moment that the rumor was true.

"Would you like to see it?" she asked, with one of her inscrutable Mona Lisa half-smiles. She led us into her bedroom, and there it was—wall-to-wall mirror on the ceiling. Just whom she enjoyed looking up there with, Mae never confided. For a legendary figure glorified and damned as the country's number-one siren, Mae managed to keep her personal life pretty much of a mystery.

In *Belle of the Nineties* we tried something Mae hadn't done previously: a torch ballad, "My Old Flame." She clicked with it just as successfully as she had with the "Frankie and Johnny" type of song she was identified with. Her rendition established what was to be a song standard for the next forty years. I don't suppose it hurt her one bit that she had the backing of Duke Ellington and his band in the scene. We had suggested Duke to Mae. When the studio objected because the band had become too expensive by then, Mae insisted, and got her way. Duke also accompanied her on the rest of the score, notably "Troubled Waters." The collaboration was well received by the critics. Duke, incidentally, paid me one of the greatest compliments I ever received when my present wife and I visited him at Basin Street East some years ago. We were reminiscing about the good old days when we worked with Mae, and Duke volunteered the statement that if there were one song by another writer he wished he had written, it would be "My Old Flame."

Following *Belle*, Mae continued to feature occasional songs by various writers in her pictures. But she never failed to call on us for an assist. In her next vehicle, *Goin' to Town*, I supplied "Now I'm a Lady," which I wrote with Sammy Fain and Irving Kahal. On *Klondike Annie* I collaborated with Gene Austin, who was in the film with her. Arthur Johnston had some good music in her *Go West, Young Man* the same year.

The last Mae West feature I worked on was *Every Day's a Holiday*. That assignment is a story in itself. For once, Mae was not particularly happy with her own script. Neither was her producer on that film, Manny Cohen. I had already written five songs for the script, two of them with screenwriter Barry Trivers and three by myself. (Arthur had left Paramount by that time to accept an offer from Fox.) Mae wanted to hear her numbers.

In her 1959 autobiography, *Goodness Had Nothing to Do with It*, Mae devotes a page to the playing of the songs. She tells how the first number I played, "Fifi," gave her an immediate brainstorm. She stopped me and told Manny Cohen that there was a whole plot for a new script in my lyric. Her old script was scrapped (to coin a phrase), and Mae dictated a complete new story line based on the Fifi character I had written the song about.

151

If you saw the picture, you will recall that Mae, in a black wig, plays the role of a Brooklyn gal who pretends to be a French music-hall singer, Mademoiselle Fifi.

After Mae's brainstorm, I played the other four songs. During the last one, "Every Day's a Holiday," Mae stopped me again, fairly screaming to Manny: "We've been trying to get a title for the picture. There it is—*Every Day's a Holiday!*" And that's what the film was finally called. All five songs were done in the picture in characteristic West fashion, and this time she insisted on being accompanied by old Satchmo himself, the unforgettable Louis Armstrong and his big band. Nothing but the best for Mae. And working with her was a great break for me, bless her ever-lovin' business acumen. There's never been anyone quite like her.

Belle of the Nineties was the last score Arthur and I worked on together at Paramount. It was too bad we had to end the partnership. We had rolled up a batting average of 1.000, from "Just One More Chance" to "My Old Flame." But the parting of the ways was unavoidable. I simply had no other choice.

Arthur was a troubled soul at that time. He had a stormy personal life, compounded by a hectic relationship with a girl he was in love with but couldn't make up his mind to marry. One day the affair was on; the next day they would break up in a violent quarrel. The sequence was repeated interminably, and the turmoil played havoc with his nervous system. Arthur was not a well man, frequently suffering from bouts of illness of one sort or another. To alleviate the continual stress he was undergoing, he began drinking far more heavily than usual.

The problem had already disrupted our working routine on more than one occasion. The first interruption occurred the year before, while we were doing *Murder at the Vanities.* Having hit on the idea for "Cocktails for Two," I waited more than a week for Arthur to show up at work. He had enthused over the title, but his creative faculties were numbed by emotional conflicts and daily hangovers. In desperation, I finally wrote both the music and lyrics of the first half of the chorus. Arthur patched up his romantic life in time to show up to write the tune for the middle section of the chorus ("My head may go reeling," etc.). The final eight bars were of course a repetition of the opening phrase.

Similar disruptions kept popping up, although Arthur bounced back and was in fine fettle when we worked on *Belle.* During this interval, he contributed most of the melodies, including the marvelous music for "My Old Flame."

152

On the next score we were assigned to, Arthur had another relapse. He was knee-deep in problems, Scotch, and sickness. The picture we were to work on was *Many Happy Returns,* a starring vehicle for George Burns, Gracie Allen, and the Guy Lombardo Orchestra. It was an especially important assignment for us because the Lombardo organization now ranked as the country's leading "sweet" band. As such, they could make a hit of just about any song they featured.

Scripts were sent to each of us, but Arthur was in no shape to even read his. He stayed away from the office for weeks at a time, and might as well have been in darkest Africa for all the help he was giving. I phoned him daily, getting one excuse after another, often incoherently. I was becoming frustrated and despondent over the whole thing. Then one day I was shocked into my senses. I learned that the studio had bought two songs from Cliff Friend and Carmen Lombardo to be interpolated into the score. Guy Lombardo and other members of the cast had dropped over to our office repeatedly to hear their numbers. By now I guess they were tired of the excuses I was forced to improvise.

Frantically, I phoned producer Bill LeBaron and promised to have the rest of the score ready in one week. A definite appointment was set up for Bill and the Lombardo brothers to come in on a Saturday morning especially to hear the songs. By midweek, I had not yet succeeded in shaking Arthur out of his rut. I felt I was at the end of my rope.

I went home in the middle of the afternoon, locked myself in my study with the final shooting script, and emerged two days later with four completed songs, words and music. They were in characteristic Lombardo style.

The evening before our appointment to play the songs, I drove over to Arthur's house. There I fed him a special hangover concoction of tomato juice with big splashes of Worcestershire and other ingredients. Because he was still nervous and shaking a bit, I put him to bed with a sleeping pill. Then I left word with his concerned black housekeeper to see that he had a cold shower on arising, and that he was driven to the studio at least an hour before our 10 a.m. appointment. My plan was to go over the four songs with Arthur when he was fully awake and alert, giving him an hour to familiarize himself with them before LeBaron and the Lombardos arrived.

The next morning, Arthur failed to arrive at the appointed time, though a phone message told me that he was on his way. Bill

LeBaron got there before he did. Arthur finally showed up at the same time Guy and Carmen Lombardo arrived. It was most embarrassing as Arthur glibly asked them to "take a walk around the block" or have a cup of coffee in the commissary while we gave the songs a final run-through to make sure of some "last minute revisions." I don't think the three believed him for a moment, but they were gracious enough to accede to his request. During the fifteen minutes or so before they returned, Arthur got to the piano and quickly rehearsed my hastily concocted lead sheets. With his instinctive musical flair, he could rattle off precisely the proper harmonies and musical embellishments right off the lead sheets. When he finally played the tunes, he was so familiar with them that you would have sworn he had composed them himself.

Guy and Carmen were all smiles as they listened. Quickly they okayed the songs. Three of the four songs were in the final cut of the film when it was released.

Shortly afterward, our collaborating problems were resolved. Arthur told me he had failed to agree with Paramount on a renewal of his contract and had instead signed to do a couple of musicals for Twentieth Century-Fox. His decision forestalled what would have been a crisis. Following the LeBaron-Lombardo incident I had put my foot down. I told Arthur that I would no longer stand for his name going on songs written by me alone. It was a sad finale to a fruitful collaboration, but I could no longer go on working under such conditions. My peace of mind meant too much to me, and the long waits between Arthur's trips to the office had become intolerable. I am by no means saying that my problem was as acute as Dick Rodgers' similar one with Larry Hart, or that Arthur's binges were even in the same league with Larry's. Arthur in fact eventually licked his problem. But in many ways his drinking was just as difficult to cope with. And the effect was just as deplorable as the Rodgers and Hart breakup, for in my estimation Arthur was as truly a musical genius as Larry Hart was a genius with lyrics.

"Fare Thee Well" was the standout number of *Many Happy Returns.* Of its many recorded versions that year, the one I prize most highly is the Noel Coward vocal recording, one of the rare occasions when Coward selected a song he had not composed himself.

I have a ridiculous anecdote about another song in the score called "The Boogie Man." If you saw the film, you will recall that the Lombardo outfit performed the song in a sleeping car, with members of the band in pajamas, playing their instruments in upper and lower berths. Shortly after the shooting, Esther and I left on the Superchief for a brief vacation in New York. On the first night out, somewhere in the middle of the Mojave Desert, we were suddenly awakened in our compartment by a violent jarring. The train came to an abrupt halt, and we were almost thrown out of our berths. We wondered if some sort of collision had occurred. We sleepily looked out the window. We were in the middle of nowhere. A few minutes later, another train pulled up on the track alongside ours, squeaking and grinding to a halt. After a further wait, we heard a knock on our compartment door. A voice called out: "I have a message for Mr. and Mrs. Coslow." Half asleep, I opened the door—and was greeted by a deafening blast of trumpets playing the opening bars of "Boogie Man." In the dimly lit corridor, I discerned Guy's brother Lebert and the rest of the Lombardo brass section. They played a half chorus of the song, then fled. In a few minutes, our train was on its way again.

Next morning, Esther and I awoke, wondering whether we had telepathically had the same dream. It seemed unreal. It was not until a year later, on the opening night of the Lombardo band at the Cocoanut Grove in Los Angeles, that Guy gleefully revealed to me what had occurred. The band had been en route to a one-nighter somewhere in Texas when Guy learned that his train would meet the Superchief at a small railway junction in the desert around 4 a.m. At a cost of several hundred dollars, Guy arranged to have the Superchief stalled at the junction for five minutes until it was met by his train. His train conductor then got our compartment number from our conductor, and worked his expensive practical joke. Judging by the number of music men who have told me about it since, Guy must have told the story a thousand times about scaring the daylights out of us.

Following Arthur Johnston's departure from Paramount, I must confess I felt a trifle insecure at the prospect of working alone. What would my songwriting future hold in store? My first solo assignment was to write a theme song for *Eight Girls in a Boat*. The task was made easier when the musical director of the film, Harold "Lefty" Lewis, suggested a title: "This Little Piggie Went to Market." It fit the scene in the script nicely. "This Little Piggie" proved to be an immediate success, the number-one song of the day. I rewarded Lefty Lewis for his help by giving him credit on the sheet music and a percentage of my royalties. It sold well over half a million copies.

"Piggie" was followed in short order by three more solo efforts, all of which became top-selling song hits and took their place among my best standards. All three songs—"A Little White Gardenia," "In the Middle of a Kiss," and "Mister Paganini (You'll Have to Swing It)"—have stories related to them.

"A Little White Gardenia" was the love theme I wrote for the second Carl Brisson musical, *All the King's Horses*, in which Carl co-starred with Broadway prima donna Mary Ellis. The idea for the song came from a story Carl told me about a mystery fan in London. While Carl was appearing there in his smash revival of *The Merry Widow*, an unknown female admirer pulled up at the stage door in a chauffeured limousine once every week like clockwork during the entire two-year run of the show. She would always leave a small box for Carl, and it always contained a white gardenia, nothing more. No card was ever enclosed, no note or anything—just the single flower. London newspaper writers thought it was a publicity stunt, but Carl swore up and down that he never had the slightest clue to the lady's identity. I tried to catch the essence of the story in the chorus of the lyric, which began:

> I will bring a little white gardenia,
> As refreshing as a day in May,
> You may wear it if you care
> —Or toss it away.

It became the hit of the film, so identified with Carl that it became his signature.

"In the Middle of a Kiss," which tied for first place on the Hit Parade, was written in response to a challenge. While attending a Hollywood party one night, Fuzzy Knight, a comedian who appeared in many Paramount Westerns, asked me how long it took me to write a complete song. I replied that there could be no pat answer. It could take anywhere from an hour to a month.

"One hour?" Fuzzy echoed, incredulously. "Do you mean to say you actually wrote a whole song in an hour?"

"Very rarely—but it *has* happened."

Fuzzy was skeptical. *Nobody* ever wrote a song in an hour, he scoffed. A small group that had gathered around us agreed with

156

SWEEPIN' THE CLOUDS AWAY

WORDS AND MUSIC BY SAM COSLOW

Dancing to Save Your Sole
All I Want Is Just One
My Marine
Let Us Drink To The Girl of My Dreams

Famous Music
CORPORATION
719 SEVENTH AVENUE · · · · NEW YORK

Sweepin' the Clouds Away
Any Time's the Time to Fall In Love
I'm In Training For You
Paramount On Parade

Everett Crosby, Bing's
brother and manager

*Bing took advantage of the
Paramount makeup department
for this early gag shot*

*Sam Coslow snapped this picture of director Eddie Sutherland, Fifi
D'Orsay, Skeets Gallagher and Bing Crosby at the latter's 1932 house-
warming party*

YOU CALL IT MADNESS BUT I CALL IT LOVE

SUCCESSFULLY INTRODUCED
ON THE AIR BY
RUSS
COLUMBO
"RADIO'S REVELATION"

CON CONRAD
MUSIC PUBLISHER, LTD.
SOLE SELLING AGENT
HARMS
NEW YORK

by
CON
CONRAD
GLADYS
Du BOIS
RUSS
COLUMBO
AND
PAUL
GREGORY

A rare etching of
Russ Columbo.
Artist unknown, but
he (she?) deserves
better

Esther Muir, Coslow's
second wife,
with Andy Clyde in
a 1932 comedy short

Songs were
sometimes filmed
before performers
had time to learn the
lyrics. Mae West,
anticipating TV,
solved the problem

At Coslow's summer home at Lake Sherwood, California, Sam catches a meditative Carl Brisson in profile

On the set of Too Much Harmony: *Bing, Ricardo Cortez, Jack Oakie, Shirley Grey, Charles Laughton, Kitty Kelly, Harry Green, Lilyan Tashman*

Sam snapped the last photo of Lew Cody in Lew's Malibu Beach home in 1934

Collaborator Arthur Johnston with ex-boss Irving Berlin in 1933

For Kate Smith, Sam Coslow and Arthur Johnston wrote one of her biggest hits, Moon Song. Here Kate rehearses it on the set of Hello, Everybody, as Sam listens at right and Arthur accompanies

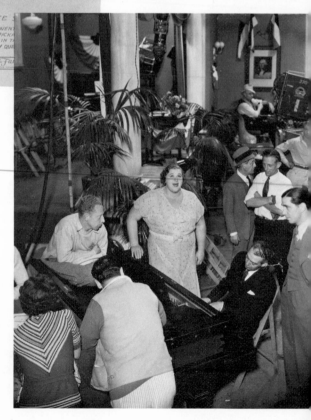

*On the set of
Limehouse Nights
in 1934, Sam joins
Jean Parker,
Anna May Wong
and George Raft*

*Sam snapped
Joan Crawford
and her husband
of that time,
Franchot Tone, at the
Cocoanut Grove
in the middle Thirties*

RESTLESS

Words and Music by SAM COSLOW and TOM SATTERFIELD

Complimentary

Publishers to Paramount Pictures • FAMOUS MUSIC CORP • 1619 · Broadway • New York City

168

Part of Guy Lombardo's band in Paramount's 1934 musical, Many Happy Returns. *Carmen is blowing his alto sax in the upper deck, and Guy is at Carmen's right*

The music staff at Paramount tossed a luncheon in 1935 for giant songwriters Jerome Kern, Oscar Hammerstein II and Sam Coslow. Front row: Coslow, Hammerstein, Kern, June Knight. Back row: Gerard Carbonaro, Irvin Talbot, Max Terr, Victor Young, Phil Boutelge, Boris Morros, Fred Hollander

GALA TESTIMONIAL PARTY

IN HONOR OF

GEORGE M. COHAN

TO BE GIVEN AT THE

AMBASSADOR "COCOANUT GROVE"

On Monday Evening, August 22nd

BY

AMERICA'S LEADING SONG WRITERS

*Composers of the Songs of Yesterday and Today
That You Have Whistled and Loved*

(FOR FULL DETAILS SEE INSIDE)

Masters of Ceremony

at the Gala Testimonial Party in honor of Mr. George M. Cohan will be...

MR. CHARLEY MURRAY   MR. WILLIAM COLLIER, SR.

Reception Committee

MR. AL JOLSON   MR. SID GRAUMAN   MR. HARRY WEBBER
MR. RICHARD CARLE   MR. L. E. BEHYMER   MR. HERBERT WEBBER

Entertainment Committee   Musical Directors

MR. FREDERICK V. BOWERS   MR. PHIL HARRIS
MR. CHRIS O. BROWN   MR. SID LIPPMAN

Choruses of the Following World-Wide Hits of Yesterday and Today Will Be Presented by Their Composers in Person:

Mr. Albert Von Tilzer - - - - "Take Me Out to the Ball Game"	Mr. Edwin Poulton - - - - - "Erminie" (Lullaby)
Mr. L. Wolfe Gilbert - - - - - "Peanut Vender"	Mr. Chris Shoenberg - - - - "Whispering"
Mr. Al Jolson - - - - - - - "Sonny Boy"	Mr. Banks Winters - - - - - "White Wings"
Mr. Edward Madden - - - - - "Moonlight Bay"	Mr. Kerry Mills - - - - - - "Georgia Camp Meeting"
Mr. Vincent Bryant - - - - - "Tammany"	Mr. J. C. Lewis, Jr. - - - - - - "I Got the Ritz From the Girl I Love"
Mr. Charles Wakefield Cadman - "At Dawning"	Mr. Sam Coslow - - - - - - "Just One More Chance"
Mr. Jimmie Hanley - - - - - "A Cottage Small by a Water Fall"	Mr. Ted Fiorita - - - - - - "Three on a Match"
Mr. James Brockman - - - - - "I'm Forever Blowing Bubbles"	Mr. Harry Akst - - - - - - "Dinah"
Mr. Charles Daniels - - - - - "Hiawatha"	Mr. Gordon Clifford - - - - - "Paradise"
Mr. Harry Tobias - - - - - - "Sweet and Lovely"	Mr. Oscar Rasbach - - - - - "Trees"
Mr. Al Dubin - - - - - - - "Many Happy Returns of the Day"	Messrs. Ruby and Kalmar - - - "Three Little Words"
Mr. J. Kernan Brennan - - - - "Let the Rest of the World Go By"	Mr. Raymond Egan - - - - - "Till We Meet Again"
Mr. Frederick V. Bowers - - - "Because I Love You"	Mr. Leo Robbins - - - - - - "Hallelujah"
Mr. Nat Vincent - - - - - - "Round Up Time in Texas"	Mr. Lee S. Roberts - - - - - "Smiles"
Mr. Victor Schertzinger - - - - "Marchetta"	Messrs. Burton and Jason - - - "Penthouse" (Serenade)
Mr. Richard Carle - - - - - "A Lemon in the Garden of Love"	Mr. Harry Warren - - - - - "You're My Everything"

Distinguished Women Composers Whose Songs Will Be Presented:

Carrie Jacobs Bond - - - - - "The End of a Perfect Day"
Cara Roma - - - - - - - - "Can't You Hear Me Callin', Caroline"
Anne Caldwell O'Day - - - - "Good Bye Girls, I'm Through"

A MEDLEY OF MR. COHAN'S GREATEST NUMBERS WILL BE PRESENTED BY PHIL HARRIS AND HIS ORCHESTRA

170

At a concert
aboard the
S. S. Champlain
in 1936, Leon
Belasco and
20-year-old
Yehudi Menuhin
are seated front,
Lily Pons is
center back,
and Sam Coslow
flanks Belasco

At an ASCAP cocktail party at the Beverly Hills Hotel, the eagles gather:
Jerome Kern, Irving Berlin, Sam Coslow, Benee Russell, Arthur Freed,
Burton Lane

A portrait of singer Frank Parker that won Sam first prize in a 1938 competition at the Beverly Hills Camera Club

Sam captures three of his bandleader friends off the California coast in 1937: Jimmie Grier, Jan Garber and Eddy Duchin

him. Johnny Weissmuller was in the group, but I cannot recall who the others were. They challenged me to sit down at the piano and write a song in an hour.

It was a dumb stunt for me to attempt, but I was goaded into it. It was the only time in my life I ever wrote a song in full view of an audience. And it didn't take an hour. I actually wrote the words and music of "In the Middle of a Kiss" in exactly thirty-five minutes! As I sat down at the piano, our group observed a couple dancing to a record player on the terrace outside. They were kissing like mad as the record ended. Fuzzy and I both thought of the title at the same time. "In the Middle of a Kiss" was born. Once I got the title and the opening musical phrase, the rest was easy. It just seemed to flow, one line leading to the next, like rolling off a log—as if some unseen force were dictating in my ear. I still can't explain how it happened, but it did. I never changed a line or a note of the song afterward.

A few weeks later the studio sent me the script of a new musical called *College Scandals.* There I found a good spot for the song. It was sung in the picture by Johnny Downs and Arline Judge (two names that crop up when Hollywood trivia addicts gather to flaunt their expertise). Perhaps partly because of the way it came to be written, it has always been one of my favorite compositions.

I surprised Fuzzy Knight by sending him a check for 20 percent of my royalties—a substantial amount to him—as a Christmas gift that year. After all, the song never would have been written if he hadn't challenged me.

The anecdote on "Mister Paganini" is really the story of how Martha Raye got her big break in Hollywood. I was called in to contribute some additional songs for Bing Crosby's first Western musical, *Rhythm on the Range.* The producer of the film, Barney Glazer, asked me to run down to a small night club on the outskirts of Los Angeles to hear a young comedienne he wanted to test for a role. The girl was Martha, and I was pleasantly surprised when I went to hear her. I could sense immediately that this was not the usual run-of-the-mill talent the studio was always testing, but a rare comedy find—and one with a spectacular singing voice to boot.

Martha was nervous as hell about her forthcoming test, and made no bones about how scared she was. There was a good reason for her jitters. She had everything except good song material, and she knew it.

I told Martha it would be a mistake to use one of the wornout

173

pop songs from her act for her first movie test, and I offered to write something tailored especially for her offbeat personality.

"Oh—*would* you?" she asked, almost in tears.

I knew that this kid could not afford special-material writers on the meager salary she received in second-rate nightclubs. Yet it was important that she have an original, funny number to show her to best advantage in the screen test. I had a strong hunch that unless I provided her with such a number, Paramount might pass up what I felt might be the comedy discovery of the year.

I dug hard for an outlandish comedy idea, and hit upon it after several days. I phoned Martha to come over to the office and hear "Mister Paganini." I had stayed up all night working on it. It was one of those feverish writing sessions where I couldn't stop once I had the idea and the start of the song. I felt I had to finish it for fear I might not be able to capture the same mood another time.

No artist I have written for ever had the instinctive feel for a song more than Martha Raye had when I first played "Paganini" for her. It was exactly what she wanted. She immediately ad-libbed some of the great jazz licks and funny little dance steps that made her rendition of the song unforgettable. I spent the next few afternoons rehearsing her at my office. When she was letter-perfect, the test was made.

Martha's test won her the comedy lead in Bing's film. The studio officials were so impressed with her "Paganini" test that they decided to make it her featured solo in the picture, building up her part greatly in the process.

At the sneak preview of *Rhythm on the Range*, something happened that I have never seen before or since at a preview. At the finish of Martha's song, the audience was laughing, applauding, and whistling so boisterously that the film could not continue. The projectionist stopped running it, and repeated Martha's number.

The next day, Martha was signed by Paramount to a five-year starring contract, at a figure she never dreamed she would ever earn. "Mister Paganini" has been her theme number ever since, and I can't tell you how many hundreds of times she has entered a nightclub stage or begun a TV appearance to the strains of the song.

Although no one has ever duplicated Martha's inimitable version, the song has served well for other performers also. Ella Fitzgerald's vocal with Chick Webb has become a jazz classic, and her later arrangement as a vocal feature was so long (seven minutes of delightful jazz improvisation) that the single was released with Part One on the "A" side and Part Two on the "B" side, a rarity in jazz annals.

While *Rhythm on the Range* was in production, Paramount's new music director, Boris Morros, came to my office one day escorting a wizened, sad-looking little man whom he was showing around the studio. Without introducing me to his friend, Boris said, "Sam, this gentleman has come all the way from Russia and has never seen a popular composer in action. So do us a favor—play your new song, the one about Paganini."

I played and sang it, somewhat reluctantly. They had been conversing in Russian as they entered my office, and I felt sure his friend would not understand a word of the lyric. To my great surprise, however, when I got to the first line of the chorus, the friend was no longer a sad little man. His eyes were twinkling, and he was enjoying it. At the finish, he clapped his hands in delight. It was not until then that Boris introduced us.

"This is one of our popular song composers, Sam Coslow. . . . and this—is my friend from Russia, Igor Stravinsky."

I damn near fell off the piano bench. Boris told me afterward that I actually blushed with embarrassment. He also revealed that the delayed introduction was deliberate, for he knew I never would have had nerve enough to play a popular tune for the great Stravinsky. He was so right. I wouldn't have dared—not for all the caviar in Russia!

The string of four successive hit songs, all of them written solo, was reassuring to me. I took on a flock of new studio assignments in the next few months. It was a busy period. I worked on *Champagne Waltz* for Gladys Swarthout, *Hands Across the Table* for Carole Lombard and Fred MacMurray, and even managed to squeeze in a couple of super-Western epics—"The Texas Ranger Song" for Paramount's *Texas Rangers* (now played whenever the Rangers get together for a shindig), and a theme song for Hopalong Cassidy called "My Heart's in the Heart of the West." This one stood me in good stead some years later during the early years of television, when the Hopalong Cassidy films were revived for a new generation of kids. Practically every Hopalong movie that was shown on TV—and they were the most widely played Westerns of the early 1950's—began with my theme number behind the screen titles. The theme was a bigger bonanza than Hoppy's gold strikes. Every time it was televised on a coast-to-coast network I received several hundred dollars in ASCAP performance fees.

Chapter Nine

TIN PAN ALLEY, LONDON

Some time around the mid-1930's I received a long-distance call from Lou Diamond, a Paramount V.P. in charge of their music publishing division in the New York home office. Lou asked me if I had a passport.

"A passport? What for?"

"Well, the company just loaned you out to Gaumont British. They're the leading film studio over there. You're going to write the songs for an important musical. You have to leave next week."

I was puzzled. "What do you mean, loaned me out?" I demanded to know. "What am I—a lawn mower or something?"

Lou laughed. "I guess it's a new thing in the film industry," he explained. "Lots of studios are now loaning out contract players and stars to other studios. The other studio takes over your contract for the loan-out period and pays us a premium for supplying your services. It's the first time we've done it with one of our songwriters, but we have the right to do it. Read your contract."

I really didn't want to go abroad at that particular time. Esther and I were building a new home in Coldwater Canyon and were at the crucial final stages when so many decisions had to be made every day. But the loan-out agreement between the two studios was signed, so I bowed to the fait accompli. Paramount's foreign department had a couple of passports rushed through in a hurry for us, and booked a sailing on the Ile de France. We were on shipboard a week later, en route for Southhampton.

176

On our arrival at the Victoria Station in London, we were met by Jimmy Campbell and Reg Connelly, the young, enterprising British music publishers who, as I soon learned, had originated and engineered the loan-out deal. We were whisked to the Savoy Hotel where Gaumont British had arranged a suite for us, and where, over a sumptuous luncheon in the Savoy Grill, Jimmy and Reg filled us in on the details.

I was to write the words and music for the next musical starring Jessie Matthews, Britain's leading singing and dancing star, their answer to Ginger Rogers. Jessie's previous film had been *Evergreen,* for which Rodgers and Hart had been imported to write the score, which included the immortal "Dancing on the Ceiling." The film had made Jessie a household name all over Europe.

"Keep talking," I told the Englishmen. "You're making it all sound so easy. All I have to do is follow Rodgers and Hart, right?"

They explained the reason they were confident I could do it. Earlier that year they had set up a new publishing venture in association with Chappell and Company, England's largest publishing house, for the express purpose of publishing the British editions of the songs from Paramount's musicals. Their first two Paramount musicals released in England had several songs of mine which had topped the British Hit Parade, and they considered me their "white-haired boy" over there. Jack Hylton, in fact, who was known in London as the "British Paul Whiteman," had even recorded an unusual twelve-inch medley of the Bing Crosby hits I had composed with Arthur Johnston, and it had been a top-selling dance record.

"You simply can't miss," they assured me. "You'd be surprised at how well known your songs are over here. You've really had quite a flock of big hits in England, you know."

I didn't know, for when you are working six thousand miles away, Europe seems so remote; and you don't see your foreign royalties until a couple of years later. But I took their word for it. Sure, I can tackle a challenge like this—I kept assuring myself over and over again.

Bright and early the next morning the concierge phoned to tell me that a limousine from the Gaumont studio was waiting to pick me up. I found Reg Connelly in the back seat, ready to escort me to the lot and introduce me to the top brass.

"I like the way they do things over here," I commented to Reg. "A chauffeured Rolls, no less. No one ever took me to work like that in Hollywood."

Reg, amused, said, "We don't do that for our own writers either.

But you're a visiting celebrity. The red carpet treatment is a studio tradition at Gaumont."

We were driven to Shepherd's Bush, a section of London that was Britain's version of a miniature Hollywood. A uniformed page boy showed us to the office of Sir Michael Balcon, Gaumont's production head. Although knighted, no one ever called him anything but Mickey.

Mickey was all apologies as he greeted us. He had hoped to be all ready for my arrival with a shooting script to work from. But the usual delays and revisions had cropped up, and everyone was weeks behind schedule. Only the producer-director, Victor Saville, had any inkling of what the writers were up to, and they were off somewhere battling it out among themselves.

Mickey suggested that I enjoy London for a few weeks—lots of theater, cabaret, sightseeing. Esther and I could even run over to the Continent for awhile if we chose, he suggested. "After all, you're on salary," he pointed out, "so what have you got to lose? Relax and enjoy yourselves. We'll send you a cable as soon as we get a script."

I wondered how long this had been going on. Go out and have fun, and get paid for it—Hollywood was never like this. We spent the first week in London like a couple of tourists from Sheboygan, Wisconsin. A different show every night—West End hits like *Night Must Fall* and Noel Coward's *Conversation Piece.* Late supper afterwards at the Caprice, the Cafe de Paree, or Quaglino's. London was incredibly cheap in those post-depression days. The best seats for any London show were available at the British pound equivalent of three dollars. A good dinner at an "in" restaurant set you back no more than five bucks for a couple. I had a custom-tailored suit made in five days by the most fashionable Savile Row tailor for seventy-five dollars. The town was lively, exhilarating, challenging. We loved every minute of it— especially at those prices.

By day, we eagerly took in the places that no member of the jet set would want to be found dead in—the British Museum, the National Gallery, the Bloody Tower, Windsor Castle, and the Houses of Parliament. The things I always wanted to see. I blessed the scriptwriters, and hoped they were having lots of story trouble.

During the second week, I discovered London's Tin Pan Alley. It was the genuine thing, not spread all over town like the one in New York. Just one short block called Denmark Street, off Charing Cross Road. Every house on the block was a rickety old nineteenth-century two-story building, with a different music publisher in each one. Campbell and Connelly's establishment was across the road from Laurence Wright, flanked by Bert Feldman, Kieth Prowse, and Francis, Day, and Hunter, among others. They all seemed to be on Denmark Street except the prestigious old firm of Chappell and Company, which was headquartered in fashionable Bond Street in Mayfair.

You could hear the pianos tickling all over the little street. The songs were all American hits of the previous season. For despite their shabby-looking, dilapidated exteriors, these firms were the giants of the British pop-music industry, each one contracted as the British outlet for a major American publisher.

The smell and the atmosphere of the song factories must have done something to arouse a dyed-in-the-wool alleycat like me. I found myself getting restless and yearning to be in action. Two weeks had gone by, and still no sign of a script.

I began to haunt the Campbell and Connelly offices, revelling in the sound of the pianos at full blast as music-hall acts rehearsed. I was fascinated by the sales pitches of the songpluggers with their Cockney accents. It was like the old days in New York. Lunch at the Ivy around the corner was like the midday sessions at Lindy's on Broadway. All the music men were there, bragging about the plugs they had landed and the sales of their latest American import.

Desperate for some activity, I gave Reg and Jimmy a song I was free to have published. I had written it prior to my Paramount contract. It was the song I mentioned earlier in my story of Lew Cody's party, "The Show Is Over." For some strange reason, I had never found a spot for it in one of my Hollywood films. They gave the song to their subsidiary firm in the house next door, the Irwin Dash Music Company. Irwin had been Phil Kornheiser's righthand man at Leo Feist's in New York, a top-ranking professional man and a real hustler. Reg and Jimmy had brought him over and put him in business with a firm of his own, in full partnership with their company. Irwin's American plugging methods had made the new firm an overnight success. He was glad to get my song, and worked hard enough on it to establish it as a smash ballad hit that season. My collaborators on the number, Con Conrad and Al Dubin, were in Hollywood completely unaware that the song was clicking strongly across the Atlantic. Conrad and Dubin received a welcome surprise later when their royalty checks arrived in the mail.

But I am getting ahead of myself. A month had gone by and still no word from the studio. Reg Connelly was due in Paris for conferences with his French publishing representatives. He offered to take Esther and me along as his guests, reminding me that Mickey Balcon had suggested a visit to the Continent while waiting.

Reg introduced us to Paris and its high spots with a flair that made the trip unforgettable. We had a suite at the Crillon, sampled the wares of Europe's best chefs, and ate ourselves unconscious all over Paris.

I marvelled at Reg's lavish lifestyle and his fabulous hosting, remembering that I had heard that during the 1920's he and Jimmy were a couple of struggling songwriters knocking on all the doors in Denmark Street and being turned down. As a last resort, they borrowed a few pounds and published one of their compositions themselves. The song, "Show Me the Way to Go Home," became a worldwide hit and established Campbell and Connelly as the hottest new publishing firm in London. More bestselling hits followed, like "Goodnight, Sweetheart," which they wrote in collaboration with Ray Noble. Their firm grew so rapidly they they were forced to concentrate on being publishing executives, leaving the songwriting to others.

After a week of this paradise on the house—and with a paycheck thrown in for good measure—I was beginning to wonder if Lou Diamond's fantastic loan-out deal was going to last forever. Then I received a phone call from the studio in London. Could I report for work in ten days?

Esther and I decided to spend the last ten days of our enforced holiday on a lightning tour of the Continent. We took the Orient Express to Vienna that night. It was an uneventful train ride—no dead bodies or sinister Hitchcock characters in the corridors. I pulled up our curtain at dawn and saw a snowcapped mountain, which Esther told me was an Alp.

We were met at the train station in Vienna by Karl Berger, Paramount's general manager for Austria. He gave us a taste of what it meant to be under contract to a great worldwide entertainment complex. Karl brought with him a retinue of local newspaper photographers, Paramount press representatives, and local music people. One of them showed me a copy of the German edition of my "Little White Gardenia," informing me that it was currently the most popular song in Central Europe and the rage of Vienna. The copy had German lyrics and was published there under the title of "Kleiner Weisse Blumen."

180

Karl had us in tow during our entire brief stay in Vienna, having arranged everything for us on an hour-to-hour schedule. On the first day we were escorted on a tour of all of the standard sights, from Beethoven's home to the Vienna Woods that Johann Straus had immortalized.

Our second evening was one of the most memorable of a lifetime. Karl had arranged for his wife to dine with Esther, while I was to be the guest of honor at a special dinner that had been arranged for me, as Karl put it, "with gentlemen guests only, if you don't mind."

He took me to a private dining room in the Bristol Hotel, where I found assembled a group of illustrious Viennese operetta composers—names I had admired and looked up to all my life. The great Emmerich Kalman was there, and Robert Stolz, and one of their principal librettists, Alfred Grunewald. So was Paul Abraham, the leading Hungarian operetta composer, and Robert Katscher, composer of the most famous Viennese song hit of the 1920's, "When Day Is Done." The dean of them all, the eminent Franz Lehar, telegraphed his regrets. He had suddenly taken ill. I was toasted and retoasted, and to say I was flabbergasted and overwhelmed by the surprising tribute would be understating my emotions.

The piece de resistance of the evening was a special entertainment arranged in my honor. It consisted of a single performer, a young pianist. The young man sat down at the piano and, without any announcement or fanfare, proceeded to play a medley of the hit songs from all my musical films which had played in Austria. Following the songs, he came back to the piano to play a most astonishing encore—a selection of *background* music I had composed for some of my musicals. Little snatches of things I had written to be played behind love scenes, screen titles, even entrances and exits. Many of them I had forgotten about, and none of them had been published in sheet music form. When he returned to the table I asked him where in the world he had found these tunes. He explained that he had looked up the film cue sheets which are sent to all countries for copyright clearance. For those listed as my compositions, he had run the film sequences over and over in a screening room until he knew the tunes by heart. It was an incredibly flattering gesture, and it warmed my heart.

Following the dinner, Karl and I joined our wives at Vienna's most popular supper club, the Femina. I was introduced to the

181

leader of the dance orchestra there, a young violinist named Norbert Faconi. He had wanted to meet me because "Cocktails for Two" was his favorite violin solo. He announced my presence to the audience, and thereafter played a chorus of "Cocktails" at least once in every dance set for the remainder of the evening. As my party got up to leave, long after midnight, Norbert signalled his musicians. They proceeded to march after us, single file, playing "Cocktails for Two" all the way out to the taxi stand. As our cab pulled away, Norbert was standing there on the curb, playing the song on the violin with all the schmaltz and feeling he could command.

Riding back to our hotel, I told Karl how overcome I was by the whole evening. I never knew anyone had even heard of me over here, I explained.

"I am really touched by this amazing display of hospitality. Nothing like this ever happened to me in my own country," I went on. "American songwriters have never given a dinner in my honor. When I walk into a nightclub, the leader will sometimes wave to me, but never think of playing one of my tunes. Why is it so different over here?"

"But you see," Karl pointed out, "this is *Vienna*. Music is important to us Viennese, perhaps the most important thing in the world. Composers and musicians are our great national heroes. Beethoven's home is a national shrine, like your Washington Monument. When a man has created good music—even if he is not a Beethoven but a writer of popular music—he is appreciated and honored in this country."

I knew what he meant, having just had a demonstration of the striking difference in the standing of popular culture in our two countries.

Following Vienna, we were the guests of Paul Abraham for a day in his home town, Budapest. There we took a fast express to Berlin, which was to be our last stop before returning to London.

It was the Hitlerian Berlin of the middle Thirties, and you would have to be blind not to realize that the country was preparing for war. Wherever we went—the hotels, the theaters, the beer gardens—at least half the male patrons wore a uniform of some sort. Many of them were officers. I caught the significance of it all during our first evening there.

We were staying at the Adlon, Berlin's largest hotel, because the owner's son, young Louis Adlon, lived in Hollywood and was a good friend of ours. Louis was trying to break into the film business, and he had worked at Paramount for a time. We had cabled Louis before leaving Paris, asking him to please cable the hotel for a reservation.

On returning to the hotel after our first night on the town, we found a large basket of flowers in our suite, with a card from Mr. Adlon inviting us to breakfast with him in his top-floor apartment the following morning.

Mr. Adlon proved to be a gracious host, offering to do anything to make our stay comfortable. He was also eager for news about his son, and we were glad to bring him up to date. We strolled out on the rooftop terrace, and he pointed to several of the nearby penthouse apartments. "That one is Hitler's apartment when he is in Berlin," he said, "and the next one is Goering's." And he heaved a sigh.

Over breakfast, he said he wanted to ask a favor of us.

"Anything you say, Mr. Adlon," said Esther. "What can we do for you?"

"Well—I hope you won't mind—I first want to ask you if you are of Jewish blood."

"My wife isn't, but I am," I replied. "Why do you ask?"

He was a kindly old gentleman, and his eyes lit up with a glow of warmth as he answered me.

"You probably have heard what the situation is over here," said Adlon, "and it concerns the favor I want to ask of you, which is simply this: *Please* do not tell anyone that I entertained you at breakfast. It is my great pleasure to do so, but if the wrong people knew about it, I could be in great trouble. It is a terrible strain we are living under these days." And he sighed again. We intuitively knew he was sincere.

In the afternoon, we were invited to have tea at Paramount's Berlin offices, where the Berlin manager was an amiable individual named Phillips. During the tea, I asked how things were going with Paramount in Germany. I was just trying to make polite conversation, but I saw that I had struck a serious note. His amiable smile suddenly faded.

"Things are what you Americans call plain lousy," he said. "And do you know why? See all those empty desks out there in the main office? A few weeks ago the Gestapo walked in and told us to fire every employee who was all or part Jewish. I had no choice. Those are the desks of our salesmen, and all the best ones were Jewish. Most of them were with us for many years and had families to support. Consequently, business is lousy." Bitterness

183

was written all over his face. He could not disguise his feelings.

Phillips took us to dinner that night at a large supper club which, like the one in Vienna, was also called the Femina. It was lively and crowded. Yet I detected a note of decadence in the place, like the atmosphere in Isherwood's play *I Am a Camera.* Again we found many of the customers in uniform, heavily imbibing their steins of beer and staggering from table to table. The place reeked with a sense of false gaiety.

Phillips had wanted us to come to the Femina because it boasted Germany's most popular dance band, Oscar Joost and his Orchestra. "A Little White Gardenia" was a hit in Berlin too, and Joost had been broadcasting it nightly. Being a big radio name there, he had helped zoom the song to popularity.

I watched Joost from our table. He was a large, burly man, typically Prussian in type, with a close-cropped haircut and strictly deadpan. He never smiled once as the dancers flitted by him. He waved his baton fiercely, occasionally scowling at his orchestra of some thirty or 35 fine dance musicians.

Phillips sent the waiter up to Joost with a note asking him to join us at the table for coffee, so he could meet me. He never left the bandstand.

During the next dance set, Phillips danced over to Joost and extended the invitation in person. Joost told him he didn't mind playing my music, but he didn't care to meet me, because he had heard I was of Jewish extraction. He didn't care to meet any Jewish composers. Not even Gershwin or Rodgers or Kern, if they ever came to the place. I guess it takes all kinds, I reflected as Phillips told me about it. What a study in contrasts—the reception I received in Berlin, compared to Vienna!

My first day back in London was spent mostly attending meetings at the studio. The affable and friendly Victor Saville, who was producing and directing *It's Love Again,* filled me in on the story and described the sequences where musical numbers were indicated. We screened Jessie Matthews' *Evergreen,* and I met Jessie herself. She looked every inch the reigning queen of British musicals: a face and figure you wouldn't believe, unsurpassable style and class in her walk, her speaking voice, and the way she wore her clothes. In *Evergreen* her singing, her acting, and especially her dancing had left very little to be desired. In person she came across with great charm, sincerity, and enthusiasm. I felt I would be writing for a star who would really cooperate. My hunch proved correct.

184

I turned out four songs, words and music, for *It's Love Again*. (The studio had already purchased one other number, by Harry Woods, some months before.) Jessie was delighted when I played my little score on its completion, and Victor Saville was extremely complimentary. The principal production number I gave Jessie, "Got to Dance My Way to Heaven," fulfilled everyone's expectations and was a hit all over England soon after the film's release. The title song, "It's Love Again," also sung by Jessie, did nearly as well.

During the final days of shooting, I received a letter from Lou Diamond telling me that negotiations were on for another loan-out of my services. This one would be very close to home—right next door to Paramount, at the neighboring RKO studios. RKO wanted me to write the songs for the next Fred Astaire-Ginger Rogers musical. I cabled Lou that I was thrilled beyond words, and to please work fast on the loan-out deal.

A letdown came with the mail a few days later. Lou informed me that the team of Astaire and Rogers had just broken up—some problem or other about Ginger's contract—and the film would be called off unless RKO found a quick replacement for Ginger. A tough order indeed—someone who would look good dancing and singing with Fred Astaire. In less time than it takes to whistle a chorus of "The Carioca," I was in Jessie Matthews' dressing room asking her if I might suggest her for the part.

"Co-star with Fred Astaire?" she fairly squealed. "Do you really think I'd have a chance?"

I assured her that I knew all the prospective co-stars in Hollywood, and that her chances, in my estimation, were better than anybody's. It was certainly worth a try. I made the suggestion in a long cablegram to Lou Diamond, telling him I had just worked with a star who was made to order for Astaire and urging him to transmit my enthusiasm to the people he was dealing with at RKO. Lou cabled a quick reply that RKO would screen *It's Love Again* as soon as a print was available in New York.

Shooting on the film was finally completed. I stayed around London a few weeks longer, sitting in on the background scoring and waiting to see a final cut. During that period I was besieged with letters from a young English girl from the country. Her name was Vera Lynn and she desperately wanted to audition for the studio officials. She had read the newspaper publicity about *It's Love Again* and was sure that if I heard her sing I would recommend her for a singing part in a movie. I finally got around

185

to listening during the lull after shooting. I invited her to come over to the studio.

Vera seemed nervous and awkward when she began her audition, but there was no mistaking the classic quality of her powerful singing voice. The studio officials, however, felt that she was not a film possibility, and passed her up. It was their loss. Half a dozen years later, Vera Lynn had established herself as the most celebrated songstress of the World War II period in Britain, and she is still a lengendary star there. She is generally given credit for making "There'll Always Be an England" the country's biggest hit of the war years.

During my final week in London, I managed to squeeze in a "farewell concert" of my songs on the BBC radio network. I sang to the superb arrangements of the Henry Hall Orchestra, England's finest light-music aggregation at the time. I also worked in some recording sessions for His Master's Voice Records (RCA-Victor's British arm) and Columbia with two great London bands, Ray Noble's and Geraldo's. The Ray Noble session was a story in itself, which I will go into in the next chapter.

We were back in Hollywood a week later. My first task was to find out what had transpired on my Jessie Matthews-Fred Astaire suggestion. I was told that RKO representatives in London had screened a few sequences from *It's Love Again* while I was en route to Hollywood, and they were greatly impressed by Jessie's performance. They had contacted her new manager in London about possibly bringing her over for the film. The RKO studio bosses were now waiting to find out what sort of deal her manager wanted. I kept my fingers crossed.

After a few suspenseful days, RKO received word from their London office. Jessie's new manager, it turned out, was her husband, British comedian Sonny Hale. Sonny had a featured role in *It's Love Again,* although he received second billing below Robert Young, Jessie's leading man in the film (and known to TV fans today as Dr. Marcus Welby). Sonny had just learned that *It's Love Again* was booked to premiere in the U.S. at Radio City Music Hall, New York's largest first-run film palace. He was playing that up for all it was worth. First of all, he asked an exceedingly high salary. This didn't bother RKO. They never spared the expenses in Fred Astaire's features, which were the highest-grossing musicals of their day. But the next condition threw them for a loop. Sonny insisted that the film must contain a feature role for him as well. That squelched it. There was just no role in the story that he could play.

I have often wondered how Jessie's career might have evolved if this little example of personal vanity by her manager-husband hadn't prevented her from coming here and receiving the inevitable buildup as Fred Astaire's new partner. She would have been ideal. Fate sometimes plays weird tricks that deny one the chance of a lifetime; and it happens even to the most deserving talents.

Chapter Ten

JOCKS, JUKES, RECORDS, AND BIG BANDS

Flash-back:

Although my songs had been recorded on major and minor labels starting with my first publication, "Heartsickness Blues," my first real direct exposure to the recording industry was in March 1928 during a trip to Chicago for our new publishing firm, Spier and Coslow.

I was making the rounds of the Chicago offices of various record companies. At the local branch of Columbia Records my timing coincided with a problem that had arisen there. I was at the piano singing and playing a couple of my recent songs for Eddie King, Columbia's recording head, who had also just arrived from New York. Suddenly he interrupted me to ask, "Hey, Sam, have you ever made any recordings?"

Surprised, I told him I hadn't.

"Your voice sounds like it has recording quality," he said. "I'm glad I heard it. We've been looking for the right singer, and we need him in a big hurry!"

It's strange how often the unexpected occurs in the music business. New singers make all sorts of elaborate plans to submit test recordings to record firms, going to great expense and trouble to get any kind of a break. Then again, you hear of cases like mine, where recording was furthermost from my mind. I just happened to be at the right place at the right time.

188

Eddie explained that the song "Chloe" was suddenly breaking big. Columbia wanted to be first in the race to rush out a recording. He had a recording session scheduled for that week by a new midwestern dance band, the Tracy-Brown Orchestra.

But Tracy-Brown had no vocalist. Vocalists, in fact, were a recent development with dance bands at that time. Many well known bands had not yet gotten around to hiring them. Inconceivable as it seems today, many dance recordings of hit songs were still being released as instrumentals.

I spent the next couple of days with Manny Strand, Tracy-Brown's pianist and arranger, rehearsing "Chloe" and a couple of other songs for the session, setting my keys and experimenting with test pressings.

The actual recording session was easier than I expected. Eddie King selected take two as the acceptable one. It was pretty much guesswork, because in those early days there were no playbacks. When you felt you had recorded a good take, that was it—and you were stuck with whatever was on the wax. The fabulous electronic recording techniques of today were undreamed of. My recording of "Chloe" (Columbia 1344-D) sounds like a crude affair when you play it now, but in those days it was considered to be of pretty good recording quality. The record sold surprisingly well for a new singer and a relatively unknown band. I attribute this to the great success enjoyed by the song, one of the hits of 1928.

Shortly after the record was released, Columbia offered me a contract to record exclusively for them. But in the meantime, Larry Spier had stepped in as manager of my recording activities and had come up with a much better offer from Victor Records, including the guarantee of a buildup. Victor was then the pinnacle label that all recording artists aspired to. I accepted the offer.

My first Victor recording date in August 1928 was supervised by Leonard Joy. I was accompanied by a house band featuring some of the best musicians of the time. We made "King for a Day" (Victor 21631), which also turned out to be one of the year's big numbers, backed up with "You're a Real Sweetheart." Victor really got behind it, and the royalties exceeded my expectations. By today's standards, "King for a Day" was a pretty corny recording. It included a recitation in which I really hammed it up, imitating Jolson, Richman, and Ted Lewis all rolled into one. I often play it these days for friends, and it never fails to get hysterical laughter. No one remembers that records like that were made in all seriousness back in 1928. Yet Victor advertised it nationally as a "highly dramatic rendition, the like of which you have never heard." And they weren't kidding.

I recorded eight more titles between "King for a Day" and the time I moved to Hollywood in 1929, including popular hits like "I Wanna Be Loved by You" and "Spell of the Blues," with Nat Shilkret conducting the Victor house band on most of them. I also did a novel Victor release—voice and organ—called "Just a Night for Meditation." Victor teamed me up with the country's most popular organist, Jesse Crawford, a big name in that era.

For one of my last recordings before leaving for the Coast, Victor assigned me to do the current Jolson smash, "Sonny Boy." It was an ill-advised choice. Jolson's record, just released on the Brunswick label, took off like a meteor and made recording history. To attempt to overtake it would have been futile. Victor, in a rare display of good sense, decided to shelve my version. It was just as well, because I had done such an unabashed imitation that I was actually trying to out-Jolson Jolson. It reeked of pure, unadulterated hokum.

My Hollywood songwriting activities interrupted my recording career. As I noted in an earlier chapter, I did not record again until Victor opened a Hollywood branch. There I recorded a 12-inch single (on 78) of Rodgers and Hart's "Isn't It Romantic?" in the summer of 1932. This was followed by other hits of the early Thirties like "Here Lies Love" and Irving Berlin's "Say It Isn't So." And for the first time, Victor allowed me to record some of my own compositions, starting with "Learn to Croon" and "Moonstruck" from *College Humor.* Previously the company was reluctant to let me record my own numbers. I soon realized that the company had been right. On "Learn to Croon," for example, I was bucking the man I had written the song for, Bing Crosby. Bing's Brunswick recording was such a big seller that my Victor release was eclipsed. Who could ever compete with Bing, the biggest-selling recording artist of all time? Certainly not I. All I did was create an awful lot of shellac for the scrap heap. Sorry, Bing—Victor and I should have known better.

In the middle Thirties, as I mentioned in the previous chapter, I made several vocal recordings in London. Victor's English label, HMV (His Master's Voice), scheduled a session for me to record two of my own compositions, which Campbell and Connelly were publishing over there.

The first, "A Place in Your Heart," came off without mishaps. Take one was a beauty. The B side, a hastily concocted novelty

190

whose title I have conveniently forgotten, somehow failed to jell at the session. It had been arranged in a key that was too high for me, and our first run-through sounded like a dog fight. It was one big gigantic mess. I turned to Ray Noble, who was in charge of the session and who was accompanying me with his small recording band, and asked him to scrap the second number.

Ray was then an up-and-coming young conductor, typically British in bearing and demeanor. Occasions like this left him unperturbed. I was the only one who was bothered.

"What do we do now, Ray?" I asked in consternation. "We don't have anything else prepared, do we?"

Ray, still remarkably composed and looking even slightly bored, reflected for a moment. Then he asked me, "Would you mind terribly if the B side were something you didn't write, old chap?"

I assured him I wouldn't mind at all, adding that I had recorded dozens of songs by other writers.

Ray, almost apologetically, said, "It just happens that I have a little number here I wrote myself the other night."

Quick as a flash, out of his inside coat pocket came a one-page lead sheet with the lyrics scrawled in pencil. "My boys already know the tune and can fake it," Ray assured me. "It's very simple and short. I can teach it to you in ten minutes."

I didn't believe I could learn any song that quickly, but I listened with great interest as Ray played it on the piano. He had already composed a smash hit a few years before, "Goodnight, Sweetheart," with a lyric by Jimmy Campbell and Reg Connelly, so I knew he was no slouch as a writer.

Ray had written both words and music for the new song. It was none other than his now famous "The Very Thought of You." At that time, it was just another new ditty in his coat pocket which he thought he might—or might not—"find a spot for one of these days."

By the time he was halfway through the chorus, I was enthusiastic. "Wow! Ray, that's some song!" He looked up at me in pleased surprise. I was able to learn the song—not in ten minutes, but in five.

It was the first-ever recording of what eventually became Ray Noble's foremost standard and his signature throughout his long radio career which followed. When the record was released in England as HMV B-8181, it was "The Very Thought of You" that attracted immediate attention. London record shops were so besieged with calls for the record that my song, "A Place in Your Heart," was naturally relegated to the "B" side and consigned to oblivion, as most "B" songs are. Ray was turning out dozens of new song manuscripts every month at that early stage of his career, and many of them never saw the light of day. I therefore have often wondered what might have happened to "The Very Thought of You" if it hadn't suited my singing voice, and if my second song at the session hadn't been a dud.

Shortly after the session, Ray came over to the U.S. with his manager and drummer, Bill Harty, who had secured a lucrative contract for Ray on NBC radio. Ray's first American band was an all-star aggregation if I ever heard one, numbering among his musicians such immortals as Glenn Miller on trombone, Charlie Spivak on trumpet, George Van Eps on guitar, and Claude Thornhill on piano. He later broadcast from Hollywood, where I threw a large party to welcome Ray on his arrival, introducing him to many of the American radio and film contingent. Ray was a household name to American radio audiences well into the 1950's, not only for his impeccable musical virtuosity, but in his familiar role of the dimwitted Englishman (which Ray was anything but, in person) on the Burns & Allen and Edgar Bergen-Charlie McCarthy network shows.

Although not generally realized, the disc jockey and the playing of records on radio were developments that stemmed directly from the great depression of the Thirties. I saw it all happen: slowly at first, after which it finally emerged as a full-blown music phenomenon that completely dominated the art of song exploitation by the time the 1940's arrived.

During my early Hollywood years, songs were popularized chiefly by musical films and radio artists, either staff singers and orchestras or the so-called "remotes"—dance bands that broadcast from the hotels or nightclubs where they played. Remotes provided the late-night programs on the country's networks. Starting around 11 p.m., a typical NBC scheduling might begin with a half hour of Guy Lombardo from the Roosevelt Hotel in New York, then a swing over to Ben Bernie from Chicago's Sherman Hotel, followed by Gene Rodemich from St. Louis, and finally Gus Arnheim from the L.A. Cocoanut Grove. Some stations would carry remotes far into the night. During the earlier evening hours, sponsored orchestras and singers were programmed.

This type of programming grew out of the strict regulations

192

imposed by the Musicians' Union and its "czars," James Petrillo in Chicago and Joseph Weber in New York, whose influence was felt nationally. Every station of respectable size was required to employ a full house orchestra, or else carry enough remotes to take its place. Records were played only occasionally, usually by small-town stations.

Starting around 1931 and 1932, radio stations were beginning to feel the economic pinch. House bands were gradually cut down until they became almost nonexistent. The union had to go along. At least the network stations were still carrying the big sponsored shows that emanated mostly from New York and Los Angeles, shows that featured Crosby, Vallee, and other music luminaries. But the independent stations, hard up for sponsors, were in trouble. They began to use records more and more, until record shows came to dominate the independent stations.

At first, the modus operandi consisted simply of a staff announcer carrying an armful of new releases to the turntable, announcing each title in turn. The stations in most cases received these records free, either from songpluggers who supplied their plug songs as fast as new recordings were released, or from representatives of the recording companies intent on building sales.

The rise of the disc jockey was a natural consequence of this new way of pop-music life. I watched the deejays begin their rise as key personalities in local radio. They chattered about the artists and records they played, delivering commercial spiels between recordings and attracting followings that gave them profound influence throughout the music world.

The first big-name disc jockeys I became aware of around the Pacific Coast stations were Martin Block and Al Jarvis, each of whom claimed to be the originator of the Make Believe Ballroom programming idea. I don't know who actually conceived the idea, but eventually Block forged ahead to become a fullfledged radio star in his own right, with sponsors lining up to capture his best time slots. Martin made enough out of his rapid rise to build, later in his career, a large estate in the San Fernando Valley where he installed his own broadcasting equipment and housed his own extensive record library. I visited him often in his palatial residence-studio, sitting in on some of his broadcasts while he played a flock of current recordings of my film songs. Martin was a human encyclopedia on recording artists and songs in general, and his goodhumored, breezy chatter was a delight to listen to.

In the mid-Thirties he had moved to New York to become, by

193

universal consent, the nation's top disc jockey. His Make Believe Ballroom show debuted on WNEW in 1935 and stayed there till he moved to WABC in the middle Fifties. Martin became a magnet to Tin Pan Alley songpluggers and the managers of popular bands and singers. His programs made not only song hits but stars. His format in New York boiled down to a ninety-minute morning show and a two-hour evening program in which fifteen-minute segments were devoted to the recordings of different singers or orchestras. The competition among artists to get featured on the show became frenzied.

During the 1940's, the hundreds of deejays from coast to coast came to rule the music scene. Many became household names in their regions. Some, like Steve Allen, went on to achieve stardom in other broadcast fields. Steve, when he was a young disc jockey on KFWB in Hollywood, devoted a full hour on one of his shows to interviewing me and playing a selection of recorded hits I had written. A few years later, in 1956, I was one of his first guests when he launched the Tonight Show on NBC television. My songs were performed on the show by Andy Williams, then Steve's staff vocalist, with yours truly at the piano. Steve chatted with me between numbers and we discussed the personalities I had written for.

In 1941, a music blackout descended on radio and lasted for many months. The broadcasting industry was feuding with ASCAP (American Society of Composers, Authors, and Publishers) over performance rates for our music. The network stations, whose licensing contracts with ASCAP had expired, resorted to playing Stephen Foster and other composers whose copyrights had run out. During that long barren stretch, disc jockeys assumed even greater importance. They were featured on the independent stations and were thus able to feature ASCAP songs, since most of the independents were quick to make their own agreements with ASCAP. New popular songs, of course, were still being written and recorded on all labels, though they were barred from the networks. The new songs still could be heard during this period on juke boxes, which were now mushrooming in every bar, lunch room, bus station, hot-dog emporium and ice-cream parlor throughout the country. According to trade estimates, some 200,000 juke boxes were gathering trillions of nickels and dimes by the middle 1940's.

The music business was in a state of chaos during the network ban. The songplugging fraternity was deprived of its regular net-

194

work outlets. It was all very hit-or-miss, and a weird bunch of songs were topping the bestseller charts, for no one could possibly predict what would click—a song by one of the ASCAP veterans, or one by a new composer represented by Broadcast Music, Inc. (BMI), the new licensing group whose songs were approved for network broadcast.

Peace was eventually restored between our organization and the National Association of Broadcasters. By late 1941, things were again starting to take on a semblance of normalcy in the Alley.

In my own personal treasure house of recollections, I have reserved a special place for the Big Band era of the Twenties and Thirties. It gives me a warm feeling to know that this marvelous music was an integral part of the world I lived and worked in. I have always felt that the magic of the wonderful Big Band sound was in large part the songs they played: the finest popular music that has ever been created. The music of Berlin, Kern, Gershwin, Porter, Rodgers and so many others gave the period an aura that has never been equalled. All the other eras in popular music suffer by comparison. It was a rare privilege for me to have worked in the Golden Age of popular song. I, like all nostalgia buffs, will always look back at those superb interpreters of that great music with the deepest affection. Many of these musicians were close friends of mine, since I naturally gravitated to those who satisfied my craving to hear my work performed in the best style. To them, I owe a profound debt of gratitude. Without their memorable renditions and recordings, I surely could not have gone very far as a songwriter.

I've already related some of my experiences with Whiteman and Lopez, who were the earliest of the Big Band conductors. Paul Whiteman was the first. He brought a new dimension to dance music and revolutionized it overnight. Before Whiteman, even the best-known dance bands in New York, such as Earl Fuller's Society Orchestra, were small outfits who played stock orchestrations (printed by the music publishers for mass consumption). When you heard one you heard them all, lifeless and undistinguished. Paul, with the background of a violinist in the Denver Symphony (his home town), was the first to offer something new and different: *special arrangements*—unheard of in dance bands at that time—that bordered on the symphonic; an orchestra with twice as many men as the average dance band; all

195

of them individual stars whose solos were the epitome of virtuosity (immortals like Busse, Gorman, Beiderbecke, Pingitore, the Teagardens, Bargy, and both Dorseys); and impeccable taste and showmanship at all times.

Formed on the West Coast in 1919, they were such an immediate sensation that they were quickly signed to open the new Palais Royale restaurant on Broadway. They became the talk of New York by the end of their opening week. Nothing like it had ever been heard before, and the Palais Royale became the rendezvous of the dancing rich. Many a Vanderbilt, Rockefeller, and Whitney foxtrotted to Paul's baton in those days, and the historic Big Band craze was under way. It was only natural that the band would quickly attract the attention of the major recording companies (there were as yet no radio bands). In mid-1920 Victor Records, after giving the band a try-out at their Camden, New Jersey home studios, awarded Paul the juiciest recording contract any dance orchestra had ever received.

The first release was the renowned Whiteman recording of "Japanese Sandman" and "Whispering," the latter a song Paul had discovered while playing in California. Both were hit sides, and the record exploded like a ton of dynamite on the music scene. Now, through the mighty Victor sales organization, millions became aware of the new revolution in dance music. "Avalon" was the second release, and Henry Busse's celebrated "Wang Wang Blues" came next.

My "Grieving for You" was the fourth Whiteman release. Like the first three, it was a number-one record seller. All four sold so many that they still turn up often in the junk shops.

Other favorite compositions of mine that Whiteman recorded were "Lonely Melody," with the unforgettable Bix Beiderbecke cornet solo, "Down the Old Ox Road," which sounds as fresh today as when it was released, and "Now I'm a Lady," one of my Mae West tunes. Until the advent of the great swing bands in the middle 1930's, Whiteman reigned supreme, the emperor of the Big Band world. His influence on good popular music, ranging from jazz to his Aeolian Hall concert to introduce Gershwin's "Rhapsody in Blue," will probably never be surpassed.

In person, I always found Paul congenial, cooperative, courteous, and bursting with enthusiasm for everything he was involved in. I was proud to count him among my good friends until he passed away about ten years ago, at the age of 77. The only unhappy recollection I have of this personable giant occurred in

196

the late 1940's when Paul, after a long period of inactivity, attempted a comeback as a disc jockey on a Hollywood radio station. He called me for an interview during the first week of his program. Of course I dropped whatever I was doing at the time and hurried over to the station. I remember how it saddened me to sit alongside him, answering his questions absentmindedly. All I could think of was what this great man represented in American musical history. He was a titan, a legend—yet here he was asking me trite, banal questions like "What are you working on now, Sam?" and "How do you get your ideas for new songs?" and spinning platters of my songs between questions. Paul was pushing sixty at the time, and he looked tired. Most of the old sparkle was gone. Suddenly, something clicked inside of me, and I surprised him by turning the program around from a Coslow interview to a tribute to Paul Whiteman. I found myself unable to answer his questions. All I could talk about was that wonderful yesterday when Paul ruled the airwaves, what a great inspiration he had been to me and my contemporaries, and how much it had meant to have the Whiteman band feature my songs. There was a brand new generation of radio listeners out there, and I wanted them to know all about him—his fame, his stature, everything he had been and still was. At the conclusion of the half-hour show, I could see there were tears in his eyes. He turned to me after the signoff, embraced me, and mumbled a husky "Thank you, Sam."

Vincent Lopez was the first orchestra leader who was alert enough to sense what was happening to radio in the early Twenties, and he climbed on the Big Bandwagon without delay. His band made history as the first dance orchestra to do a remote broadcast, back in 1921. Expanding his band from a five-piece combo that opened in a Times Square chop suey joint (the Pekin) to a larger ensemble frankly patterned after Whiteman's, Vince, who had been my colleague on the Charles K. Harris songplugging staff, produced a stage-band show for big-time vaudeville. It soon became a headline act. He invested in flashy arrangements and high-priced soloists. He played to capacity audiences at the Pennsylvania Hotel in New York for several seasons, then at the St. Regis, and finally at the newly opened Taft Hotel, where he established an all-time longevity record by remaining on the same job for 27 consecutive years. Like Whiteman, Vincent was a friend, a booster, and a plugger throughout his lifetime. He finally retired in his seventies, moving to Miami Beach where he and his wife were occasional visitors at my Palm Island winter home. Always one jump ahead of the mob, he was a rare combination of astute businessman, innovative genius, and talented musician.

After Whiteman and Lopez, a host of other Big Bands sprang up around the country. On the West Coast, where it all started, the orchestras of Art Hickman, Abe Lyman, Gus Arnheim, Earl Burtnett, and Eddie Elkins became familiar names on records and radio. In the Midwest, two bandleaders who also composed many hit songs, Isham Jones and Ted Fio Rito, gathered big followings. Around the same time, New York was hearing the likes of Waring's Pennsylvanians, George Olsen, Ben Bernie (who had started as a violin-playing vaudeville comic), Jan Garber, Phil Spitalny (without his all-girl orchestra), and others. They, along with pioneers Whiteman and Lopez, were the vanguard of the Big Band vogue which lasted for some 35 years and which has not yet completely died out. They were my buddies, and they plugged, broadcast, and recorded my songs throughout their long careers—bless 'em all!

Next came the first Big Bands in the jazz field, most of them black. I have mentioned "finding" Ellington in a previous chapter. The Duke became probably the most renowned of the jazz greats who emerged in the Twenties. At the time he was probably surpassed in popularity by Fletcher Henderson, whose band played at the Roseland Ballroom on Broadway and who recorded some highly collectible jazz classics. Louis Armstrong, fresh from New Orleans, was beginning to attract attention with his raucous voice and his creative trumpet improvisations.

The best big-band white jazz I ever heard was Ben Pollack's. I don't think any real jazz addict would argue the point. Ben stands out as the greatest collector of marvelous jazz musicians ever known in this business. When I tell you that his outfit included, at various times, Benny Goodman on clarinet, Glenn Miller and then Jack Teagarden on trombone, Charlie Spivak on trumpet, Eddie Lang on guitar, and Harry James on trumpet, you may realize what all-star really means.

The Pollack band played at the Park Central Hotel around 1928 and 1929. Before I moved out to Hollywood it was my favorite late-night haunt. I used to sit there in a trance, too fascinated by the incredible sound to go home. You had to hear it to believe it. Glenn Miller wrote many of the arrangements, and they were about twenty years ahead of their time. I don't think Benny ever realized how great his band was. He rarely conducted, at that time, preferring to sit in with the band playing drums, which he did with a good deal of style and competence.

A chattery, thoroughly likable little guy, he would sit at the table with me, guzzling down countless cups of coffee between dance sets until far into the night. For some strange reason that I will never understand, the band never really made it big with the public, although they deserved to on sheer class alone. Ben's recording of my "True Blue Lou" is a particular favorite of mine.

I saw Ben again in the middle Thirties when he migrated out to the West Coast. There he formed another great band, which Bob Crosby eventually took over. In time, eleven of Ben's former sidemen had Big Bands of their own, and most were far bigger names than their erstwhile boss had ever been. I was profoundedly shocked about five years ago when I read that Ben had committed suicide, in Palm Springs, by hanging himself. He had always seemed like such a happy-go-lucky sort, brimming over with good humor and exuberance. There must have been a side to him that I never knew; or perhaps some personal tragedy befell him in his later years.

By the early 1930's, a new crop of so-called "sweet" bands appeared on the horizon. Of these, the undisputed kings were Rudy Vallee on movie-house stages and Guy Lombardo in hotels and ballrooms. The Lombardo outfit, whose dynasty will soon pass the half-century mark, included four brothers (and sometimes a sister), all outstanding specialists in the fine art of schmaltz. At the Edgewater Beach Hotel in Chicago, Ted Weems became a byword. He featured a sleepy-eyed young vocalist named Perry Como, who sang practically everything I wrote in those days. Eddy Duchin, presiding from the keyboard, was a new name in Boston and New York hotels. Lawrence Welk had recently started, and was the Prime Minister of Polka. Tommy and Jimmy Dorsey had graduated from Whiteman's band to head their own Dorsey Brothers Orchestra. Which just about brings me to the start of the great Swing Era of the 1930's, the musical miracle that will always be associated with that decade. The Dorseys bridged the gap between the preceding melodic years and the new swing fad. They were part of both worlds, making the transition as smoothly as one of their subtle modulations.

As I stated earlier, the Dorseys had started their own orchestra back in 1928, quickly attracting national attention with their first hit record, their two-sided concert version of my song, "Was It a Dream?". Tommy and Jimmy were new at the conducting game at that early stage, so they prevailed upon their friend, Dr. Eugene Ormandy, to conduct the recording session—the same Eugene Ormandy who, as I mentioned before, later conducted the Philadelphia Symphony for so many years.

The first Dorseys' band never got much farther than the recording studios, and the brothers themselves became studio sidemen much in demand in the early Thirties. In 1934 they formed another band, smaller and swingier. It was this band that helped pioneer the new swing vogue, which the Dorseys capitalized on to the hilt. Jimmy, with his great alto sax and clarinet improvisations, was by far the swingier of the two brothers. Tommy was more of a soloist on the sweet side, noted for his virtuosity on the trombone.

The Dorseys were soon overtaken by the rapid rise of a new luminary named Benny Goodman, who soon won the label of King of Swing through his classic clarinet renditions of early swing hits. The King has never been dethroned even to this day, although a few like Artie Shaw and Glenn Miller gave him quite a run for the money in the late Thirties and early Forties.

For the sake of the record, I must say that as far as I am concerned the same brand of music was being played in the middle Twenties, although nobody called it swing then. Ellington was playing authentic, marvelous swing almost a full decade before it got its name. Later, in 1930, an exciting swing recording of my "Sing, You Sinners" appeared on a new label called Hit of the Week. As I mentioned earlier, these records were merchandised through newsstand sales. The song was recorded by a band called the Harlem Hot Chocolates, which was easily recognizable as the Ellington outfit under a *nom de disque*. It was the first recording I ever recall that was referred to as a swing number. And certainly the sounds by Cab Calloway around the same time were pure swing if they were anything.

The great swing musicians were all remarkable stylists, the like of which we may never hear again. They were sidemen with the Big Bands in the late 1920's and early 1930's—memorable artists like Bunny Berigan, Jack Teagarden, Miff Mole, Bud Freeman, George Van Eps, Glenn Miller, Harry James, and the great B.G himself. In those years, they drifted from band to band. Whoever came up with the most prestigious engagement and the highest pay usually got them. They were all chummy, and accustomed to playing with each other. Being individual stars in great demand, most of them eventually wound up leading their own bands in the Thirties.

Glenn Miller was one of the last to venture out on his own, waiting until 1937 before fronting his own organization in a Boston ballrom. By then, he was already known as one of the best arrangers in the business, having orchestrated for Ben Pollack, Ray Noble, the Dorsey Brothers and other big outfits. This was the era of Glen Gray's Casa Loma Orchestra, Bob Crosby and his Bobcats, and the great black swing maestroes like Count Basie and Jimmie Lunceford, all frontrunners in the swing race of the Thirties.

It was also the era of inimitable swing vocalists: Martha Tilton and Peggy Lee with Goodman (Peggy's rendition of "My Old Flame" on the Goodman record is one of my prize possessions); Helen Forrest with Artie Shaw, Goodman and Harry James; Connie Haines and Edythe Wright with Tommy Dorsey; and Helen O'Connell and Bob Eberly with Jimmy—all of whom were to become historic recording names.

I also recall—with some pleasure and pride—that two great vocal names began their recording careers with songs I had written. The Andrews Sisters started as a vocal trio with the Leon Belasco Orchestra, and their very first recording was "Jammin'," which I had composed for the film *Turn Off the Moon.* Then there was Rosemary Clooney, who began her dynamic recording career as vocalist for Tony Pastor's Orchestra. Her debut on record was a revival of "Grieving for You," my first hit of 25 years before.

I was friendly with many of the swing idols. The two I knew best were Tommy Dorsey and Artie Shaw. Tommy, who had recorded around a dozen of my compositions, did a two-hour coast-to-coast broadcast in my honor in the early 1940's from the Astor Roof in New York City. His vocalists at the time were Frank Sinatra, Connie Haines, and the Pied Pipers, a group that included Jo Stafford. I spent an enjoyable afternoon rehearsing on the Roof their vocals of my songs. On the broadcast, I sang a few of the songs myself.

Tommy owned a country estate in Bernardsville, New Jersey. His Sunday afternoon parties there were festive occasions attended by the Who's Who of the music world—star performers, songwriters and publishers. Tommy was a genial host who was never really satisfied until most of his guests were thoroughly swacked. In that condition, some of them engaged in the wildest and most inspired jam sessions I ever remember hearing. Oh, to have had a portable tape recorder in those days!

I met Artie Shaw, Benny Goodman's chief rival, during one of my trips to New York. We became good friends. I played "I'm in

Love with the Honorable Mr. So-and-So" for Artie at the RCA-Victor studios one afternoon, and he insisted on recording it at his next session. Artie's clarinet solo, plus the remarkable vocal by Helen Forrest, made it a memorable platter. Later, in Hollywood, he recorded my "Dreaming Out Loud" with equally satisfying results.

During his Hollywood sojourn Artie, who had all of his hair at that time, was far and away the handsomest bandleader the town had ever seen. He was not only goodlooking; he was an individualist and a raconteur, possessed of great personal charm. I have had friends, like Steve Allen and Noel Coward, who had a great variety of talents, but Artie certainly rivals them in the range of his accomplishments. He played one hell of a clarinet, composed many of the swing tunes he recorded, acted in big Hollywood musicals, produced box-office movie hits, wrote successful fiction, and, judging from his nine marriages, probably excelled in the hay. It was therefore inevitable that some of the film colony's most glamorous females would clamor for his company. It seemed that every time I picked up the *Hollywood Reporter* I would read about Artie marrying somebody or other—Lana Turner, Ava Gardner, and Evelyn Keyes were among his nine brides.

But he never married the one girl that I always thought fell for him the hardest of all, Judy Garland. He would bring Judy over to my house in Coldwater Canyon on Sunday afternoons. I guess she was about seventeen or eighteen then, and she kept looking up at him with her big, soulful eyes, doting on his every word. Her mad teenage crush never reached the marrying stage. I guess Artie felt she was too young for him. I don't know how long Judy carried her torch, but a couple of years later I was invited to her wedding—to another fine musician, conductor-composer Dave Rose. Talented music personalities always had a great attraction for her.

I thought that Stan Kenton had the best swing band of the 1940's. Stan's outfit had a new and mystic quality all its own, one that haunts me to this day. Just before he attracted attention nationally, I hired the Kenton band to appear in a series of musical shorts I was producing. Stan created a sensation. Another big swinger to come along in those years was Harry James, who had been Benny Goodman's star trumpet soloist for two years. Harry went out on his own in 1939 and exploded like a meteor in 1941 with never-to-be-forgotten recorded solos like "You Made Me Love You" and (a bit earlier) "Ciri-Biri-Bin." For some strange reason, my path never crossed Harry's, although I had written many film songs for his wife, Betty Grable, and in fact knew her quite well. (Betty was in my weekly poker game for awhile.)

Along with the great swing bands, there was also a new crop of important sweet bands emerging at the same time. Ray Noble gathered together probably the best aggregation of the lot, and took New York by storm at the Rainbow Room. On radio, commercial orchestras like those of Kay Kyser, Sammy Kaye and Shep Fields were reaping rich rewards. On the West Coast, Freddy Martin, who tooted a mean sax himself, ruled the roost at the Cocoanut Grove for many years, later employing a good-looking young vocalist named Merv Griffin, who used to sing most of my new songs and bombard me with all sorts of questions about how I came to write them and what it was like writing for film stars, and so forth. I should have sensed at the time that Merv was cut out to be a big-time interviewer delving into the lives of personalities on the air. But I guess his talents as an M.C. were obscured by his vocalizing, which used to delight me no end.

Many of the Big Band personalities starred in Hollywood musicals in the Thirties and Forties. I wrote the scores for some of these, including *Coronado* for Eddy Duchin, *Many Happy Returns* for the Lombardos, and films that featured Duke Ellington and Louis Armstrong. Film biographies of Paul Whiteman, Eddy Duchin (portrayed by Tyrone Power), Benny Goodman (played realistically by Steve Allen), and the Dorseys also served as box-office musicals. I also produced musical shorts starring Ellington, Armstrong, Kenton, Les Brown, and Spike Jones during the early 1940's. As you may have surmised, I relished being part of the Big Band era, and I loved every minute of it.

The Big Band vogue began cooling down during the 1950's, knocked for a loop by new sounds that were being played by much smaller combos. The sounds were first called rhythm and blues. Around the middle Fifties the label was changed to rock and roll. Although I had written my share of swing and jazz standards, these sounds were foreign to my ears. They seemed a far cry from the great American and European songs the Big Bands had played for more than three decades. The new sounds had dynamic drive, an irresistible beat, and a crude, mind-blowing quality that appealed mostly to subteenagers. But I never could quite make up my mind whether it was music or just noise. And yet, despite the inroads rock has made on the pop-music scene, there is still some life left in the older and more melodious world of the Big Bands. The great standards are still played, year after year, and seem to outlive all the other varieties. I firmly believe that fashions in music run in cycles, and that good songs are once again on the ascent.

Chapter Eleven

HOLLYWOOD AND TIN PAN ALLEY IN THE LATE THIRTIES

Nineteen thirty-seven and 1938, my ninth and tenth consecutive years at the Paramount studios, were busy ones for me. Come to think of it, that is quite an understatement. By actual count, I turned out sixteen film scores in those two years! Yes, I said sixteen. Because I know a statement like that may be challenged, here are the titles of the sixteen films, all of them made and released in those two years:

> *One Hundred Men and a Girl* (for Deanna Durbin)
> *Double or Nothing* (Crosby film; I added songs)
> *The Buccaneer* (DeMille film)
> *Swing High, Swing Low* (Carole Lombard)
> *True Confession* (Carole Lombard)
> *Hideaway Girl* (Martha Raye)
> *Mountain Music* (Martha Raye)
> *St. Louis Blues* (Dorothy Lamour)
> *Romance in the Dark*
> *Turn Off the Moon* (Betty Grable)
> *Give Me a Sailor*
> *This Way, Please*
> *Thrill of a Lifetime* (Dorothy Lamour)
> *Love on Toast* (Do you believe that title?)
> *You and Me*
> *Make Way for Tomorrow*

One Hundred Men and a Girl was another loan-out assignment. Paramount farmed out my services, teamed up with Freddy Hollander, to Universal to write songs for Deanna Durbin. Although Deanna tried very bravely, she simply was not cut out to do popular songs. She was far more at home in classical and operatic selections, so the songs landed on the no-hit parade. Nevertheless, the film received the Academy Award for the best score of the year—although Freddy and I, due to some sort of a procedural mixup, never received an Oscar. The statue went instead to Leopold Stokowski, who appeared in the film and conducted the orchestra that accompanied Deanna. The explanation given us was that Deanna's familiar operatic arias were considered part of the score, even though "best score" included the four numbers we had written for her. I suppose I should have raised a fuss, but I was just too busy to argue the point, working on five scripts at once.

Mountain Music was a hillbilly musical starring Martha Raye as a mountain lass opposite Bob Burns, one of the leading radio comedians of the day. I did the words and music, including "Good Morning," which turned out to be Martha's second popular hit after "Mister Paganini." "Good Morning" later turned out to be a real bonanza for me. It became the familiar jingle used in the Kellogg Corn Flakes commercials, and I received a sizable annual fee from the Kellogg Company for more than twenty years, under a deal Paramount's New York office worked out for me.

My next two releases were pleasurable assignments because they were starring vehicles for Paramount's up-and-coming songstress, Dorothy Lamour, one of the nicest and most cooperative ladies I ever wrote for. Dorothy, a rare human being, was a complete contrast to the usual self-involved, affected young starlets that the town was overridden with in those years. She was as friendly to the lowliest grips and messenger boys as she was to the higher-ups, and was at all times the most popular player on her set. Everybody loved her. We have remained good friends ever since, and I still receive long, chatty letters from Dottie every couple of months or so.

Her film, *St. Louis Blues*, in which I collaborated with Hoagy Carmichael and Leo Robin, contained one of my favorite compositions, "Kinda Lonesome," which Dottie did full justice to. I wish I could say that she is still identified with the song, but as luck would have it, Jimmy Dorsey stole the show by coming out

206

with a brilliant clarinet job on his recorded version before the movie was even released.

Turn Off the Moon (oops—there's that word again) was a musical film remembered chiefly because it contained the Andrews Sisters' "Jammin'" and a number I wrote for Phil Harris called "Southern Hospitality," which Phil became identified with and repeated forever after in innumerable radio performances.

You and Me was a difficult assignment because the studio teamed me up as lyricist with the celebrated German composer Kurt Weill for his first American film score. Kurt insisted that I write the complete lyrics first. It was the only way he could work. In my previous collaborations, I generally needed the inspiration of a good tune to write to, or at least the opening strains, whether it was mine or a collaborator's. I found it rough going working in this manner, the more so because Fritz Lang, who was to direct the film, insisted that I base the lyrics on ideas that the writers had injected into the script. Thus I found myself struggling with situation numbers whose titles had to be things like "Song of the Cash Register" and "The Door-Knocking Ballad," titles with very little chance for popularity. Weill and I actually managed to concoct songs out of nine such script situations, but I couldn't wait to get off the assignment and on to something more interesting. With all the flair of two surefire screen writers like Virginia Van Upp and Norman Krasna, plus Fritz Lang's directorial genius (he had directed the classic suspense film *M* for UFA in Berlin, which led to Paramount importing him), and despite noteworthy performances by two popular stars, George Raft and Sylvia Sidney, the film failed to jell and received only lukewarm notices. They were trying to come up with something offbeat and different, part opera and part gangster-style movie, but it was neither fish nor fowl. It just never came off.

My next job was far more rewarding, even though it was a one-song film, the Carole Lombard starrer, *True Confession*. Freddy Hollander and I were asked to write the title song. Carole was then the highest-paid actress in Hollywood, and *True Confession* was her final Paramount vehicle. She was co-starring with the great John Barrymore and Fred MacMurray. The director was Wes Ruggles, for whom I had done *Honey* and Bing's *College Humor*. Wes had specifically asked for me to do the title song.

Freddy and I knocked out "True Confession" in a single afternoon. Like most songs that come with such ease, it fairly flew to the top spot. It topped the chart in *Variety* for three consecutive weeks, and the agency that represented me, Artists and Authors Corp. of America, took a full-page ad in the trade paper *Hollywood Reporter* to proclaim:

WE ANNOUNCE WITH PRIDE
THAT OUR CLIENT
SAM COSLOW
IS THE NATION'S NUMBER ONE SONGWRITER
FOR THE THIRD CONSECUTIVE WEEK. AS TAB-
ULATED IN *VARIETY*, MORE COSLOW SONGS
WERE PLAYED ON THE MAJOR NETWORKS
THE PAST 3 WEEKS THAN THE WORKS OF ANY
OTHER WRITER OR TEAM. ASIDE FROM "TRUE
CONFESSION" SAM COSLOW WAS ALSO TIED
FOR FIRST WITH THE MOST TITLES ON THE
LIST (5).

And then, just when I was sitting so smugly on top of the world, I was abruptly knocked off my perch—and right on my can.

I will relate the story without the comments and sour grapes that one might expect. It came about this way:

A few years before, when I still owned a piece of the publishing firm I had founded, Famous Music, I had my eye on a songplugger who seemed like a real dynamo. His name was Abe Frankl. He was well known in the music business as assistant professional manager for Irving Berlin's company. I explained to Abe how Paramount was trying to build up our new publishing company, and asked him how he felt about coming over with us as professional manager for Famous, in charge of exploitation. He named a high salary for those depression days, $400 a week. I gasped, but told him I'd see what I could do. No songpluggers made that kind of money in the Thirties. I nevertheless told Larry Spier to try and "steal" Abe from the Berlin firm; so we entered into a longterm contract.

For several years, Abe seemed to be doing one hell of a job. Famous had more smash hits, consistently, than any other publisher in Tin Pan Alley. I honestly don't know whether it was due to Abe's highpowered song promotions or to the quality of the songs he promoted. Paramount scores were written by Rodgers and Hart, Frank Loesser, Robin and Whiting, Hoagy Carmichael, and Freddy Hollander, besides myself. But Abe got the credit for launching hit after hit for Paramount.

208

On the set of Copacabana, *around the table: Chili Williams, columnist Louis Sobol, Toni Kelly (Mrs. Jan Murray), columnist Earl Wilson, Variety editor Abel Green and Tommye Adams. Standing: director Alfred E. Green, columnist Jimmy Starr, Copa owner Monte Proser*

The cast of Copacabana, *and the United Artists brass*

210

At the London premiere of Coslow's 1955 British film musical, As Long as They're Happy, Sam is flanked by star Jack Buchanan and BBC producer Denis Main-Wilson

Sam Coslow portrayed the great composers in his Academy Award-winning musical, Heavenly Music: Beethoven, Tschaikovsky, Bach, Wagner, Paganini and Brahms. The Old Masters seem not to be enjoying Sam's serenade

211

Coslow in his London flat, 1955

Sam discusses As Long as They're Happy with singer (Sweet?) Georgia Brown, BBC producer Denis Main-Wilson, and the film's musical director, Stanley Black

Liberace and Frances King Coslow at the same bash

Sam auditions his score for An Alligator Named Daisy *for star Diana Dors and producer Raymond Stross*

At a party at the Coslows' Regent Park flat in London, 1960: Shirley Bassey, Liberace and his vocalist Janet, and the Coslows

Wife Frances, under New England painter Henry Sutton's portrait of her

*Sam's daughter
Jackie with
Donald Gantry in*
The Merry Wives
of Windsor
*at the 1965 San Diego
National Shakespeare
Festival*

Jackie Coslow as Anne Page
Donald Gantry as Fenton in
"THE MERRY WIVES OF WINDSOR"

*Coslow wrote George
McGovern's campaign
song in 1972, so
the Senator drops by in
Florida to say thanks*

216

Sammy Cahn, President of the Songwriters Hall of Fame, congratulates Coslow at the Beverly Hilton Hotel on his election in 1974. Sam is holding a replica of Irving Berlin's first piano, symbol of the Hall of Fame honor

ASCAP honors its oldest living member, 94-year-old Eubie Blake, in March 1977. Flanking Eubie are Mitchell ("Stardust") Parish, Sam Coslow, Bud ("Once in a While") Green, ASCAP president Stanley Adams, unidentified guest, jazz pianist Billy Taylor, Harold ("Wish You Were Here") Rome, Kay ("Fine and Dandy") Swift, Johnny ("Rudolph, the Red-Nosed Reindeer") Marks, Gerald ("All of Me") Marks

217

Sam with Lena Horne and Tony Bennett at a 1975 party in Miami Beach

The 1976 Christmas card from Buddy Rogers and Mary Pickford depicts them and Pickfair

Mary

Christmas
Wishes

Buddy

In Hollywood, money talks louder than anything. By 1937 Paramount executives were greatly impressed by the tremendous net annual profit their music publishing subsidiary was earning for the company. As a result, some bright bigwig—I never found out whom—conceived the notion of bringing Abe out to work at the studio. He was installed in a plush new office suite and given some fancy title like Executive Music Coordinator—I have forgotten the exact wording. His job was to tie in the studio with the publishing company to achieve maximum results. Abe was to read all new scripts and decide which of the contract songwriters were most suited for each assignment. And, as they wrote their scores, Abe was to have the last word on which songs were to be promoted.

Abe loved his new job, and seemed to fit in very well. I naturally found him very friendly. He spent most of his time with the writers—listening to each new song, pepping us up, and offering suggestions. He was at our music table in the studio commissary for lunch every day, and he took us to Big Band openings in the evening. We attended the Los Angeles openings of Benny Goodman, Tommy Dorsey, and Guy Lombardo, as I recall.

Then the guillotine hit me, right smack in the middle of my stretched-out neck, and right in the midst of all this friendliness and good feeling. By that time, I was taking for granted that the annual option in my studio contract would be picked up, and with it the $250-per-week raise. I just never gave it a thought. They had been picking up the option year after year, and I thought I deserved it. I had had ten years of consecutive hit songs in each year—including at least four or five in the preceding twelve months, and I was certainly working far beyond the call of duty. Eight scores in a year certainly ain't chopped liver.

During the third consecutive week that "True Confession" made the number-one spot on the bestseller list, the little note came from the front office. It read, very simply: "We regret exceedingly that we will not exercise your option this year." It was signed by Eugene Zukor, assistant to the President.

I stared at the note in disbelief, feeling a little bit sick inside. I suppose I had begun to think it would last forever, with the annual raise and all. I guess I was in a state of shock; it was all so unexpected. I suddenly came to, and sprinted over to Gene Zukor's office as if I were training for the Olympics. He opened the door for me as soon as my name was announced.

Gene was the son of Adolph Zukor, Paramount's founder and

guiding genius at the New York home office. Gene had only recently been installed in the studio job. He was a quiet, industrious young man, completely dedicated to his job. I had known him for a number of years and had always found him warm, sympathetic and appreciative of my efforts.

He was visibly embarrassed as he ushered me into his office, and he beat me to the punch.

"I know how upset you must be, Sam," he began, "but I simply had no choice—none at all."

"What do you mean you had no choice, Gene?" I demanded to know. "Whose decision was it, anyway?"

"Well, you know we hired this guy Abe Frankl, and we agreed to abide by any decisions he made about songwriters. It's strictly his bailiwick, and none of us know very much about the subject."

"Gene, you've got to be kidding. I'm the guy who brought Frankl into this organization. I can't believe he'd *do* that to me. What possible reason—?"

"Well, I'm violating a confidence, because I wasn't supposed to tell you it was Abe's decision. But you've been here a long time, and I've got to be fair with you. Your next option brings you up to $1500 a week, and Abe said no songwriter is worth that kind of money. I believe it was his sincere opinion, strictly from a dollars-and-cents standpoint."

I was furious. "A dollars-and-cents standpoint? What's it worth to Paramount to have the biggest song hit in the country? How about the fact that I've done the same thing every year for ten years, after handing the company my publishing firm—practically for peanuts?"

At that moment George Bagnall walked in. George was the studio manager, and he had the adjoining office to Gene. George greeted me with a big show of exuberance.

"Hi, Sam," he fairly shouted, clapping me on the back. "You're certainly red hot, aren't you? I just saw where you've got five songs on the *Variety* chart. Isn't that some kind of a record?"

It was obvious that George hadn't been told about the axe that had fallen in the middle of my back.

"Yeah, George," I replied. "I'm so hot I just exploded myself out of a job."

I guess he detected the bitterness in my voice. I walked out, leaving Gene to explain to him what had happened.

As I said above, I wanted to relate the facts without making any comments about Abe Frankl. Maybe it *was* his honest opinion,

220

and maybe no songwriter *was* worth $1500 a week in 1938. At any rate, I never said a word to him about it. In fact, I never saw him again, ever. As the lyric writers say, "C'est La Vie"—at least in the music business. Or is it "Que Sera"?

My agent had set up several appointments to talk about film-score assignments at other studios. But I was, at the moment, disgruntled and angry at Hollywood, so I chose instead to take a much-needed long vacation. I hadn't had a breathing spell between pictures for many months. I was physically and mentally tired. So Esther and I boarded the Superchief for a trip to New York, saw all the hit shows, and went to the clubs and hotels where my bandleader pals were playing.

After about a month of this, I relaxed enough to visit some of the music publishers who had been calling me. I even began to feel like writing again. At one publishing office I ran into my former collaborator of fifteen years before, Abner Silver. He was writing a song with Eddie Heyman, who wrote the lyric of "Body and Soul." The song they were working on was called "Have You Forgotten So Soon?".

That evening, Abner phoned and asked if I would consider finishing the song with them. He had told Eddie that I was always lucky for him as a collaborator, and Eddie had agreed to make it a three-way song. Actually, their song was almost completed—just a few rough spots to smooth out. I smoothed and provided a few punch lines, feeling a bit guilty at getting in on a raincheck. "Have You Forgotten So Soon?" was accepted for publication by Irving Berlin, and became the firm's chief plug song. Irving's new professional manager was my old friend Harry Link (see "Animal Crackers" and "Hello Swanee" in an earlier chapter). Harry was, in my opinion, the most fabulous songplugger the music business has ever seen. He swore he would get "Have You Forgotten" up to the number-one spot in *Variety* in exactly thirty days. He even named the precise date. He was right on target. I have never seen anyone before or since who could do it. He was phenomenal.

On the same trip, Larry Spier introduced me to a Viennese composer who had recently arrived over here, Will Grosz. Will had composed the melodies of "Red Sails in the Sunset," "Isle of Capri" and other big ones. He played a couple of new tunes for me. I loved them. The first one I wrote up I called "Tomorrow Night," and I immediately felt that I had another hit on my hands. I brought Grosz over to play it for Harry Link, and Harry repeated the same performance. Thirty days of network promotion, and "Tomorrow Night" was on top of the chart. The song, which became one of my top standards, was successfully revived twice: by Elvis Presley in the 1950's, and by Charlie Rich in a country version in 1973, when Charlie and I each received one of the coveted ASCAP Country Music awards in Nashville. "Tomorrow Night" was the title of the first popular Charlie Rich long-playing album, and helped to establish him as the hottest new country artist in the land.

The other Will Grosz tune I liked was "Make-Believe Island." I first called it "Panorama Island." Then Will ran into columnist Nick Kenny, who wrote lyrics in his spare time. Nick suggested he change the title to "Make-Believe Island," and immediately called publisher Jack Robbins to rave about the song. I had intended bringing this one to Harry Link also. But before I had a chance to, Will agreed to let Robbins have it—for a hefty advance. It did almost as well as "Tomorrow Night," reaching number three on the Hit Parade and selling around 400,000 copies. Nick Kenny, who had altered a few lines to fit his new title, received a third of the royalties and co-writer credit.

We returned home to California, and I felt that my few months in New York had been most productive. Three hits in that short space of time had restored my confidence and provided a much needed lift to my bruised morale.

Back on the Coast, I received a call from my old boss, Nat Finston, who had left Paramount awhile back to become head of MGM's music department. Nat signed me to do a couple of MGM films, the first an assignment to write one song for Virginia Bruce in a film called *Society Lawyer*. I didn't actually have to write this one, for I had it in my "trunk." It was called "I'm in Love with the Honorable Mr. So-and-So." I had written it earlier with Helen Morgan in mind. Helen had asked me for a song for *Ziegfeld Follies*, which she had signed to co-star in. There was no *Follies* that year because Harry Kaufman, who had bought the *Follies* title from the Ziegfeld estate, couldn't find any backers. Helen loved the song nevertheless, and had featured it in her act at the Helen Morgan Club on New York's East Side.

I hadn't given it to a publisher, and it seemed just right for the spot in the MGM film. It was later recorded by a number of girl vocalists who were popular at that time, including Frances Langford, and later Jeri Sothern, and I have already mentioned Helen Forrest. It is one of my personal favorites, and it eventually became another standard.

Chapter Twelve

"ANYONE CAN BE A PRODUCER"

To explain the title of this chapter, I will jump ahead of my story a few years to the middle 1940's, when I was a contract producer of musical films with United Artists.

I was sitting in my office at the Samuel Goldwyn studios staring at the pile of work on my desk and wishing I were back in my former capacity at Paramount, when all I had to do was turn out forty or so songs a year. My secretary walked in.

"Your cousin is outside. He'd like to see you."

"My cousin? What cousin? I don't have any relatives out here."

"He says he hitchhiked all the way from New York to see you."

I have about two or three dozen cousins, so I came out to see which one it was, mostly out of curiosity to learn who was that fond of walking.

It was my Uncle Louie's young son, age about twenty, and looking quite peaked after his three-thousand-mile trek. He had been following my career by long distance, even carrying a small scrapbook in which he had pasted various press writeups about my activities. I asked him what I could do for him. Haltingly, he stammered out that he had made the long hike because he had decided that he too would like to work in the movie business, make it his life's work.

Uncle Louie was my favorite uncle, so I delved into it further. "Well, what sort of a job are you after? I mean, what branch of the movie business are you attracted to?"

"I dunno. What branches are there?"

"Well, for instance, are you interested in photography—working with a movie camera? Or, have you studied music?"

"No, not really."

"Do you aspire to be a writer? Or an actor, perhaps?"

"Nope."

"Are you interested in the mechanical side—like the electrical department, or set construction?"

"I don't think so."

I went through the whole gamut of possible studio jobs. He didn't really lean toward anything, had no special interests.

I was becoming impatient, even exasperated. "It's all very well to come out here and say you want a job in the movie industry," I pointed out, "but you've got to know what you want. This is a highly specialized business. You must have a specific goal—any one of the twenty or thirty different crafts involved in the making of a picture. You must be interested in *some* category."

My cousin looked right at me and, without batting an eyelash, said, "Can't I be like you? *You* don't have to know anything. You're a *producer*."

It was quite a comedown. I had won an Oscar the year before, for producing, and I felt like hitting him over the head with it. So this was how the lay public viewed the role of producer—after I had been knocking my brains out!

I gave my cousin the only job he was equipped for with his lack of experience or training. We needed a doorman, to prevent strangers from wandering on to the set. He got the job. It was as far as he ever got in the movie industry. But the incident has an astonishing P.S. Today, more than thirty years later, my cousin is a widely quoted Wall Street expert. I suppose that proves something, although I've never figured out exactly what.

I never really had the producing bug, but studios were not employing many contract songwriters by 1940, the trend being mostly to film Broadway musicals with their original scores intact. So when an opportunity came along in the producing game, it seemed like a nice timely idea.

Jack Votion, who had been casting director for Paramount, had left to join the Joyce and Selznick agency. He became my agent. He was getting only spasmodic assignments for me during the musical-film lull, one song at a time here and there. Among Jack's other clients were Lum and Abner, the country's second highest-paid team of radio comedians, just behind Amos and Andy.

224

Jack asked me to lunch with him at the Brown Derby one day, to discuss a project. He thought that Lum and Abner had a large enough following nationally to warrant starring them in a movie, and the boys had agreed to let Jack explore the idea. He felt that the project should be a musical, including other radio personalities to support Lum and Abner. He therefore wanted to set up a deal whereby I would co-produce the film with him. He knew very little about how musicals were made, and I had been involved in fifty or sixty of them. I decided to give it a try, and joined Jack as a full partner.

The first step was to get a major release commitment, which would make it easy to get the backing. To achieve this, we went to New York to see an attorney we both knew quite well, Bill Fitelson. Bill had made numerous releasing deals for independent producers. We hadn't even the germ of an idea for a script, but Bill liked the notion of Lum and Abner doing a film. So he put together a deal for us which included an RKO release, backing from the General Finance Corporation for a low-budget musical, and enough "front money" to enable us to get a brief story outline. If RKO should approve the story idea, General Finance agreed to supply the necessary funds, for which they would receive half of our profits. They agreed to include in the budget a modest producers' fee, plus another fee for whatever songs I wrote.

Tailoring the right vehicle, especially for an offbeat team like Lum and Abner, was no easy assignment. But two of my friends who were well known screen writers, Barry Trivers and Bob Andrews, agreed to tackle the job. They wrote an untitled story outline which was immediately approved by RKO head George Schaeffer, and we moved into the Goldwyn studios to get started. We cast popular songstress Frances Langford, veteran Broadway stage star Frank Craven, and Phil Harris in featured roles to support Lum and Abner.

With Frances Langford in a leading role, I decided to write a song for the film, a ballad called "Dreaming Out Loud." When I played it for Harold Young, whom we had engaged to direct, he insisted we also make it the title of the film.

Lum and Abner, who were really a couple of young men despite their familiar radio roles as lovable old hicks, came off like two troupers, although they had never faced the cameras before. A superb makeup job was a big help, aging them considerably. Another surprise was Frances Langford in her first leading role.

225

The only problem we had was with Phil Harris, who we thought would breeze through his part like an old hand after years of being featured on Jack Benny's radio show.

Phil had the part of a typical "city slicker," a fast-talking salesman trying to sell his merchandise to Lum and Abner, owners of the general store in Pine Ridge, Arkansas. On the day Phil was scheduled to do his big comedy scene, I received a call to rush over to the set.

I found they were still trying to get the first take after three hours. Every time Phil began his opening lines, he fluffed—over and over again. The director was pacing up and down, muttering under his breath. Votion kept looking at his watch, mentally figuring out what sort of a dent an unproductive half day would make in our skimpy budget. I could see that Phil was both nervous and embarrassed over blowing his lines repeatedly, so I suggested the company break for lunch to give Phil a chance to calm down. Phil spent his lunch hour in his dressing room going over his lines. After lunch, Harold Young broke Phil's lines into very small segments, and we finally got a take in the can by midafternoon.

It was not until a couple of months later that I learned the reason for the costly delay. I ran into one of the boys in Phil's band at a restaurant, and we discussed Phil's strange performance on the set. "You remember Phil's wife, don't you?" the musician asked me.

I told him I did indeed. Phil was married to a very attractive dark-haired girl who looked like Joan Crawford's twin sister. I had seen her around town with Phil at various social gatherings. Phil always seemed extremely devoted to her. They looked the picture of an ideal couple very much in love.

Phil's musician told me that on the morning of Phil's big scene with us, he awoke to find his wife gone, leaving only a short note to say she wanted a divorce. They hadn't even had an argument the night before. Phil had gone to bed with no inkling of what was to come. Until he saw her note, Phil was still under the impression that he was a happily married man. Her sudden departure came as a complete surprise, and Phil arrived at the studio in a state of shock. That, of course, explained everything.

Dreaming Out Loud never broke any box-office records, but it received extensive bookings as the second film in double features. It yielded a fair profit for all concerned.

We received a commitment from RKO for a second Lum and

Abner feature, but I bowed out and let Jack make it on his own when I was offered something that sounded much more exciting.

James Roosevelt, whose illustrious father was then sitting in the White House in his third term in office, was greatly fascinated by the movie industry. He decided to become part of it, full time. The Mills Novelty Company of Chicago, second largest manufacturers of juke boxes, had developed a new invention called the Panoram. It was a glorified juke box that ran films instead of records. It looked like an oversized TV set (TV was still in the experimental stage) with a viewing surface about two feet square in the center of the box. You dropped in a dime and saw a musical film that ran about four or five minutes.

The Mills people had designated young Roosevelt to line up product, but there was practically nothing around of that nature. He thereupon decided to find someone who could produce a regular program of short musical films for the new medium. He decided that my background was right for the post. I had twelve years' experience with musicals, writing songs and special material, recording and scoring, and, more recently, producing a feature film which had received favorable reviews.

Jimmy's office was down the hall from mine in the Goldwyn studios, and we had a number of talks. He finally arranged for me to fly to Chicago to meet with Ralph Mills, president of the Mills outfit. We agreed to set up a new production company called Roosevelt, Coslow and Mills, Inc., later shortened to R.C.M., Inc.

I was named as production head of the new outfit, with a term contract calling for $1,000 a week and one-third of the stock. Jimmy Roosevelt was chief executive, mainly concerned with sales and marketing.

I was to turn out three shorts a week in Hollywood, plus another three a week at a studio in New York. The juke boxes gave you the choice of ten different films, so a steady flow of new product was essential.

The Mills people, with about a thousand boxes initially scheduled to go into various locations, provided the financing to make the films. We took over a small studio, Eagle-Lion, which was next door to the Goldwyn plant on Santa Monica Boulevard in Hollywood. I engaged a complete staff which included Ben Hersh, who performed competently as our unit manager on *Dreaming Out Loud.* Ben engaged a full shooting crew, because three musical shorts a week meant that we would be in continuous production throughout the year. It was, in its way, a large

227

undertaking for a new Hollywood enterprise. At the New York studio, Jack Barry was in charge of another shooting crew.

I called the short films Soundies, and at first tried to make them like illustrated phonograph records. One of the first things we did was a series with Louis Armstrong. The first Armstrong release was his familiar theme, "Sleepy Time Down South." We photographed Louis singing with his band, then cut away to shots of black plantation workers harmonizing against a backdrop of cotton fields. Later, we expanded from illustrated songs to a wider range of subject matter, from Sally Rand's fan dance to a Hillbilly Grand Opera. In addition to producing, I was also the idea man for the company. It was a continuing challenge to keep coming up with new backgrounds, and plots and ideas that were not repetitious. But it was all intriguing. I loved it.

Another challenge was finding a steady flow of good talent. At first I played it safe by using established musical names who happened to be around Hollywood or New York. Besides Louis Armstrong, I hired Duke Ellington and his Orchestra for a notable series that included "Take the A Train," "Mood Indigo" and other familiar Ellingtonia; Spike Jones in a series of comedy subjects; and bands like Les Brown's and Stan Kenton's.

What was more notable about the talent used in the Soundies, however, was the fact that I found an array of great performers who were destined to become top names in the entertainment world. Like Doris Day, for instance. Her very first appearance before the cameras was as the vocalist for Les Brown's Orchestra in a series of Soundies. I also hired a small group I had seen in nightclubs called the King Cole Trio, which featured a young singer named Nat "King" Cole just starting out in the business. Cyd Charisse had her first screen appearance as a featured solo dancer for us, as did Yvonne De Carlo. In fact, Yvonne was in our chorus line, and she photographed so well that I gave her a small part.

The two girls who clicked most strongly for us and became the outstanding Soundies favorites were Gale Storm and Dorothy Dandridge. They developed a great following, and were responsible for more dimes being dropped into our juke boxes than anyone else we had under contract. Gale later became the co-star of the popular early TV series, *My Little Margie,* playing the title role opposite Charlie Farrell. Dorothy, undoubtedly the most beautiful black singer of her generation, made screen history in *Porgy and Bess* for MGM.

228

In December 1941, our entry into World War II brought about some radical changes in the Soundies operation. James Roosevelt immediately joined the U.S. Marines and shipped off to the South Seas, leaving me as the sole executive, in charge of all the divisions of the company. We temporarily converted from an entertainment firm to a film unit for the government. The first year of the war we entirely devoted to making training films. I flew to Washington and received contracts from the U.S. Merchant Marine, the Army Air Force, and the Office of War Information. We turned out dozens of short films which were screened throughout the armed forces. While I suppose it is true that the Roosevelt name may have opened a few doors for us in Washington, a far more important reason was that we had an established, fully equipped, professional production unit with skilled personnel, a studio at our disposal, and the knowhow to turn out miles of film fast. There was no profit for the company. I agreed to turn out the films for actual cost as our contribution to the war effort.

The war brought about another big change for R.C.M. War shortages made it impossible for the Mills factory to obtain parts for the Soundies machines, so production of the juke boxes was halted. In order to keep intact what I considered to be one of the most efficient production units in Hollywood, I looked around for other outlets to keep us going. Jerry Bresler, who headed the shorts division for MGM, had screened a number of our Soundies, and was impressed enough to invite me to produce a two-reel musical. It was to serve as a sort of pilot film for our unit; if it turned out well I was to produce six a year for MGM.

One of our directors, Reginald Le Borg, came up with an idea and a script for the pilot. It was called *Heavenly Music,* and was a fantasy about a young songwriter who was killed in the war and was trying to gain admission inside the Pearly Gates. His entrance depended upon approval from a Board of Immortals that included Beethoven, Brahms, Bach, Wagner, Mozart, and Liszt. I hired good actors who, however, didn't particularly resemble the great composers. But with the aid of MGM's amazing makeup department, the results were positively uncanny. Steven Geray, using an ear trumpet, looked like every picture you'd ever seen of Beethoven. The others were made up with equal precision and skill. I gave the film a title song, which Perry Como recorded with great flair.

Heavenly Music was previewed by MGM at a theater in the outlying suburb of Inglewood, California, in conjunction with the first Lassie film, a B picture in which Elizabeth Taylor, then thirteen, made her screen debut. It was, and still is, the custom for studio people to gather in the theater lobby after a preview to discuss the pros and cons of the film and weigh its chances for success. After this preview, to my great surprise I found the entire studio buzzing about my short, and saying very little about Lassie or Liz Taylor. Studio head Louis B. Mayer rushed over to congratulate me, throwing his arms about me and saying, "My boy, you'll go a long way with our company!"

A couple of days later, the daily trade paper *Hollywood Reporter* came out (on March 26, 1943) with a special editorial on the front page written by the paper's editor, W. R. Wilkerson, entirely devoted to my short. The article began:

> At MGM yesterday, in Jerry Bresler's shorts department, I saw a two-reel musical, produced by Sam Coslow, titled *Heavenly Music.* It is the best musical short your reporter has ever seen.

Several months later, the Academy nominations were announced. *Heavenly Music* was one of the five films nominated as the best two-reel short subject.

I honestly thought I had very little chance for the award. The other four nominated films had been highly touted and were made by impressive names in the shorts field like Pete Smith and others. Nevertheless, I decided to attend the Academy Award ceremonies at Grauman's Chinese Theater because the annual Awards affair was always an exciting and glamorous occasion, and win or lose I didn't want to be cheated out of it.

As a nominee, I was given four tickets for the event. Esther was sure I had no chance, and declined to join me, so I brought three friends. It was a rainy night, and we were bottlenecked by a traffic jam on the way to the theater. The four of us rushed inside, raincoats over our arms, and found the ceremonies had already started. The usher showed us to our seats, which were in the second row. We found four people—obviously gate crashers—occupying them! The people refused to leave, protesting that they paid for the seats. The usher argued loudly with them while my friends and I stood in the aisle with egg on our faces.

In the midst of it all, I suddenly heard Walter Wanger on the stage announcing the winners. "For producing the best two-reel short, Sam Coslow for *Heavenly Music.*" I was still befuddled over the seat mixup, but on hearing my name I snapped out of my fog and rushed up on the stage, still carrying my hat and raincoat. I don't suppose anyone else ever received an Oscar under such circumstances. I took the statue and mumbled something about the great crew I had worked with—much too flustered and out of breath to think of anything original. Today, when people see the Oscar on my piano and ask me what it feels like to receive one, I just smile and say, "I'll never really know."

With Jack Votion now producing for RKO, I had a new agent, Frank Orsatti. Soon after the Awards he phoned me to meet him at Louis B. Mayer's office at MGM. He said Mayer wanted to see me right away, probably to take up MGM's option to have me produce six shorts a year. Instead, Mayer, beaming profusely when I got there, surprised us. "I'm going to take you out of shorts. From now on, you'll produce some of our big musicals. My boy, you'll go a long way with MGM!" Apparently Louis B. had forgotten he said the same thing to me at the preview. Or maybe he said that to everybody he hired. He then turned to Frank and told him to see MGM Vice President Lou Sidney to work out terms for a five-year contract.

Within a few days, the contract was signed, calling for yearly options for a five-year period. Orsatti assured me that I would be the fairhaired boy among the new MGM producers, and everything possible would be done to make my new job a bed of roses. In fact, these were orders from Louis B. himself, who happened to be Orsatti's close pal socially as well as in business.

I was moved into an imposing office suite on the MGM lot in Culver City. It was lavishly furnished with a supersize executive desk, etchings on the wall, and even a casting couch. A studio secretary who looked like a Powers model was assigned to me. I arrived at work bright and early the first morning, ready to conquer the world.

It didn't take me many weeks to realize that I was working in some kind of glamorous madhouse. The first of the MGM insanities that I was exposed to was my first weekly visit to the paymaster's window, to pick up my salary check. I knew the paymaster well. He had formerly held the same job at Paramount. As I arrived at his window, a man wearing an open sport shirt, red shorts, and tennis shoes was picking up a check while a chauffeured limousine waited for him. As he got back into his car and sped away, the paymaster asked me, "Do you know who that guy was, Sam?"

231

I replied that I had never seen him before, adding, "Why do you ask?"

"Well, he's been coming over here every Wednesday for more than a year now, the same as today. His chauffeur drives him up, I hand the guy a weekly check for $3,500, and he drives right away. As far as I know, he's never set foot inside the studio. Somebody told me he's a foreign producer with a contract here, but so far nobody seems to know of any picture he's produced."

"Nice work if you can get it," I said, amazed. "Any more like him around here?"

"Oh, we have a whole flock of mystery men like that, all with contracts and king-sized paychecks. There's one of your colleagues, Jerome Kern. I handed him a weekly paycheck for five thousand bucks for a long time. I hear he was finally assigned to do a picture and is working on it back East."

The first intra-studio call I received was from Jerry Mayer, Louis B.'s brother. Jerry was the studio production manager, a nice, friendly soul. I walked over to his sumptuous office.

"This is just a routine thing," said Jerry. "I do this with all new producers we sign up."

He pulled a large photo album out of a desk drawer, and began thumbing through it.

"These are the photographs of our contract players," he explained. "You'll be making pictures here, and I'm supposed to brief you on who these people are, so you can use them as often as possible. In other words, give first preference to our talented young contract people before you look on the outside."

"Seems reasonable enough," I agreed. "Like, for instance?"

Jerry went through the book, a page at a time, giving me the credentials and credits of each one. After four or five of these, the next was a photo of a beautiful, sexy blonde. He said nothing, turning hurriedly to the next page.

"Hey—who was that?" I asked.

"That one you don't touch. She has a contract here, but she's the property of so-and-so"—he named one of the senior MGM producers, a name to conjure with in the industry.

Every fifth or sixth face in the book was a similar case. Somebody's property, mustn't touch. I found myself wondering how many MGM hit pictures I had to make before getting into that category. A girl friend, with the studio footing the whole tab. Nice going.

Before I left his office, Jerry said, "Oh, just one more thing.

232

Here is a list of young writers we have under contract. They cost very little, and we'd like you to give some of them a break once in awhile. Try them out on a story treatment or something."

I glanced over the list. None of the names rang a bell, but the last one on the list attracted me because it had a sort of magical sound to it.

"Tennessee Williams . . . they must be kidding," I said. "Nobody's got a name like Tennessee Williams."

"Oh, that really *is* his name," Jerry assured me. "I don't know a thing about him, but why don't you try him on a script some time? He will add very little to your budget."

How often I later wished I had taken Jerry's suggestion!

The office next to mine was occupied by Ben Hecht and Charles MacArthur, probably the most talented scriptwriting team in the business—but I doubt whether anyone at MGM really knew how great they were. Not having a film assigned to me as yet, I got into the habit of dropping into their office and kibitzing. They too were between assignments. They were not very happy about working there, and hated most of the scripts they had been assigned to.

One day I was idly looking over some of the photographs on their walls when I spotted one that made me roar with laughter. It was a small French postcard—one of those dirty ones sold by hawkers on the streets of Paris. It was the usual bedroom scene— a naked man and woman in the act of fornicating, no holds barred. Ben and Charlie had cut out and pasted the heads of Louis B. Mayer and another studio big-wig, Eddie Mannix, over the faces of the two French participants. It was a real eyebrow-lifter, fiendish and diabolical. Only Hecht and MacArthur would think of a joke like that.

"It's just something we did to while away some of our idle moments around here," Ben remarked. "We find it's become a real conversation piece."

One day I walked in and the picture was gone.

"What happened?" I asked. "You guys gone respectable?"

"No, not at all. Louis B. dropped in here the other day and spotted the picture on the wall. He looked it over very closely, and never said a word to us. He just turned around and walked out, mad as hell. The guy just has no sense of humor!"

I used to arrive at my office promptly at 10 a.m. each day, read my mail and the *Hollywood Reporter,* and wait for something to happen. I would spend about two hours at the studio commissary starting at noon, eating a long, leisurely lunch and tablehopping to everyone I knew on the lot. In the afternoon, I would make the same routine phone calls, two or three times a week. To Sam Katz, who was in charge of the younger producers, for example. "Just wanted to remind you that I'm still waiting to be assigned to a picture," I would say.

"Relax, Sam," he would answer. "We'll find one for you that's right up your alley. Just be patient."

Or I would call the story department to find out if they'd read any good scripts lately. Sure they had. But the real plums always went to Pandro Berman or Mervyn LeRoy or Arthur Hornblow, senior producers who could call their shots. If something was scheduled for the Book-of-the-Month Club, or if a new Broadway show opened to rave notices, it always went to someone in the so-called "country club set"—the top producers.

After about two months of this, I received a call from Arthur Freed, MGM's leading producer of musicals. Arthur, like myself, had started as a songwriter and was an old pal from way back when. He used to tell me it had taken him years to get to the position where he could make important musicals, and urged me to be as patient as he had been.

On this particular occasion, Arthur phoned to tell me he had been discussing a really important musical with Sam Katz and had suggested that they turn it over to me because Arthur had three other scripts in preparation and couldn't get to this one for at least a year. It was to be a remake of an old hit film, and he was sending a messenger over with the original script.

When the script arrived, I found it was *Good News.* I mean that was the name of it, for it was really bad news. I had seen it as a Broadway show back in 1927, then in the first movie version starring Bessie Love a few years later. I read it quickly. It was so stale and antiquated it made me slightly ill.

Sam Katz phoned me to find out if I had read the script.

"Yes, I've read it, and I must be honest and tell you this is not the vehicle I should have for my first MGM feature. I'd be starting out with two strikes against me."

Sam was astonished. He was not accustomed to having new producers turn down assignments.

"Two strikes against you—how can you possibly say that?" he demanded.

"Well, Mr. Katz, you know I was signed here because I had produced something highly original and different, an Academy Award winner. How can I do justice to a creaky old heirloom like

234

Good News? You know, there's a world war on, and I feel anything we make should be vital and significant. Who the hell cares about a story concerning the outcome of a football game, in this day and age?"

Katz hung up on me. I guess he called Arthur Freed to complain about me, because in a flash Arthur was phoning me.

"I think you're making a big mistake turning down *Good News.* It could be a real biggie. By the time you shoot and edit it, the war will probably be over. Better think about it, Sam."

I read it again, and it seemed even more trite and insipid than the first time. I stuck to my guns.

They never sent me another script. I tried suggesting a few projects of my own, like a revue based on Irving Berlin's song hits, to be called *Say It with Music.* I felt sure that "IRVING BERLIN'S SAY IT WITH MUSIC" over a marquee would mean millions at the box office. I even called Berlin long distance and found out what he would ask for the title and the film rights to his songs. A half million bucks, which to MGM would have been peanuts for a title and score of that magnitude. Sam Katz turned it down without even taking a moment to think about it.

"Too damn expensive," he snapped. "And who the hell does Berlin think he is to demand a half a million bucks?" I tried to tell him.

After awhile, complete boredom began to set in. Nothing was happening, absolutely nothing. I began taking afternoons off, going to the Hollywood Park racetrack near the studio. I saw a lot of important MGM people there, like Mervyn LeRoy, who was one of the owners of the track.

One day a messenger came to my office with the new studio directory. I looked idly through it for want of something better to do. I remember counting the names of 51 contract producers, all on high salaries. The studio had recently announced a program of 44 features for the 1943-44 film schedule. Knowing that Freed, LeRoy and Berman each had three new scripts on their agendas, I mentally figured out—without the aid of a calculator—that the other producers would make an average of seven-tenths of a film apiece that year. I recalled the foreign producers who showed up at the studio only once a week to get their paychecks. I began to wonder if that was to be my fate too.

In desperation, I went to see Orsatti. I told him I wanted out. He was my agent, and should be able to get me a release. The situation was becoming unbearable.

A few days later, lunching at Lucey's Restaurant in Hollywood,

I ran into Buddy DeSylva. His publishing firm, DeSylva, Brown and Henderson, used to occupy the floor above Spier and Coslow back in the Twenties, and we often lunched together at the Brass Rail, which was on the ground floor of the building.

In the intervening years, DeSylva, Brown and Henderson had become legendary names in the business, with a string of musical successes a mile long. After the trio broke up, Buddy began producing Broadway and Hollywood musicals on his own—*Panama Hattie* and a host of other hits. He had just joined Paramount as production chief in charge of the whole works. I congratulated him.

"How are you doing at MGM?" asked Buddy. "I saw *Heavenly Music* a few months ago and loved it. You did one hell of a job."

My reply was hesitant. I wasn't exactly happy there, I explained, and told him about some of the frustrations that were bugging me. I even told him about turning down *Good News,* which Buddy himself happened to be the writer of!

He laughed. "You did the right thing there. It was fine when I wrote it, seventeen years ago. Today, I wouldn't touch it with a ten-foot pole. It would be like making *East Lynne.*"

Later, as Buddy was leaving the restaurant, he stopped at the table where I was lunching with a friend.

"I've been thinking," he said. "Why don't you get a release from your contract and come back to Paramount? I need some new blood around here, producers with fresh ideas."

I told him my agent was trying to get a release but that nothing had happened so far.

"Well," he assured me, "just in case you get the word, you can count on having a home with us—at the same salary MGM is paying you."

It gave me a nice feeling to know that, even if I didn't get the release. A real ace in the hole, I thought.

The following week, Orsatti told me he had worked out the release deal. He was a smart cookie, and he had maneuvered it so that the MGM officials thought they had to buy me off. They had agreed to give me the balance of my first year's salary in a lump sum—about $45,000—and to release me from the contract. I would have signed the release without a cent in settlement, had they asked me to. Or even paid *them* for the release!

I made a beeline for Culver City and cleaned out my desk in a hurry, putting my few belongings into a briefcase. On the way out, I ran into Louis B. Mayer, who was just arriving at the execu-

236

tive building. It was the first time I had seen him since the day he hired me. In a big factory like MGM, you can work for years without running into some of the key people—especially higher-ups like Louis B., who ate his lunch only in the executive dining room, screened all film in his private projection room adjoining his office, and seldom ventured outside his own domain. He stared at me, trying to place me. I refreshed his memory.

"Hello, Mr. Mayer. I'm Sam Coslow—remember me?"

"Oh yes—you made that wonderful short for us. My boy, I'll see to it that you go a long way with MGM. This is a great opportunity for you!" And, as before, he clapped me on the back, beaming effusively.

I just didn't have the heart to tell him. And I seriously doubt that anyone else ever did.

Buddy DeSylva kept his word. I signed with Paramount again, with the starting date set for the following month. It was like coming home after a five-year absence. I felt good being there again and renewing old friendships.

The atmosphere was as congenial as ever. I especially enjoyed the daily luncheon sessions in the commissary. At noon each day, Buddy presided at the head of a long table which for some unknown reason was called the Board of Directors' table, although few directors ever sat there. The regulars who sat at the table were an assorted bunch that included two other producers besides myself, Paul Jones and Ed Leshin (Ed was Stephen Sondheim's stepfather); Gary Cooper, who enjoyed listening to all our lively patter but never said a word himself except an occasional "yup"; playwright-director Preston Sturges; Buddy's assistant, Sammy Ledner; and several screenwriters.

I recall one luncheon session when Pauline Kessinger, the popular hostess at the commissary, handed Buddy a note which she said was urgent. Buddy read it and roared with laughter. He then passed it around for all of us to read. The note was from H. Allen Smith, the celebrated humorist who had written the bestseller *Low Man on the Totem Pole* and who had recently signed with the studio to write screenplays. A photocopy of a check was attached to the note, which, as nearly as I can remember, read: "I've been here over a month and I don't know what it takes to make me qualify for inclusion at your lunch table. I am therefore enclosing a photostat copy of my salary check, just in case that is the criterion you use. Please let me know if I can join you, or if my salary is not high enough let me know how much I have to earn to qualify, and I will instruct my agent to ask for the necessary raise."

Buddy sent me a half dozen stories and books that the studio had purchased as possible musicals. But before I had a chance to read them, I thought of an idea myself that intrigued me. I told Buddy about it, and he sparked immediately. "That will be your first production. Put the story idea on paper—just a couple of pages or so—and we'll get a good scriptwriter to work on it with you."

The brainstorm I had come up with, to state it very briefly, was to do a satire on the Sinatra legend, swooning bobbysoxers and all. That was the year that Frank became a national craze, making the front pages all over the country. There had been rumors that several different people owned a "piece" of Sinatra, and that he was paying out more than half his salary on various percentage deals. The rumors, of course, were completely untrue, but they were such a widespread topic of conversation that they served as the basis for my story idea. The story centered on a Western Union messenger boy with a great crooning voice whose manager had sold his contract to five different people. The original title, suggested by Buddy, was *Divided by Five.* But after the script was under way it was changed to *Out of This World,* a popular hipster phrase of that period that has gone into the language.

I put Walter De Leon and Artie Phillips, a couple of real screenwriting pros, on the script, sweating it out with them for several months. I asked for Eddie Bracken, the hottest young comedian on the lot, to play the crooning messenger boy, and I got him. Eddie had just starred in Preston Sturges' box-office winner, *The Miracle of Morgan's Creek,* and had developed a big following. To co-star with him, I selected Veronica Lake, who was then in her heyday, and Paramount's child star Diana Lynn, in her first grownup role. Diana had just turned sixteen and was a natural for the role of the swooning bobbysoxer.

The script called for Eddie to sing a half dozen crooner songs, and that is where I chickened out. I got a mental picture of the screen titles reading: "Original story by Sam Coslow . . . produced by Sam Coslow . . . words and music by Sam Coslow," and I became a little panicky.

I went to Buddy's office and told him, "This is my first major musical production, and I don't want to stick my neck out too far. I would be quite content to get producer and story credit. How would you feel about hiring someone else to write the score?"

238

Buddy, astonished beyond belief, protested. "We are entitled to get songs from you under your contract, without going to the added expense of hiring other songwriters. Whom would you suggest?"

"Well, I feel that if I can use Harold Arlen and Johnny Mercer, I'd be in great shape. I'd be sure to have a hell of a score, and nobody would say I'm trying to do everything myself."

After a little persuasion, Buddy saw the point. Johnny and Harold were, at that time, the hottest songwriting team in Hollywood. They could do no wrong. Their recent hits like "Blues in the Night" and "That Old Black Magic" had topped the Hit Parade, and Harold had also composed (with Yip Harburg) the much-talked-of score for *The Wizard of Oz* a few years before.

I phoned their agent and he said yes, the boys were available, but their fee had gone up to $60,000 a picture. I had to do a massive selling job on Henry Ginsberg, business head of the studio. I practically stood on my head, and in the end I got Paramount to hire the boys.

They earned their $60,000 fee in something like five days, coming up with a flock of great songs that included their marvelous title song, which has since become one of the great Mercer-Arlen standards.

I sent mimeographed copies of the songs to Eddie Bracken and asked him to learn them. I knew he couldn't sing worth a damn, but I wanted him to learn them well enough to mouth them so the dubbing would not be detected. I had already arranged for the actual singing to be done by—none other than Der Bingle, Crosby himself. Can you imagine Eddie Bracken playing Frank Sinatra with Bing Crosby's voice coming out of him?

At long last, we got a final draft of the shooting script. Buddy named a starting date for shooting, and sets were built on Sound Stage Five. We were three days away from shooting, when all hell broke loose.

Eddie Bracken walked into my office looking very grim and determined, but pretty nervous as well. He came right to the point.

"I'm walking off the picture, Sam. I can't do it."

I suddenly felt faint. "What do you mean you're walking, Eddie? Why—how—what—?"

Eddie pulled a letter out of his coat pocket. "Just read this," he said.

It was a fan letter, from a girl who was not only Eddie's fan but a fan of Sinatra's as well. She had read the press releases about Eddie poking fun at her Frankie boy in his next film. She just wanted Eddie to know she would never again go to one of his movies, and would tell all her friends to stay away as well.

"This is my career that's at stake," Eddie continued. "I can't jeopardize it by making fun of crooners. It could ruin me."

I could scarcely believe what I was hearing.

"Come on, now, Eddie," I said, "you don't really take yourself *that* seriously, do you? I saw Sinatra the other night and he doesn't mind. In fact, the whole idea tickled him. So why the hell should you?"

I couldn't budge him, so I tried another approach.

"Besides, how can you possibly do a thing like that to *me*? Here I am, ready to go to bat with my very first production here—and the star walks out on me! Have you forgotten that you have a contract with Paramount?"

Despite all my pleading and cajoling, nothing worked. He really did take himself that seriously, incredible as it seemed. And out he walked.

When I broke the news to Buddy, he exploded. "That bastard! We've got a million bucks tied up in this picture, and he's ready to put five hundred people out of work! I'll have the Screen Actors' Guild bar him from show business!"

Buddy told Marie, his secretary, to get Bracken on the phone. He still refused to budge.

In desperation, Buddy began calling a few agents, frantically. Danny Kaye was not available. Red Skelton was, but MGM refused to loan him out. Kenny Baker, who was right for the part, had just opened on Broadway in *One Touch of Venus*. My future suddenly began to look bleak.

Despondent, I went back to my office. Edith Head was waiting for me with sketches for Veronica Lake's gowns. I looked at them, but my heart wasn't in it. We were interrupted by Preston Sturges, who had strolled in from his office next door. Edith left, and Preston, very much concerned, yelled, "What's this I hear about Bracken behaving like a horse's ass? Is the story true?"

I told him it was, and brought him up to date. Preston was a friend of long standing. I had known him back in New York, before coming to Hollywood. Besides, in a way we were brothers-in-law. He was planning to marry the sister of my ex-wife Dorothy.

Preston had been responsible for Bracken's success, having

240

written, directed and produced the film that made Eddie such a hot property, *The Miracle of Morgan's Creek.* Now he offered to come to my rescue. "Will you let me handle the sonofabitch? I think I know him better than anyone."

"Please do." I was grasping at straws. "My office is about to turn into a disaster area."

Preston invited Eddie to his house for dinner that night and began working on him. He worked on him far into the night. At about 6 a.m. Eddie threw in the towel and agreed to do the picture. I don't know exactly what did the trick, but Preston told me afterwards that he had almost scared Eddie to death by the time he left, convincing him that his career was far more certain to end if he walked out than if a few silly fans blackballed him. Eddie showed up to work on the first shooting day, oozing with sweetness and light, meek as a lamb. He never again mentioned his fan mail or his "career."

Under Hal Walker's fastpaced direction, the picture came in on schedule, under budget and with no further mishaps. I even had enough left over in the budget to add a big number in the last reel. At the last minute, I conceived the idea of reprising the Arlen-Mercer score with five pianist-bandleaders at five grand pianos: Ray Noble, Ted Fio Rito, Carmen Cavallaro, Henry King, and Joe Reichman. It looked and sounded beautiful.

Out of This World premiered at the New York Paramount Theater in the summer of 1945 and won unanimously favorable reviews from the critics. Financially, it was a real winner for Paramount. I had brought it in for $1,100,000. When all the returns were in, it had grossed more than four million dollars worldwide.

My next production was to be *Princess on the Warpath.* Based on an original story of mine, it was announced by the studio as a starring vehicle for Dorothy Lamour. But halfway through the writing of the script, Paramount refused to renew Buddy DeSylva's contract. A rival faction had seized the reins at the studio. When the axe fell, it hit not only Buddy, but the whole array of producers he had hired, including Ed Leshin, myself, and a few others. It was pure studio politics, so when the new faction took over, they wanted no part of what they called "Buddy's boys." Unfortunately, I was one of the boys.

If you have heard many times that so many Hollywood deals have originated impromptu at parties and social affairs, my next producing job proves that this is really so.

241

I ran into Mary Pickford and Buddy Rogers one night at some-body's home. I can't remember whose home it was, and it doesn't really matter. But the meeting led to an interesting deal. Buddy was an old pal from my early Paramount days. I had not only written songs for some of his films, but had also helped him rehearse them on the piano, sax, trombone, trumpet, clarinet, banjo, and a few of the other instruments he played. He was no virtuoso, but could play all of them well enough to get by in the one-man-band act he liked to do occasionally between pictures. I wrote some of the special material he used in his act, which he performed in stage shows in key Paramount theaters.

On this occasion, the conversation got around to the picture business, of all things. (What else?) I have yet to attend a Holly-wood party where anything except shop talk was the principal topic of conversation. In New York, it's different. Show people usually talk about themselves. In Hollywood, it is show business that preoccupies them.

It seems that Buddy and Mary had seen both *Heavenly Music* and *Out of This World.* After mentioning this, they followed with the inevitable question: "What are you going to make next?"

I replied that next I would make a beeline for the office where you collected unemployment checks. I wasn't kidding. Everyone in Hollywood did that between jobs. They didn't need the money, of course, any more than I did. But it was always deducted from our paychecks when we worked, so why not collect it when it was coming to us? The Unemployment Insurance office in Hollywood was, without a doubt, the snazziest one in the land. You would be just as apt to see a scattering of celebrities there as a studio clean-ing woman. It is no exaggeration to say that some jobless stars would run in for their weekly check while their chauffeurs waited outside in their Lincoln Continentals.

Anyway, Mary perked up at my unexpected reply. She asked me if I would be interested in coming over to join her at United Artists. Before I left that evening, an appointment was made for my agent and me to lunch at Pickfair to talk about it.

Mary was one of the two owners of United Artists (Charlie Chaplin was the other one), and she was itching to get back in action, aside from merely owning half of this giant organization. I don't mean as an actress. By 1945 America's Sweetheart was no longer interested in starring in her own films, although she still looked as lovely as ever. But she did want to be involved in production. She had not made a film since the musical, *Gay Des-*

perado, which U.A. had successfully released a few years before.

Frank Orsatti sent his brother, young Victor, to join me at the luncheon. Mary came right to the point. She wanted me to head a new production unit for her, and offered a pretty fair salary plus ten percent of the profits of any pictures we made. When Mary told us she was interested in buying some important properties— plays and books—that could be filmed as musicals, I accepted her offer. It sounded inviting, exciting—especially in writing.

The first thing we did after signing the contract was to embark for New York on the Superchief to see what was available among the Broadway shows. The one we liked best was *One Touch of Venus,* then in the second year of a successful run. It had not yet been sold for films. The asking price was too high. By this time John Wildberg, the show's producer, was beginning to fear that time was running out on him, so I was able to buy the show on terms that were surprisingly reasonable because they included a participation in the profits, which Wildberg jumped at.

We returned to Hollywood and I moved into Mary's suite of offices at the Goldwyn Studios—which she also happened to be part owner of.

I spent the next couple of months working with various writers on a film adaptation and trying to line up a cast worthy of an important property like *Venus.* Mary herself preferred working at home, and my time was divided between studio preparation chores and daily conferences with Mary at her home, Pickfair.

Despite her demure America's Sweetheart image, Mary was sharp and astute as a businesswoman. She had to be. How else could she have wound up as half owner of one of the largest film distributing companies and a large Hollywood studio, becoming in the process the wealthiest lady in town? She was keenly interested in every move I made in the preparation of *Venus,* frequently offering suggestions that were as sound as a dollar. Occasionally, however, we failed to see eye to eye on some aspect or other. On those occasions she was somewhat obstinate, sometimes petulant, always holding her ground firmly. But with it all, always lovable. She could charm the daylights out of me and make me fume at the same time. I could see why she had captured the imaginations of hundreds of millions of fans around the world, the greatest screen idol in film history.

Like Will Rogers, she liked practically everybody she ever met. The only person I ever recall Mary disparaging was Louella Parsons, whom she always blamed for breaking up her celebrated

243

marriage to Douglas Fairbanks, Senior. Doug had engaged in a quickie extramarital affair with Lady Ashley in London. Mary was quite willing to forgive and forget, but Louella blew it up so out of proportion day after day in her Hearst newspaper column that divorce became Mary's only choice.

Pickfair was the zenith of the Hollywood social scene at that time. To receive an invitation to a Pickfair party was like being asked to a White House dinner. Mary was a hostess par excellence, the Perle Mesta of the film colony. There one could meet almost anybody, from the newest crop of starlets to members of royalty like Lord Mountbatten and others. Sitdown dinners for twenty or thirty people at the long table in the mammoth formal dining room were held regularly. I remember once trying hard to converse with a bored, morose-looking gentleman on my right whose name I didn't catch. When he left the table, I glanced at his place card. It was the Baron de Rothschild.

On the quiet nights when Mary was not entertaining, I would pass by Pickfair on my way home and give Mary a blow-by-blow description of everything that had occurred at the studio that day. We were sometimes interrupted by unexpected visits from some of Mary's oldest and closest friends. One was Lillian Gish, who was very devoted to Mary. Another was D. W. Griffith. I suppose I am a sentimental soul—as you may have gathered from some of my songs. Griffith's visits always brought me to the verge of tears. He dropped over once a week or so, always for a touch. Mary would quietly slip him a couple of hundred bucks or so, which he accepted as a "loan." It was the most pathetic sight I have ever witnessed. The spectacle of this genius, the great pioneer director who was more responsible than anyone for Hollywood being what it is today, being reduced to handouts from old friends to keep from starvation, is a deplorable commentary on the gross ingratitude of the film industry. Although Mary never told me so, I found out from some of her friends that she alone was responsible for keeping David Wark Griffith in comparative comfort in the sunset years of his life. Why the industry itself did not see fit to give this great man, one of its founding fathers, some sort of an endowment or annuity to reward him for all he had done for them, is something I will never be able to fathom. They should have built a monument to him in his lifetime. The callousness of Hollywood is sometimes beyond belief.

In the Forties, most box-office names were still under contract to the major studios. Very few were available to independent producers. Nevertheless, after sweating out dozens of hours talking to agents and hopping back and forth between California and New York a few times, I was finally able to come up with a cast for the film treatment I had prepared for *One Touch of Venus*. It seemed to me that the principals I had in mind virtually guaranteed box-office success for the movie version. Mary Martin was to play the original role she had created on Broadway—Venus herself; Clifton Webb to play the effete socialite John Boles had portrayed. And, what I thought was a real inspiration, Frank Sinatra as the bouncy young singing lead that Kenny Baker had done. Plus Bert Lahr—the Cowardly Lion himself—in the featured comedy role. I thought it was a surefire cast, one that couldn't miss. They were offered to us at salaries that were not prohibitive.

Yet it was one of those occasions when Mary and I could not agree. We discussed it for days, but she just could not make up her mind. She was afraid the names were a bit chancy for a two-million-dollar film investment (the budget Mary had agreed to provide), and she felt that of the four names, only Clifton Webb had proved himself as a film-theater draw. Maybe she was right, but I finally threw up my hands. I told her it was the best that I or anyone else could come up with in the way of a cast. There was no point in trying any longer. It was *her* money, and two million is a lot of bread to supply when you are not sure you have the right ingredients.

Mary—bless her heart—would simply not hear of my quitting her and United Artists. She insisted on setting me up in a new unit, strictly on my own, to make musicals for U.A. First, however, we sold our film rights to *One Touch of Venus* to Lester Cowan, since Mary was convinced she'd never get a cast strong enough to satisfy her. Lester made the film sometime later, starring Ava Gardner as Venus. She was the only important name in the cast.

To keep her word with me, Mary attended a U.A. directors' meeting in New York and got them to approve a contract for me that provided a United Artists release for my films, with my own choice of story, stars, and the other ingredients. After the meeting, Mary phoned the news—not to me, but to my mother in Brooklyn. It gave her the thrill of her life. Mother, then in her seventies, had been a staunch Pickford fan for more than a quarter of a century.

Nowadays, only a few of her closest cronies ever see Mary at Pickfair. She and Buddy still live there, but in comparative seclusion. I still get a card from them every Christmas, with a friendly note scrawled on it. The festive, gala parties are now mere memories. The great halls of Pickfair are quiet now, but they are still haunted by the glamorous phantoms I used to see there. There go Clark Gable, Carole Lombard, Marion Davies, Sam Goldwyn, Elsa Maxwell, Ronald Colman, Gertrude Lawrence, Errol Flynn, Vivien Leigh, and the whole parade of beautiful people bedecked in their formal finery, and so indelibly photographed on my mind. Surprisingly, Matt Kemp, who runs Pickford Enterprises today, told me very recently that Mary still follows her business affairs closely. Her mind is still as alert as ever. Her old films are still featured in museums and colleges, and a year never goes by without a Mary Pickford Festival being held in some corner of the globe. They are fitting testimonials to a great lady whose grateful public has never forgotten her. As far as I am concerned, she is still America's Sweetheart.

While all this was going on, I still managed to squeeze in a certain amount of song activity. Walt Disney, an old song buff himself, thought it might be a good stunt to revive the Coslow-Johnston team. He asked Arthur and me to write the title song for that year's big Disney feature, *Song of the South*, which we did. I also had written words and music for "Beware My Heart." I sold it to Boris Morros, my former Paramount music boss, because I had no picture to use it in. Boris was producing *Carnegie Hall* for United Artists. It was the only pop song in the film; the rest were all classical. I sent it for publication to Harry Link, who had left Berlin to become general manager for Leo Feist in New York. Harry did his usual good job, getting the song on the Hit Parade by the time *Carnegie Hall* was released. Then too, a song I had contributed at the last minute to *Out of This World* (because Mercer and Arlen had gone to New York to do a show) was starting to break big on records. The song was "I'd Rather Be Me," which Eddie Cherkose and I had written to a tune by Felix Bernard, composer of the famous "Dardenella." The big record was by Bing Crosby, whose voice had sung it (through Eddie Bracken's silent lips) in my film. Over a million were sold—but not because of our song. The other side of the record was the Johnny Mercer-Harry Warren smash, "On the Atchison, Topeka, and the Santa Fe."

I set up my new United Artists production unit at the Goldwyn studios and began reading the scripts that agents were submitting. They were good stories for the most part, but they didn't read like musicals. So I went to New York to look over the new

246

Broadway musicals. There I was contacted by Monte Proser, one of the owners of the Copacabana nightclub. He said he had a hot idea for a musical.

Monte's idea was for a film called *Copacabana*, then the country's most celebrated club. I had no immediate reaction to the idea. But a few nights later, having dinner at the Copa and watching Monte's spectacular floor show with the famous Copa girls, bells suddenly began to ring inside my skull. I agreed to explore the idea.

Back at the studio, I hired Hungarian playwright Laszlo Vadnai, who had recently emigrated from Budapest after writing several successful stage musicals, to dream up a story about the nightclub. Vadnai was inventive and fast. In no time he came up with a 25-page story treatment. It sounded fresh and amusing, and provided the perfect springboard for a flock of production numbers. I decided to use it as the basis for my first release.

The next step was to line up the financing. Under my new deal, United Artists was to release the film but not finance it. Gradwell Sears, U.A.'s New York head, had told me that any bank would finance a picture that had a United Artists release deal. I found this was one of those half truths that drive independent producers up the wall. The only man I knew in the banking world was Bernie Gianinni, son of the founder of the Bank of America. Bernie's function at the bank was to run the division that financed films.

I took Bernie to lunch, showed him my U.A. release contract and the story treatment, and told him I wanted to borrow a million dollars.

Bernie laughed out loud. "Just like that? Only a million bucks?"

Except for the Lum and Abner quickie, I'd had practically no experience in this end of the business. Digging up financing was foreign to me, and something I didn't particularly relish. I was more attuned to the creative side of filmmaking.

Bernie explained to me that a U.A. release was a valuable asset. But before the Bank of America would lend me a million dollars, he would have to know who the stars were; and he warned me that they had better be box-office draws.

My work was cut out for me. The story called for a glamorous foreign comedienne who could sing and a male comedy star to play opposite her in the role of a manager whose heart was full of larceny.

The girl was no problem. Carmen Miranda was ideal for the

247

part, and her manager, George Frank, read the story and gave me an immediate commitment. Finding a male star, however, proved to be a headache. No one I wanted seemed to be available at the time. I contacted agents and studio casting directors for many weeks, without success.

Then one morning I got a letter from Gummo Marx. Gummo managed the Marx Brothers, and they were available for a new film. There was, of course, no way I could fit all three into the script, but something clicked in my mind. I phoned Gummo.

"Groucho would be the ideal star for *Copacabana*," I ventured. "How about it?"

I could hear him breathing hard over the telephone mouthpiece. There was a brief silence. Finally he spoke.

"Did I hear you right? Are you telling me you'd like to break up the Marx Brothers? People have been trying to do that for the past thirty years!"

He kept protesting that there was just no way, but he did agree to let Groucho read the treatment. I sent a copy over by messenger. I will let Groucho's son, Arthur, take up the story from here. In his 1954 biography entitled *Groucho*, Arthur writes:

> Groucho got a picture offer to star in a picture without his brothers—from songwriter Sam Coslow, who had turned independent producer to make a musical called *Copacabana*. It was Groucho's first solo attempt at picture making, and he considered it quite a challenge. It was what he had always wanted to do—play the part of a normal human being who spoke funny lines, but who didn't wear a grotesque, phony moustache.

I called Bernie Gianinni and told him I had succeeded in breaking up the Marx Brothers and now had two box-office stars for the film.

"You're doing great," he said. "Now find a good commercial director who has some top-grossing musicals under his belt."

It was like trying to fill a bottomless glass with water. But in building a movie, filling in one ingredient often supplies the next one automatically. I was able to get Alfred Green, who had recently directed the blockbuster *Jolson Story*, merely by telling him I had Groucho Marx as a solo star, plus Carmen Miranda. The bank loan came through.

We set a shooting date about three months away. I began working at a furious pace. Vadnai began turning out pages of dialogue

248

based on his treatment. I began writing songs to fit the various situations. Groucho insisted on interpolating one song, a bit of tomfoolery called "Go West, Young Man" by Harry Ruby and Bert Kalmar. I got the film rights for $2,000. We hired the rest of the cast and began building sets. I had Monte Proser send on his Copa girls from New York—the original ones, direct from the club. Each of the twelve flew out here convinced she would soon be a movie star.

One important scene in the film called for a group of well known newspaper columnists to attend the opening of a new Copa floor show. There was about half a page of dialogue for the group. I thought it might be a smart stunt to inject a bit of realism, so I engaged columnists Earl Wilson, Louis Sobol, and Abel Green to play themselves. They practically came out for the ride. I gave each of them a roundtrip plane ticket, a week at the Beverly Hills Hotel, and, if I remember rightly, $100 apiece for one day's shooting. It was just a lark for them, and they enjoyed being movie actors. Besides, they were big hams at heart. Each one tried to build up his part with extra lines.

Everyone told me Groucho would be a big temperamental headache with his continual demands. Actually, he was very little trouble. He did insist on a clause in his contract stating that he wouldn't be called on to kiss Carmen Miranda at any time. He never explained why. I think the fiery Carmen would have smacked him in the kisser had she known about the clause.

At the start of each day's shooting, Vadnai would arrive at my office with a final corrected draft of that day's dialogue. Al Green and I would read it, then send it over to the set for the players to learn. Groucho invariably took his lines and injected jokes galore. They were all very funny, but sometimes sacrificed plot to continuity to get a laugh. Vadnai would get furious, but it was impossible to control Groucho. But except for these problems, Groucho cooperated beautifully—besides being a lot of fun to work with.

The picture was released in early 1947 and was well received by the critics. But it just barely broke even on theater bookings. However, four years later, when television was new and sweeping the country, *Copacabana* became perhaps the most-played movie on the late shows. The picture turned out to be quite profitable when all the TV returns were in. Before this happened, however, it afforded me some degree of satisfaction to repay the Bank of America's million-dollar loan plus six percent interest. At least my credit stayed good.

I had one song hit, "Je Vous Aime," which Andy Russell sang

in the film. The song did even better in Europe than here. It was the top seller of the year in France, and still ranks as an important standard there.

Chronologically, the next event in my life was the arrival of D-Day—the "D" standing for divorce. Esther and I had just not been compatible for several years, and that may be the biggest understatement in this book. The only thing that really held our marriage together was Jacqueline. Jackie was our daughter, born in 1943. For years I was much too infatuated with our baby to think of leaving home. But when Jackie was five, early in 1948, Esther and I decided we'd never make it. We were just worlds apart on too many things. I left home and rented a small house in the Malibu beach colony. Jackie spent every weekend with me, enjoying the beach and the ocean. Her visits enabled me to live through the ordeal of separation from a gorgeous child I loved very dearly.

Esther was granted a divorce later that year. Under the California community-property laws, it was the costliest court decision I ever encountered. It not only gave me a separation from her, but from most of my life's savings as well. She had a hell of a good lawyer.

These were the early days of television. As a producer, I was naturally attracted to the new medium. I found out that NBC in Hollywood wanted to experiment with original half-hour musical shows, something that hadn't been done so far. When I volunteered to try producing one, they accepted my proposal. Thus far, it hadn't occurred to them that they could get a real live movie producer for the job. At that early stage, Hollywood was afraid TV would keep the public away from theaters. TV was a dirty word in the movie industry. So the NBC crowd really rolled out the red carpet for me. I therefore became, to the best of my knowledge, the first man to produce a filmed musical show for network TV.

I gave them exactly what they wanted, a half-hour revue with an original score, production numbers, and comedy skits. It was strictly an experiment, so they gave me a shooting budget of only $10,000. That meant I couldn't afford any names. I brought it in for $12,500, a miracle even for those low-cost days. There was nothing left for my services. The same film produced today would cost at least $250,000.

The film was broadcast and was well received. NBC offered me a deal to produce a series of 26 more. But there was one big hitch.

250

Until a sponsor could be found, I would have to bring them in for $10,000 each. I told them to forget it. I loved the medium, but I also loved to eat.

As I look back at it now, it was the dumbest decision I ever made. As a TV pioneer, I had the inside track at the network, and undoubtedly could have gone on from there. A year or two later, the industry was mushrooming. Sponsors were waiting on line to buy shows. But, at a time when hardly anybody I knew even *owned* a TV set, something must have gone wrong with my usual 20-20 vision. I didn't even get the message when I observed that CBS, being short of product, was renting all my old Soundies and broadcasting them from New York morning, noon, and night. Incidentally, it was TV that finally killed the Soundies business. All the cocktail bars and juke joints that housed the Soundies machines had now installed their first TV sets. They were a great curiosity then, and nobody bothered to put a dime in the Soundies box when he could sit there and watch hours of free TV.

The only other film I produced for TV was one I did later for the Bell Telephone Hour. I dramatized a true story Hoagy Carmichael had told me about one of his songs, "I Get Along Without You Very Well." Hoagy had written the tune to a poem he had clipped out of a newspaper. The song swept the country early in 1939—but Hoagy could never find out who had written the poem. Finally the author came to light after Walter Winchell aired a desperate plea on his Sunday night radio broadcast. In the film, I starred Hoagy and Walter as themselves.

Chapter Thirteen

THAT'S HOW THE BALL BOUNCED-IN TWO DIFFERENT DIRECTIONS

After more than a score of years in Hollywood, a strange restlessness overcame me in the early 1950s. When I stopped to analyze it, I knew I was fed up with the town.

I was in the midst of setting up a deal to film a script by Vadnai that I liked called *Champagne for Everybody.* But I woke up one morning and decided to chuck the whole thing. I realized I didn't really like the producing game. I seemed to be endlessly going around in circles. I still had a United Artists release deal, and another one in the offing at Columbia Pictures. But the financing end was a bloody bore. I hated it, for I couldn't get money without stars. And I couldn't get the stars I wanted without money. And so on, ad infinitum.

I began to recall how satisfying it used to be when I was just writing scores, without all the other headaches I was now involved in. "Who needs all this nonsense?" I asked myself. I envied the boys I knew who were writing scores for important shows in New York and London. I longed to be part of that scene again.

Moreover, my personal life at that time left much to be desired. I had discovered an extremely attractive young actress with a German-sounding name, renamed her Carol Brewster, and helped her land her first few parts in films. In the process, I had become romantically involved with her. But it was all wrong for

252

me. She was barely twenty and filled with driving ambition, while I was ready to stop knocking my brains out and live a more relaxed life. It was inevitable that we would break up.

I was ready for a complete change of scene, so when I woke up on that particular morning, I quickly convinced myself that twenty-odd years in Hollywood were enough for anyone. I determined to set out for greener pastures. That afternoon, I dictated letters calling off negotiations I was in the midst of with banks, film companies, writers, and players. I then gave my office staff a month's severance pay and let them go. The next day I was en route to New York.

During my first week in the Big Town, I came within an inch of writing the biggest musical hit of the century. No, make it a sixteenth of an inch, and two centuries. I'm not kidding. Talk about fate being cruel! Listen to this story, and weep with me:

I phoned a few friends to let them know I had arrived in New York and was planning to leave soon for London. One of the first I spoke to was Jean Dalrymple, who was producing lavish stage productions for the City Center. Jean urged me not to be in a hurry to go overseas. She invited me to be her house guest for the weekend at her country place near Danbury, Connecticut. She said I had arrived in New York just in time for something I would find really interesting.

Arriving in Danbury, I found that Jean had a houseful of congenial guests, mostly from the Broadway stage crowd. Among them was the man she particularly wanted me to meet, a Hungarian producer named Gabriel Pascal. He was my roommate for the weekend on Jean's top floor, which she had fixed up as a sort of dormitory.

On the first night of the weekend, Pascal talked and talked—until the roosters began crowing in the early dawn. He was a fascinating character. In his heavy accent he unfolded a series of grand plans. He also threw in his life story, including how he had obtained the film rights to all of George Bernard Shaw's plays—for ten shillings. For some reason or other, Shaw had taken a fancy to the picturesque Hungarian.

Shaw was now deceased, but Pascal still was the fairhaired boy with the estate executors. He had just closed a deal with them for something he considered the most ambitious undertaking of his career. He was going to convert Shaw's *Pygmalion*—which he had produced in films back in 1938—into a spectacular Broadway musical. As he described the idea, he waved his arms with dra-

253

matic gestures. His eyes gleamed like flashlights. He was really carried away with his concept, and had me thoroughly sold on it from the word go.

His biggest hurdle so far was getting writers. He wanted nothing but the best. The name playwrights he had contacted had turned him down. They couldn't see *Pygmalion* as a musical. For the score, he had approached Cole Porter, Dick Rodgers, and Irving Berlin in turn. They were too busy to take it on, and Pascal couldn't wait another year or two until they were free.

"And this is where you might come in—maybe, perhaps," he went on. "Jean tells me you wrote some of my favorite songs— "Cocktails for Two," "My Old Flame," and "Mister Paganini," which I love very much. They could all have been hits in Broadway shows. You should write my *Pygmalion* score."

I told him I would be delighted to. I had forsaken Hollywood to find something just like this.

"Do you have an agent?" he asked.

I said I had one in Hollywood, but when it came to a stage show I would prefer using a New York agent, someone like the William Morris Agency.

He told me he was leaving for London in a couple of days for a meeting with the Shaw estate attorneys. On his return in a few weeks, he promised to meet with whomever I decided to have represent me.

And that's where fate stepped in. If this book were a movie, the background music would be "Hearts and Flowers" at this point. With schmaltz. Gabriel Pascal dropped dead of a heart attack a few weeks later. His widow inherited his stage and film properties, and I had no idea how to reach her. I was told she was somewhere in Europe. Even if I had found her, it is doubtful that I could have conveyed her husband's wishes to her. Eventually, I read that her attorney had sold the *Pygmalion* musical rights to Herman Levin, and that he had engaged Lerner and Loewe to write the book and score. It was, of course, renamed *My Fair Lady*.

Although it has only two letters, *if* is a mighty big word. I've spent a lot of time since then wondering what sort of a score I might have written for the show *if* Pascal had lived to carry out his plans. Maybe I wouldn't have composed a "Street Where You Live" or "I Could Have Danced All Night." But then again, maybe I would have. Who knows?

You may now put away your crying towel and quote the old

cliché, "That's the way the ball bounces." But balls or no balls, it bounced in a happier direction soon afterward. Late in 1953, just before my departure for London, I was on a blind date in New York. Two film writers I knew, Clark and Marion Smith, were in town. They asked me to join them and a young lady for dinner. They promised I would find the young lady good company. They were right. The young lady was charming, adorable, and loads of fun to be with. Her name was Mary Dowell, but everyone called her Stuttering Sam. Despite her obvious assets, I knew immediately that she was not for me. Not because of her stuttering, but because she towered six inches above my own six feet. In high heels, she looked eight feet tall. Mary had been one of Billy Rose's Diamond Horseshoe showgirls. The midget producer had a fetish for tall gals, and the Diamond Horseshoe boasted the world's tallest showgirls.

After dinner, Mary asked us to go to a popular nightclub known as Number One Fifth Avenue. Her roommate, a singer named Frances King, was opening that night. At the mention of Frances King, my batteries began charging. As a member of the well known singing team of Noble and King, she had struck me as a girl I would like to know. I had seen Noble and King at the Hotel Pierre in New York, at the Bar of Music in Hollywood, and at other leading niteries. It was not only her looks, manner, and style that attracted me. I thought Frances delivered a ballad better than anyone I had ever heard in thirty years of listening—and I've heard thousands of singers.

At Number One Fifth, Fran's singing stopped the show. I was completely captivated. She joined our table following her act, and I met her for the first time. Now take the lyrics of any ten of the best love songs I've written, and you will get a slight glimmering of how I felt on that first meeting. I can even do better than that, and sum it up in one short word: WOW!

Fran and Mary shared an East Side apartment. It became my daily headquarters for a good long time. After a few months' courtship, we were married in Arlington, Virginia, on October 30, 1953. I didn't know it at the time, but it was the smartest move I ever made. As the old saying goes, "The third time is the charm." After two marriages that were failures, this time I really hit the jackpot.

We have now been married for 23 years, and they have been the happiest years I've known. We have practically everything in common. I not only gained a mate, but the finest demonstrator of

255

my songs that I could possibly ask for. Now, early in this year of 1977, we are still as much in love with each other as we ever were. What more can I say?

Fran and I have one child, Cara, who at this writing is in her freshman year at Sarah Lawrence College in Bronxville, New York. She often goes to visit her half-sister Jackie, who lives in nearby Katonah with her husband, Ted Sorel. Jackie is a graduate of the Royal Academy of Dramatic Art (RADA) in London, and has played the lead in several Broadway shows. Cara has similar leanings and is majoring in drama. I know I'm prejudiced as hell, but I feel she just might make it.

Shortly after our marriage, the Morris Agency reported that there was some interest in my doing a stage musical in London. The agency suggested that I go over at once and look into it. I had planned to go anyway, so I sailed for England in January 1954. Fran had to finish a singing engagement at the Boca Raton Hotel in Florida, so she joined me a month later. We rented a stunning two-story flat overlooking Hyde Park. I was to work there for the next two years.

On my arrival in London, I called on the William Morris British representative, Harry Foster. Harry placed me under the wing of his righthand man, Max Kester. Max was the ideal agent to handle me. He was a former songwriter himself and had written lyrics for several of Ray Noble's tunes. He knew all about me and how to sell me.

I first did the show I had come over to discuss, a revue called *Cockles and Champagne,* produced by Cecil Landeau. Frances demonstrated, for Landeau's approval, the first few songs I wrote for the show. As soon as Landeau heard her sing, he added her to the cast. She got a few rave notices when the show opened at the Saville Theater that summer, which is more than I can say for my score. The songs I wrote were all comedy songs, special revue material, and the British audiences frequently didn't get the point. I found out what I should have known all along: Britons and Americans do not laugh at the same things. The show ran until late in the year. Did I say ran? Actually, it just crept and sputtered.

Kester arranged for me to do a more important musical, *Romance in Candlelight,* for West End producer Emile Littler. But we knew there would be a long wait for the book, which had not yet been started. To fill the gap, I was signed by Britain's leading film studio, J. Arthur Rank Productions. There I spent the next

256

twelve months writing the words and music for several musicals for producer Raymond Stross. They were lavish by British standards. The first was *As Long as They're Happy* starring Jack Buchanan, Britain's foremost musical-comedy star. This was followed by *An Alligator Named Daisy,* a silly title but a hilarious comedy featuring Diana Dors and Jeannie Carson. I also contributed several songs to *For Better, For Worse,* an Associated British picture starring Dirk Bogarde.

I finally received the book, written by Eric Maschwitz, for Littler's *Romance in Candlelight.* I enjoyed working with the show's two personable stars, Sally Ann Howes and Jacques Pils.

Jacques was the husband of French chanteuse Edith Piaf. Under an odd clause in his contract, his songs had to be approved by Piaf. Fran and I flew to Paris one weekend, and I played the songs for Piaf in her apartment. Her comments were all in rapid-fire French. Despite my three years of high-school French, she spoke so fast I didn't catch more than a word or two. But I could easily translate her big approving smile.

The show opened at the Piccadilly Theater, which is in the middle of Piccadilly Circus, in the early fall of 1955. Between London and the British provinces, it ran about six months—falling into that grey area, neither a hit nor a flop. Or shall I say, "No hit, no run, no error"?

During our two-year stay in London I did two West End shows, three films, and two popular songs which landed high on the British record charts. One was "Our Dream Waltz," which Mantovani recorded in 1954. This beautiful recording, with about a zillion shimmering strings, is still selling. The other song was "Blue Mirage," a German tango hit for which I wrote the English lyric.

Chapter Fourteen

WALL STREET!

Fran and I left London after the opening of *Romance in Candlelight* and took a month's holiday touring France and Italy. We then sailed for New York via the Mediterranean on the S.S. Independence. In New York we sublet Joel Grey's East Side apartment, and I spent the first few weeks taking a long, hard look at the American music scene. I had heard rumblings in London about big changes in Tin Pan Alley. But I was quite unprepared for what I found.

The year was 1956, and an amazing revolution had taken place overnight. Big bands had given way to small groups. Melodious popular songs—my kind of music—had taken a backseat to strange new sounds called rock and roll. The big hits had titles like "You Ain't Nothin' but a Hound Dog," and most of the melodies seemed to have only two chords—and I cannot resist adding Tony Bennett's succinct comment: "both of them wrong."

I was shocked and dismayed. So apparently were most of my ASCAP songwriting colleagues. The top writers were just not writing. They were sitting back waiting for it all to blow over.

I am the sort of person who always tries to roll with the punches. But this new trend baffled me. My publisher friends suggested that I try to write some rock songs. I wanted no part of it. I never even tried. I learned that even Hollywood musicals were coming out with rock-and-roll themes, so there was no point in going back there.

I finally decided to ape the other writers and sit it out. It can't last, we kept assuring each other at our daily lunch sessions at the Friars Club and Jack Dempsey's restaurant. We were all whistling in the dark.

Three years later, I was still waiting for it all to blow over. The tide has to turn before long, I kept telling myself. Fashions in music have *always* changed every few years, haven't they? Just be patient, ride out the storm. . . .

I was not completely inactive, for I had an avocation that had diverted me for the past dozen years or so. Now I was in a position to devote more time to it. I haven't mentioned it in the book so far, because I was saving the story for this chapter.

The avocation was the stock market, as you must have guessed from the title of this chapter. A few years of enforced idleness had given me an opportunity to make an intensive study of what made it all tick. I read everything I could find on the subject and burned the midnight oil many a night studying figures, charts, market trends and cycles.

However, despite my preoccupation with the world of investment, if anyone had told me in 1959 that I would become a professional Wall Streeter for the next ten years, arriving at a position in the Street analagous to having a *My Fair Lady* on Broadway or a number-one song on the Hit Parade, I think I would have doubted his sanity. But it really happened, to my own astonishment. This is how rock and roll drove me into a completely new career, as far removed from music and show business as this earth is from Mars.

I must preface the account by pointing out that while it is indeed rare for someone in the popular music field to also successfully pursue a career in the world of finance, it actually *has* happened. Billy Rose parlayed his song royalties and his Diamond Horseshoe and Aquacade profits into a stock portfolio that ultimately made him the country's largest holder at AT&T stock. Billy sat next to a stock ticker in his home for five hours every day and was astute enough to leave an estate that included over thirty million dollars worth of blue-chip stocks.

Then there was Paul James, whose story was even more incredible. I have never seen it in print, so this may be a surprise to a great many people who used to see him around Broadway in the late Twenties and early Thirties. When I met Paul he was around thirty years old and was writing songs with Kay Swift. At least three of their songs, all Broadway show interpolations, have become among our most familiar standards: "Can't We Be

Friends?", "Fine and Dandy," and "Can This Be Love?". What Broadway didn't know was that Paul James was a *nom de plume* for James P. Warburg of the famous Warburg banking family. He eventually became a renowned figure in international finance. He was the author of a number of standard financial books like *The Money Muddle*, was Chairman of the Board of the Juilliard School of Music, and headed the giant banking firm of Warburg and Company at the time of his death a few years ago. And yet, when I knew him, all he wanted out of life was to write a big song hit.

With the music business becoming less and less inviting every day, I began devoting a major portion of my working hours to my market activities and studies. In some years, it had provided me with extra income to supplement my royalties. I now began to wonder whether it could provide a real living if I worked at it full time.

I had become aware of one element in the stock market which seemed to give me a considerable edge over most people: my discovery of market indicators and what they revealed about future movements of stocks and bonds. Nobody paid much attention to indicators in those days. Even the professionals on the Street seemed hardly aware of them. But for me, they opened up a whole new world. I researched them for hours upon end, and it really paid off. My researches made me feel like an insider because they revealed, in an uncanny manner reminiscent of ESP, what the market was about to do.

By the time I became thoroughly absorbed in the indicators, I soon realized that I was taking on a backbreaking job. I was subscribing to several market advisory services, each of which concentrated on a different indicator; and I was spending many hundreds of dollars in this fashion, in order to follow the indicators intelligently. There was *Drew's Odd-Lot Service*, for example, which attempted to time the market cycles by following the purchases and sales of odd-lotters, the little investors who could afford to buy only odd lots of stocks (10, 25, or 50 shares instead of a 100-share "round lot"). The odd-lotters were usually wrong, so you could in most cases beat the market by doing the opposite of what they were doing. I took Richard Russell's *Dow Theory Letters*. Russell based his market advice on the Dow Theory, which in most cycles has been an almost infallible indicator. Then there was the *Bank Credit Analyst* of Canada, which kept track of all the banking indicators, and about a dozen more I was following. The sum of them all told you when to buy and sell: not infallibly, because some often contradicted others. But when I listened to the message the *majority* of indicators was sending, the big picture came into sharp focus.

I began to wonder why no one had ever thought of supplying information on *all* the principal indicators, an all-in-one service that smart investors really needed. By this time, I had learned so much about them that I thought I could supervise such a publication myself, an advisory service that would save hours and hours of time each week for large investors and Wall Street institutions. I wasn't entirely sure there would be a broad enough market for the service, but I felt the idea was worth experimenting with.

In 1960, I began planning such a publication in earnest. I decided to call it *Indicator Digest.* I spent a few months playing with a dozen different ideas for a format, and wrote countless memos about what the contents should consist of. By the end of that year, I was ready to launch my brainchild. I planned to run one ad in *Barron's* weekly, the Wall Street paper that most advisory services advertised in. If the ad pulled, I would launch my service. If I found I was wrong, I would immediately refund the money to anyone who had subscribed and forget the whole thing.

The first hurdle I ran into was that *Barron's* refused my ad. They had strict rules about their advertising. Unless you had some kind of professional background in Wall Street and 24-karat-gold references, your ad was unacceptable. I had no background in the business at all—nothing more than a million-dollar concept that many months of research told me would work. They didn't believe a word of it.

Racking my brain for some way to overcome this obstacle, I met with a friend named Sol Meyer, who was a partner in a brokerage firm that had a seat on the New York Stock Exchange. Sol, a fullfledged pro, thought I had come up with a fantastic idea and wondered why no one had thought of it sooner. He offered to become a partner in my enterprise. He would put up his share of the money to get us off the ground, and would provide the professional background the media required. I accepted his proposal, having no other choice. We formed a corporation in which Sol had one-third ownership.

We ran the ad in *Barron's* in early 1961, one-quarter of a page for $300. Then we sat back to await the results. I had no office as yet. I worked out of the large basement of my home in Westchester, where Fran and I had recently moved because we didn't want

261

our new daughter Cara to grow up on the city streets.

Barron's came out on Saturday. On Monday the postman came with an armload of mail. Every envelope had a check for a trial subscription. On Tuesday, he came with two armloads. By the end of the week, the mail was stacked up about a yard high in my basement. I couldn't believe it was happening.

All I had said in my ad was that I would shortly issue a bi-weekly advisory service that would be a digest of thirty different indicators, and I named all thirty in the ad. No hard sell, nothing like that. Just an honest announcement describing my idea. It was an idea whose time had come. I clicked with it because I had beaten everybody to the punch.

I had no employees, but Fran and I, Sol, a parttime secretary in the neighborhood, and a young assistant I immediately took on named Yale Hirsch were working around the clock opening envelopes, sorting out checks, and entering subscribers on our books. The $300 ad had paid for itself tenfold by this time.

Now we were faced with getting out issue number one of *Indicator Digest*. We of course had dozens of sources of information. I was a subscriber, long before we started, to about $1,500 worth of assorted indicator services. Yale, Sol and I, plus a parttime chart-maker and statistician Sol sent up from his Wall Street office, were furiously posting charts of the indicators five days a week.

A week after the ad appeared, I rented a suite of offices in nearby Eastchester, New York, and knocked out the first issue. We were still interviewing secretaries but hadn't decided on one yet. So I typed the first issue myself, six pages of copy I had written including a front-page market summary wrapping up what all the indicators were saying that week. A friendly neighborhood printer put his entire plant at our disposal, and the issue was rushed out and mailed to subscribers.

We ran the same ad again, this time in the financial section of the *New York Times* on a Sunday. The results equalled those on the first ad. It was obvious that we had a "better mousetrap," something that everyone in the market had been waiting for. Now they could get it all in one package without having to subscribe to a score of expensive services. Moreover, I livened up the reading matter by trying to inject a little style. Most of the other services and the brokers' newsletters were dull and stodgy "tombstone" affairs. Numerous letters from subscribers told me our service was far more readable, so I knew I was on the right track. This $300 was all we ever invested, although we were prepared to go

262

much further. But we were in the black two days after the ad appeared!

By the time our second issue come out, we had hired, out of necessity, an office full of employees: office workers, mailroom help, and people who were keeping up with all the voluminous figures and charts that I had to interpret and write about.

During my first month in business, my new secretary came into my office one morning and said, "Look at this one, Mr. C.—a subscription just came in from *The Wall Street Journal*! And here are two more in the same mail—one from Lehman Brothers and one from Bankers Trust Company."

"Let me see them," I broke in, snatching the envelopes away from her. It seemed beyond belief, but it was true. Imagine *The Wall Street Journal* and Lehman Brothers paying good money to find out what *I* thought about the stock market! In rock-and-roll language, "Crazy, man."

Yale walked in and said, "I don't know why you're even surprised. You're saving *them* a lot of time and manpower too. They have to keep track of the indicators like everybody else."

The trial subscriptions called for only four issues. At the end of that time, 85% of the trials converted to more expensive one- and two-year subscriptions. We had passed the acid test. Now we were really making it.

The following year, the historic 1962 stock market crash began in March. The Dow Jones average dropped like a lead balloon, a couple of hundred points in a few weeks. Some people thought it would put us out of business. Instead, our subscribers tripled by the time the crash was over. Why? In January of that year, two months before the crash, I got out a special New Year issue with bold headlines warning that a major crash was imminent.We advised our readers to get out of the market in a hurry. The indicators had told me it would happen. Later, a major new bull market started just before the end of that year. We were right on target with that one too.

A host of imitators began to pop up, most of them with the word "indicator" somewhere in their names. Before I had started my publication, the word was rarely seen on the financial pages. Now everyone was getting on the bandwagon. But we kept forging ahead, regardless.

Wall Street was really sitting up and taking notice of us. *The Wall Street Journal* ran a front-page feature story about me, informing its readers that the editor and founder of *Indicator Digest*

263

was in reality the writer of "Cocktails for Two" and other song hits. They gleefully scooped the newspaper world with that one. *Newsweek* then interviewed me and ran a story about me as a two-career man. BBC Television sent a camera crew to my office and filmed a documentary, which was flown to London and aired the following week—all about how the composer of several London shows and films was now advising Wall Street.

I bought out Sol Meyer's interest in 1964, becoming sole owner of *I.D.* By 1968, it had the largest circulation of any technical market service in Wall Street by a huge margin. By that time we had a family of six different services, having added an *I.D. Chart Service,* a *Daily Market Letter,* a service for gold investors, and others. I had a separate company called Investors' Press that published financial books. It started out with a pretty good seller, an anthology titled *A Treasury of Wall Street Wisdom* compiled and edited by Harry Schultz and myself.

During the process, I had invented a number of important market indicators myself, some of which are frequently used in Wall Street today. One of these was IDA (the Indicator Digest Average), in which I set out to improve on the Dow Jones average of thirty industrial stocks. IDA is the average of *all* the 1,400-odd stocks on the New York Stock Exchange, and is figured daily by computer. Before the devastating 1973-74 crash, IDA turned down sharply many months before the D.J. average began its descent. Any average of 1,400 stocks is bound to tell the market story far more accurately than an average of only thirty. IDA is still widely quoted in the financial press, usually anticipating market movements well in advance.

I also originated the Odd-Lot Trading Ratio (a new wrinkle on an old theme), the Volume Momentum Index, the Dow-Jones Individual Stock Index, the I.D. 233-Key Stock Index, and several others that market analysts use today. I made some refinements on an old one and gave it a name: the "Overbought-Oversold" Index, a name which is today in wide usage throughout the investment community and is frequently referred to in Wall Street literature.

For almost ten years, I worked like a perpetual-motion machine —nights, weekends and holidays. By that time, we had over 42,000 subscribers, and our rates had gone up to $65 a year. We had a staff of sixty. We occupied three stories of our own office building in New Jersey, and had a separate building that housed our printing plant. By that time, as you may have guessed, I was getting pretty tired, physically and mentally. I hadn't written a song or produced a musical in those ten years. After all, I'm not superhuman. In fact, I had no inclination to. All I felt like doing now was sitting around in the sun somewhere for a year or two. Which is exactly what I wound up doing. I sold my company—I.D. and all the other services—went down to Florida with my family, and built a home overlooking Biscayne Bay, on Palm Island near Miami. *Indicator Digest* is still going strong under its new ownership, and remains a prestigious Wall Street service that most of the country's stockbrokers and many large investors still subscribe to.

I didn't plan to retire permanently. All I wanted was to relax in the sun for a few years, forget about deadlines, and recharge my batteries. I had worked incessantly since I was a teenager, and felt I owed this to myself.

In 1974, I was elected to the Songwriters' Hall of Fame, a mark of recognition I am indeed proud to possess. Fran and I flew to California for the annual dinner at the Beverly Hilton to receive the award, a bronze replica of Irving Berlin's old honkytonk piano. The principal speakers were Frank Sinatra, Jack Benny, George Burns, and Milton Berle. The Hall of Fame elects five new members each year. My corecipients that year were Leonard Bernstein, Johnny Green, Harry Ruby, and the team of Jay Livingston and Ray Evans. It was good seeing some of my old buddies again. I felt like I was back in my own world.

What now? I can answer this best with a little anecdote. I am an inveterate notemaker. I don't have a memory like an elephant, so I am forever writing little notes to myself on odd pieces of paper that I stuff in my pockets. Otherwise, I'd forget a lot of important things. Sometimes they are song titles, or the opening bars of a musical phrase, or something I think of doing, like getting my hair cut. Once, a long time ago in Hollywood, an idea for a story popped into my mind while I was driving home from the studio. It was an idea for a stage musical. By the time I was halfway home I had most of the plot worked out, leading characters and all. At the next stoplight, to make sure it wouldn't slip my mind, I jotted down just three words on a small scrap of paper in my pocket: "Write musical comedy." I naturally didn't have time to write down any details, but all I needed were those three words to refresh my memory.

Arriving home, I found Herbert Marshall and his wife there, ready to go out to dinner with us, as per plans we had made earlier. We had a quick drink in my den first, and Bart took out a cigarette. While I was fumbling in my pocket for a lighter, the scrap of paper flew out and fell to the floor. Bart reached for it, glanced at the three words, and said, "I don't believe it. 'Write musical comedy.' I've never in my life heard of a man who had to make a note to remember to write a musical comedy!" For years afterwards, Bart Marshall told the story to everyone he met— about what a bad memory I had.

And so, what now? Fran and I have sold our Florida home. I've *had* the relaxation bit, all the way up to my bifocal sunglasses. We just bought a new apartment on the East Side of Manhattan, and at this moment are kneedeep in packing cases and cartons, ready to make the move. In a few weeks, I will be looking out at the lights of New York high up on the 32nd floor of a 57th Street skyscraper, dreaming again and planning. What about?

Well, I'm getting restless. I just wrote another note to myself. It reads: "Write musical comedy—"

Appendix I

MY PERSONAL FAVORITES

I am frequently asked which of my 500-odd published compositions I personally prefer. I am almost always enamoured of the song that I am working on at the moment. But on looking at them in retrospect, the ones I like best comprise the following list. Some were hits, and some are virtually unknown, but these are what I consider the bulk of my best work, listed alphabetically:

Title	Collaborator	Identified with
AFTER YOU (1937; from *Double or Nothing*)	Al Siegel	Jimmy Dorsey Tommy Dorsey
BEBE (1923)	Abner Silver	Al Jolson Eddie Cantor
BEWARE MY HEART (1947; from *Carnegie Hall*)	None	Margaret Whiting
BLACK MOONLIGHT (1933; from *Too Much Harmony*)	Arthur Johnston	Bing Crosby Perry Como
BLUE MIRAGE (1955; U.S. version of German tango hit)	Lotar Olias	Guy Lombardo
BOO BOO BOO (1933; from *College Humor*)	Arthur Johnston	Bing Crosby

267

LAS CHIAPENECAS (1940; Mexican folk tune)	(My lyric)	
COCKTAILS FOR TWO (1934; from *Murder at the Vanities)*	Arthur Johnson	Carl Brisson Kitty Carlisle Spike Jones
CRAZY LITTLE MIXED UP HEART (1955)	None	Georgia Brown
DARLING, THEY'RE PLAYING OUR SONG (1954)	None	Frances King Jimmie Young
THE DAY YOU CAME ALONG (1933; from *Too Much Harmony)*	Arthur Johnston	Bing Crosby
DON'T TAKE THAT BLACK BOTTOM AWAY (1926)	None	Ann Pennington
DOWN THE OLD OX ROAD (1933; from *College Humor)*	Arthur Johnston	Bing Crosby
DREAMING OUT LOUD (1940; from *Dreaming Out Loud)*	None	Frances Langford Artie Shaw Benny Goodman
EBONY RHAPSODY (1934; from *Murder at the Vanities)*	Arthur Johnston	Duke Ellington
EVERY DAY'S A HOLIDAY (1937; from *Every Day's a Holiday)*	Barry Trivers	Mae West Fats Waller
FARE THEE WELL (1934; from *Many Happy Returns)*	None	Guy Lombardo Noel Coward
FIFI (1937; from *Every Day's a Holiday)*	None	Mae West
FIRST LOVE (1956; from *First Love)*	None	Dickie Valentine
FIVE LITTLE MILES FROM SAN BERDOO (1951; from *His Kind of Woman)*	None	Jane Russell
GOOD MORNING (1937; from *Mountain Music)*	None	Martha Raye
GOTTA DANCE MY WAY TO HEAVEN (1936; from *It's Love Again)*	None	Jessie Matthews
GRIEVING FOR YOU (1920; my first major hit)	"Three Joes"	Al Jolson Paul Whiteman

268

HAVE YOU FORGOTTEN SO SOON? (1938)	Abner Silver Ed Heyman	
HEART OF THE WEST (1936; theme of Hopalong Cassidy films)	Victor Young	Hopalong Cassidy
HEAVENLY MUSIC (1943)	None	Perry Como Tony Martin
HELLO, SWANEE, HELLO (1926)	None	Al Jolson
(I'M IN LOVE WITH) THE HONORABLE MR. SO-AND-SO (1939; from *Society Lawyer*)	None	Helen Morgan Virginia Bruce Helen Forrest
HOT VOODOO (1932; from *Blonde Venus*)	Leo Robin Ralph Rainger	Marlene Dietrich
I KNEW IT WOULD BE THIS WAY (1945; from *Practically Yours*)	None	Fred MacMurray
I NEVER KNEW (WHAT THE MOONLIGHT COULD DO)	Abner Silver	
I'D RATHER BE ME (1945; from *Out of This World*)	Felix Bernard Ed Cherkose	Bing Crosby
I'D RATHER LOOK AT YOU (1938)	None	Fred Astaire
IF I WERE KING (1930)	Leo Robin Newell Chase	Dennis King
IN THE MIDDLE OF A KISS (1935; from *College Scandals*)	None	Connie Boswell
IS IT LOVE OR INFATU-ATION? (1937; from *This Way, Please*)	None	
IT'S LOVE AGAIN (1936; from *It's Love Again*)	None	Jessie Matthews
IT'S RAINING SUNBEAMS (1937; from *100 Men and a Girl*)	Fred Hollander	Deanna Durbin
JAMMIN' (1937; from *Turn Off the Moon*)	None	Andrews Sisters
JE VOUS AIME (1947; from *Copacabana*)	None	Andy Russell Carmen Miranda

JUST ONE MORE CHANCE (1931)	Arthur Johnston	Bing Crosby
KINDA LONESOME (1938; from *St. Louis Blues)*	Hoagy Carmichael Leo Robin	Jimmy Dorsey Benny Goodman Dorothy Lamour
KISS AND RUN (1953; from *Love from a Stranger)*	None	Jane Russell
KITTEN ON THE KEYS (1922; vocal edition; my lyric was added for the second edition)	Zez Confrey	Zez Confrey
LEARN TO CROON (1933; from *College Humor)*	Arthur Johnston	Bing Crosby
A LITTLE WHITE GARDE-NIA (1935; from *All the King's Horses)*	None	Carl Brisson
LIVE AND LOVE TONIGHT (1934; from *Murder at the Vanities)*	Arthur Johnston	Carl Brisson Kitty Carlisle
LONELY MELODY (1927)	Hal Dyson Benny Meroff	Paul Whiteman-Bix Beiderbecke
MAKE-BELIEVE ISLAND (1940)	Will Grosz Nick Kenny	
MARIJUANA (1934; from *Murder at the Vanities)*	Arthur Johnston	Bette Midler (revival)
MIDNIGHT MUSIC (1952)	None	Merv Griffin Freddy Martin
MISTER PAGANINI (1936; from *Rhythm on the Range)*	None	Martha Raye (her theme)
MOON SONG (1932; from *Hello, Everybody)*	Arthur Johnston	Kate Smith
MOONSTRUCK (1933; from *College Humor)*	Arthur Johnston	Bing Crosby
THE MORNING AFTER (1936)	None	Red Norvo & Mildred Bailey
MY HEART SAYS YES (1955; from *Romance in Candlelight)*	None	Sally Ann Howes
MY LITTLE GUY (1972)	None	McGovern Campaign Song
MY OLD FLAME (1934; from *Belle of the Nineties)*	Arthur Johnston	Mae West Peggy Lee Billie Holiday

270

ONE KISS AWAY FROM HEAVEN (1957)	None	Tony Bennett
ONE SUMMER NIGHT (1927)	Larry Spier	Roger Wolfe Kahn
OUR DREAM WALTZ (1955)	None	Mantovani
RESTLESS (1935)	Tom Satterfield	Benny Goodman
THE SHOW IS OVER (1935)	Al Dubin Con Conrad	Al Bowlly
SING, YOU SINNERS (1930; from *Honey)*	Franke Harling	Lillian Roth Tony Bennett Sammy Davis, Jr.
SOMEONE CARES (1921)	Charles K. Harris	Van & Schenck
SONG OF THE SOUTH (1946; from *Song of the South)*	Arthur Johnston	
SOUTHERN HOSPITALITY (1937; from *Turn Off the Moon)*	None	Phil Harris
SWEEPING THE CLOUDS AWAY (1930; from *Paramount on Parade)*	None	Maurice Chevalier
A TABLE IN A CORNER (1939)	Dana Suesse	Artie Shaw
TEA ON THE TERRACE (1936)	None	Tommy Dorsey
TEXAS RANGER SONG (1936)	Harry Behn	Texas Rangers
THANKS (1933; from *Too Much Harmony)*	Arthur Johnston	Bing Crosby
THIS LITTLE PIGGIE WENT TO MARKET (1933; from *Eight Girls in a Boat)*	Harold Lewis	Eddy Duchin
THRILL OF A LIFETIME (1937; from *Thrill of a Lifetime)*	Fred Hollander	Bob Crosby Dorothy Lamour
TOMORROW NIGHT (1939)	Will Grosz	Charlie Rich Elvis Presley Patti Page
TOMORROW'S ANOTHER DAY (1925; from *Artists and Models)*	Romberg, Coots & Grey	
TROUBLED WATERS (1934; from *Belle of the Nineties)*	Arthur Johnston	Mae West Helen Merrill

TRUE BLUE LOU (1929; from *Dance of Life)*	Robin & Whiting	Ethel Waters Russ Columbo
TRUE CONFESSION (1937; from *True Confession)*	Fred Hollander	Carole Lombard
WANITA (WANNA EAT?) (1923)	Al Sherman	Al Jolson
WAS IT A DREAM? (1928)	Spier & Britt	Mantovani Dorsey Brothers Fred Waring
WHEN HE COMES HOME TO ME (1934; from *You Belong to Me)*	Leo Robin	Helen Morgan
YOU BLEW IT (1974)	None	Danny Street
YOU DIDN'T KNOW THE MUSIC (1931)	None	
YOU LITTLE SO-AND-SO (1932; from *Blonde Venus)*	Leo Robin	Marlene Dietrich
YOU WANT LOVIN' BUT I WANT LOVE (1929)	Jack Osterman Larry Spier	Rudy Vallee

Appendix II

SELECTIVE DISCOGRAPHY OF SAM COSLOW SONGS

A complete discography of all the recordings that have been made on my songs—if it were possible to compile such a list— could fill a small book by itself. The following list, therefore, is confined to those that impressed me most at the time they were released, plus some others that are listed because of their importance or historical interest.

VOCAL RECORDINGS

Andrews Sisters   *Jammin'*—Brunswick
      Comment: The first Andrews Sisters recording, released in 1937 when they were vocalists with Leon Belasco's orchestra.

Gene Austin   *Thrill of a Lifetime*—Decca

Mildred Bailey   *The Morning After*—Brunswick
      Comment: Accompanied by husband Red Norvo's band, Mildred Bailey was in my estimation one of the greatest female vocalists of all time.

Belle Baker   *Sing, You Sinners*—Brunswick

Tony Bennett   *True Blue Lou*—Columbia

	Sing, You Sinners—Columbia
	One Kiss Away from Heaven (with Percy Faith Orchestra)—Columbia
Connie Boswell	*In the Middle of a Kiss*—Brunswick
	True Confession—Decca
	Love or Infatuation—Decca

Comment: Connie's great *Love or Infatuation* was made with the illustrious Ben Pollack Orchestra.

Al Bowlly	*This Little Piggie Went to Market* —HMV (English)
	Moonstruck—Decca (English)
	Learn to Croon—Decca (English)
	Thanks—HMV (English)
	The Show Is Over—HMV (English)
	A Little White Gardenia—HMV (English)

Comment: Al Bowlly was the most popular of all British vocalists in the 1930's. He must have recorded at least twenty of my compositions. Those above are my favorites. The four listed as HMV (His Master's Voice, which was the British affiliate of RCA Victor) were done as vocalist for Ray Noble's Orchestra. Al's very last recording, tragically, had a prophetic title: *When That Man Is Dead and Gone*. It was recorded on April 2, 1941. Fifteen days later, he was killed during an air raid over London.

Carl Brisson	*Thanks*—Decca (English)
	Cocktails for Two—Brunswick
	Live and Love Tonight—Brunswick
	A Little White Gardenia—Brunswick
	Be Careful, Young Lady—Brunswick
Georgia Brown	*My Crazy Little Mixed-Up Heart* —Decca (English)
Jean Carson	*I Don't Know Whether to Laugh or Cry*—HMV (English)
Maurice Chevalier	*Sweeping the Clouds Away*—RCA Victor
June Christy	*Beware, My Heart*—Capitol
Perry Como	*Black Moonlight*—RCA Victor
	Heavenly Music—RCA Victor
Correll and Gosden	*I Never Knew (What the Moonlight Could Do)*—RCA Victor

Comment: Correll and Gosden were top radio stars of the 1930's, better known as Amos and Andy. This was their only song recording and thus rates as a collector's item.

Noel Coward   *Fare Thee Well*—RCA Victor
> *Comment:* One of the rare occasions when Coward recorded a song he didn't write himself. He was accompanied by the popular Carroll Gibbons Orchestra of London.

Joan Crawford   *(I'm in Love with) The Honorable Mr. So-and-So*—RCA Victor
> *Comment:* Joan's only recording.

Bing Crosby   *Just One More Chance*—Brunswick
Moonstruck—Brunswick
Learn to Croon—Brunswick
Down the Old Ox Road—Brunswick
Thanks—Brunswick
The Day You Came Along—Brunswick
Black Moonlight—Brunswick
I Guess It Had to Be That Way —Brunswick
I'd Rather Be Me—Decca

Doris Day   *Pumpernickel*—Columbia
Moon Song (with Paul Weston Orchestra)— Columbia

Morton Downey   *A Little White Gardenia*—Rex (English)
In the Middle of a Kiss—Rex (English)

Duncan Sisters   *Sweet Onion Time in Bermuda*—RCA Victor
> *Comment:* The Duncans also recorded the same number for Parlophone in London in the late 1930's.

Deanna Durbin   *It's Raining Sunbeams*—Decca

Ruth Etting   *Just One More Chance*—Banner

Gracie Fields   *Just One More Chance*—HMV (English)
Have You Forgotten So Soon?—Rex (English)

Ella Fitzgerald   *Mister Paganini* (Both sides of record, with Sy Oliver's Orchestra)—Decca

Mary Ford & Les Paul   *Just One More Chance*—Capitol

Helen Forrest   *(I'm in Love with) The Honorable Mr. So-and-So* (part of an album)—Capitol

Erroll Garner	*Cocktails for Two* (piano solo)—Columbia
The Happiness Boys	*Sweet Onion Time in Bermuda*—Columbia
(Billy Jones & Ernie Hare)	*Animal Crackers*—Domino
Marion Harris	*Grieving for You*—Columbia
Dick Haymes	*Stranger Things Have Happened*—Decca
	Je Vous Aime (with Gordon Jenkins Orchestra)—Decca
Billie Holliday	*My Old Flame*—MGM
	Just One More Chance—MGM
Herb Jeffries	*Was It a Dream?*—Coral
Al Jolson	*Wanita (Wanna Eat?)*—Columbia
Kitty Kallen	*Star Bright*—Decca
Dennis King	*If I Were King*—RCA Victor
Dorothy Lamour	*Panamania*—Brunswick
	I Hear a Call to Arms—Brunswick
	Kinda Lonesome—Brunswick
Frances Langford	*Moon Song*—Bluebird
	(I'm in Love with) The Honorable Mr. So-and-So (with Harry Sosnik at the piano) —Decca
	Dreaming Out Loud—Decca
Peggy Lee	*My Old Flame*—Capitol

    Comment: A revival, from one of Peggy's 1973 albums. As good as her original recording with Benny Goodman.

Jessie Matthews	*It's Love Again*—Decca (English)
Marian McPartland	Album of Coslow Standards—Dot

    Comment: The album, titled *My Old Flame*, features Marian's jazz piano artistry.

Bette Midler	*Marijuana*—Atlantic
Helen Morgan	*When He Comes Home to Me*—Brunswick
Jane Morgan	*Once More My Love*—Kapp
	C'est la Vie, C'est l'Amour—Kapp
Billy Murray	*Wanita (Wanna Eat?)*—RCA Victor
	Dumb Dora—RCA Victor

Patti Page   *Tomorrow Night*—Mercury
      Comment: I believe this is Patti's first recording.

Oscar Peterson   *My Old Flame* (piano solo)—Verve

The Platters   *My Old Flame*—Mercury

Dick Powell   *Was It a Dream?*—Vocalion

Elvis Presley   *Tomorrow Night*—RCA Victor

Martha Raye   *You'll Have to Swing It (Mister Paganini)*—Brunswick

Charley Rich   *Tomorrow Night* (also title of album)—RCA Victor

      Comment: 1974 revival. It got me an ASCAP Country Music Award.

Andy Russell   *Je Vous Aime*—Capitol

Ginny Simms   *(I'm in Love with) The Honorable Mr. So-and-So*—Vocalion

Frank Sinatra   *Moon Song*—Reprise

Kate Smith   *Moon Song*—Brunswick
                                Twenty Million People—Brunswick
                                My Queen of Lullaby Land—Brunswick
                                Make-Believe Island—Columbia

Whispering Jack Smith   *When Autumn Leaves Are Falling*—RCA Victor
      Comment: One of the earliest radio singing stars of the 1920's, Jack's famous recording of *Cecilia* sold in the millions. Abner Silver was at the piano for the above record.

Jeri Southern   *Romance in the Dark*—Decca
                                (I'm in Love with) The Honorable Mr. So-and-So (with Dave Barbour Trio)—Brunswick (English)

Jo Stafford   *My Old Flame*—Columbia

Aileen Stanley   *I Ain't Got Nobody to Love*—RCA Victor
                                  Positively Absolutely—RCA Victor
                                Nay, Nay Neighbor—RCA Victor

Danny Street   *My Little Guy*—Decca (English)
                                  You Blew It—Decca (English)

Maxine Sullivan	*Down the Old Ox Road*—RCA Victor
	Kinda Lonesome—RCA Victor
	Restless (with Bob Wilber)—Monmouth-Evergreen
Sylvia Syms	*Never a Day Goes By*—Columbia
Art Tatum	*Cocktails for Two* (piano solo)—Decca
Mel Torme	*The Day You Came Along*—Capitol
Sophie Tucker	*You'll Have to Swing It (Mister Paganini)*—Parlophone (English)
Dickie Valentine	*First Love*—Decca (English)
Dinah Washington	*Just One More Chance*—Mercury
	My Old Flame—Emarcy
Ethel Waters	*True Blue Lou*—Columbia
	Shoo, Shoo, Boogie Boo—Columbia
	Do I Know What I'm Doing?—Columbia
Margaret Whiting	*Beware My Heart*—Capitol
	Sing, You Sinners—Capitol
	This Little Piggie Went to Market—Capitol
Jimmy Young	*Darling, They're Playing Our Song*—Decca (English)

DANCE BAND RECORDINGS

Gus Arnheim and his Cocoanut Grove Orchestra	*Just One More Chance* (Donald Novis vocal)—RCA Victor
	Red, Red Roses (Dave Marshall vocal)—RCA Victor

Comment: Not generally known is the fact that Fred MacMurray was in the Arnheim band on these recordings, playing tenor sax.

Roy Bargy and the Benson Orchestra	*Deedle Deedle Dum*—RCA Victor
Charlie Barnet Orchestra	*Buckin' the Wind* (Helen Heath vocal)—Oriole
	Ebony Rhapsody—Bluebird
	You and Who Else? (Larry Taylor vocal)—Bluebird

278

Count Basie	*My Old Flame* (Lynne Sherman vocal)—Okeh
Les Baxter Orchestra	*I Never Had a Dream Like This*—Capitol *Blue Mirage* (also title of album)—Capitol
Ben Bernie Orchestra	*She's Still My Baby*—Brunswick *Hello, Swanee, Hello*—Brunswick
Henry Busse Orchestra	*Have You Forgotten So Soon?* (Don Huston vocal)—Decca
Cab Calloway Orchestra	*A New Moon and an Old Serenade* (Cab Calloway vocal)—Vocalion
Carmen Cavallaro Orchestra	*Cocktails for Two*—Decca
Larry Clinton Orchestra	*True Confession* (Bea Wain vocal)—RCA Victor *Romance in the Dark* (Bea Wain vocal)—RCA Victor *A Table in a Corner* (Terry Allen vocal)—RCA Victor
Bob Crosby Orchestra	*Thrill of a Lifetime* (Kay Weber vocal)—Decca *Every Day's a Holiday* (Bob Crosby vocal)—Decca
Dorsey Brothers Orchestra	*Was It a Dream?* (2 sides)—Okeh
Jimmy Dorsey Orchestra	*After You* (Don Matteson vocal)—Decca *Kinda Lonesome* (Lee Leighton vocal)—Decca *A Table in a Corner* (Bob Eberly vocal)—Decca *Tomorrow Night* (Bob Eberly vocal)—Decca
Tommy Dorsey Orchestra	*Tea on the Terrace* (Edythe Wright vocal)—RCA Victor *Jammin'* (Edythe Wright vocal)—RCA Victor *Turn Off the Moon* (Jack Leonard vocal)—RCA Victor *Good Mornin'* (Edythe Wright vocal)—RCA Victor

279

Mountain Music (Edythe Wright vocal)—
RCA Victor
The Morning After (Jack Leonard vocal)—
RCA Victor
Cocktails for Two—RCA Victor
An Old Curiosity Shop (Jack Leonard vocal)—RCA Victor
A New Moon and an Old Serenade (Jack Leonard vocal)—RCA Victor
After You (Edythe Wright vocal)—RCA Victor

Comment: Note that both Dorseys recorded *After You*. I would say the contest was a draw.

Eddy Duchin Orchestra	*This Little Piggie Went to Market* (Lew Sherwood vocal)—RCA Victor *You Took My Breath Away* (Lew Sherwood vocal)—RCA Victor *Kinda Lonesome* (Stanley Worth vocal)—Brunswick *Adios Americano* (June Roberts vocal)—Columbia
Duke Ellington Orchestra	*My Old Flame* (Ivy Anderson vocal)—RCA Victor *Live and Love Tonight*—RCA Victor *Cocktails for Two* —RCA Victor *Troubled Waters* (Ivy Anderson vocal)—RCA Victor *Ebony Rhapsody* (Ivy Anderson vocal)—RCA Victor
Shep Fields and his Rippling Rhythm	*Kinda Lonesome* (Hal Derwin vocal)—Bluebird
Dizzy Gillespie Orchestra	*My Old Flame*—Esquire (English)
Benny Goodman Orchestra	*My Old Flame* (Peggy Lee vocal)—Columbia *Kinda Lonesome* (Martha Tilton vocal)—RCA Victor *Dreaming Out Loud* (Helen Forrest vocal)—Columbia *Restless* (Helen Ward vocal)—RCA Victor
Glen Gray and the Casa Loma Orchestra	*Sweeping the Clouds Away* (Jack Richmond vocal)—Okeh *Last Night's Gardenias* (Kenny Sargent vocal)—Decca
Jimmie Grier Orchestra	*Music in the Moonlight* (Jimmie's theme;

280

	Donald Novis vocal)—RCA Victor *Learn to Croon*—RCA Victor
Harmonicats	*Just One More Chance*—Mercury
Harlem Hot Chocolates (pseudonym for Duke Ellington Orchestra)	*Sing, You Sinners* (Irving Mills vocal)— Hit-of-the-Week Records
Phil Harris Orchestra	*That's Southern Hospitality* (Phil Harris vocal)—Vocalion *Jammin'* (Phil Harris vocal)—Vocalion
Lennie Hayton Orchestra	*The Morning After* (Paul Barry vocal)—Decca
Horace Heidt Orchestra	*Beside a Moonlit Stream* (Charles Goodwin vocal)—Brunswick *A New Moon and an Old Serenade* (vocal by the Heidt-Lights)—Brunswick
Fletcher Henderson Orchestra	*Say Say Sadie*—Perfect
Spike Jones Orchestra	*Cocktails for Two*—RCA Victor *My Old Flame*—RCA Victor

Comment: I am including Spike's *Cocktails* on this list although I have an aversion to it. I cannot overlook the fact that it was a multimillion record seller and made history in the business.

Roger Wolfe Kahn Orchestra	*One Summer Night* (Henry Garden vocal)—RCA Victor

Comment: One of the great forgotten big bands of the 1920's. It included great musicians like Eddie Lang, Joe Venuti, Nat Shilkret (on cello) and Vic Berton. Kahn was the son of financier Otto Kahn and the heir to a fortune worth several hundred million dollars, but preferred leading a dance band.

Sammy Kaye and his Swing & Sway Orchestra	*The Hoiriger Scottische* (vocal by the Three Kayedets)—RCA Victor
Hal Kemp Orchestra	*Restless* (Maxine Gray vocal)—Brunswick *In the Middle of a Kiss* (Skinnay Ennis vocal)—Brunswick *Got to Dance My Way to Heaven* (Bob Allen vocal)—Brunswick *You and Who Else?* (Bob Allen vocal)— RCA Victor

281

Wayne King Orchestra	*Moon Song*—Brunswick *Sleep My Love*—RCA Victor
Gene Krupa Orchestra	*An Old Curiosity Shop* (Irene Daye vocal)—Brunswick *Make-Believe Island* (Howard Dulany vocal)—Columbia
Ted Lewis Orchestra	*I Ain't Got Nobody to Love*—Columbia *My Old Flame* (Ted Lewis vocal)—Decca
Monia Liter Orchestra	*Blue Fandango*—London
Guy Lombardo Orchestra	*Fare Thee Well* (Lebert Lombardo vocal)—Brunswick *Restless*—Decca *Blue Mirage*—Decca
Vincent Lopez Orchestra	*Deedle Deedle Dum*—Okeh
Louisiana Five	*Heartsickness Blues*—Emerson
Abe Lyman Orchestra	*Was It a Dream?*—Brunswick *Just One More Chance* (Phil Neely vocal)—Brunswick
Freddy Martin Orchestra	*You Took My Breath Away*—Brunswick *Keep Your Fingers Crossed*—Brunswick *Dreaming Out Loud* (Eddie Stone vocal)—Bluebird *Midnight Music* (Merv Griffin vocal)—RCA Victor
Billy May Orchestra	*Cocktails for Two*—Capitol
Red Norvo Orchestra	*Have You Forgotten So Soon?* (Mildred Bailey vocal)—Vocalion
George Olsen Orchestra	*I Never Knew (What the Moonlight Could Do)* (vocal by Fran Frey, Bob Borger, Bob Rice)—RCA Victor *I Don't Need Atmosphere* (Bob Borger vocal)—RCA Victor *This Little Piggie Went to Market*—Columbia
Original Memphis Five	*Great White Way Blues*—Vocalion
Raymond Paige Orchestra	*When My Prince Charming Comes Along* (Marian Manfield vocal)—RCA Victor

Charlie Parker Quintette *My Old Flame*—Roulette

Ben Pollack Orchestra *True Blue Lou* (Scrappy Lambert vocal)—RCA Victor
Love or Infatuation (see Connie Boswell)—Decca

  Comment: *True Blue Lou* was recorded when Goodman, Teagarden and other star musicians were with the band.

Leo Reisman Orchestra *I Still Belong to You*—Columbia
You Didn't Know the Music (Ben Gordon vocal)—RCA Victor

Fred Rich Orchestra *Don't Take That Black Bottom Away* (Leroy Montesanto vocal)—Vocalion

Gene Rodemich Orchestra *Bebe*—Brunswick

Ben Selvin Orchestra *Learn to Croon*—Columbia

Artie Shaw Orchestra *(I'm in Love with) The Honorable Mr. So-and-So* (Helen Forest vocal)—Bluebird
If I Put My Heart in My Song (electrical transcription, for use of radio stations)—RCA Thesaurus
A Table in a Corner (Helen Forrest vocal)—Bluebird
Dreaming Out Loud (Martha Tilton vocal)—RCA Victor

Jack Teagarden Orchestra *A Table in a Corner* (Kitty Kallen vocal)—Columbia

Rudy Vallee Orchestra *You Want Lovin' But I Want Love* (Rudy Vallee vocal)—RCA Victor
Turn Off the Moon (Rudy Vallee vocal)—American
That's Southern Hospitality (Rudy Vallee vocal)—American

Fats Waller Orchestra *Every Day's a Holiday* (Fats Waller vocal)—RCA Victor

Waring's Pennsylvanians *Hello, Swanee, Hello* (Tom Waring vocal)—RCA Victor
Was It a Dream? (Tom Waring vocal)—RCA Victor

Chick Webb Orchestra *Mister Paganini (You'll Have*

	to Swing It; Ella Fitzgerald vocal) —Decca
Ted Weems Orchestra	*Buckin' the Wind* (Parker Gibbs vocal)—Bluebird *I Guess It Had to Be That Way* (Red Ingle vocal)—Bluebird
Paul Weston Orchestra	*Je Vous Adore*—Decca
Paul Whiteman Orchestra	*Grieving for You*—RCA Victor *Lonely Melody* (with Bix's famous solo)— RCA Victor *Down the Old Ox Road* (vocal by Peggy Healy and Al Dary)—RCA Victor *Now I'm a Lady* (Ramona vocal)—RCA Victor
Victor Young Orchestra	*In the Middle of a Kiss* (Milton Watson vocal)—Decca *A Day Without You* (Harlan Lattimore vocal)—Brunswick *This Little Piggie Went to Market* (Peg LaCentra vocal)—Brunswick *Thanks* (Scrappy Lambert vocal)—Brunswick *The Day You Came Along* (Scrappy Lambert vocal)—Brunswick

Comment: Victor Young assembled a dream combo for his recording sessions. Would you believe Bunny Berigan on trumpet, Jimmy Dorsey on clarinet, Joe Venuti and Lou Kosloff in the string section, and Jack Teagarden on trombone?

BRITISH BANDS

The following recordings of my compositions were made by some of London's foremost dance bands. All record labels are English.

Bert Ambrose Orchestra	*One Summer Night*—Brunswick *You Want Lovin' But I Want Love*—Decca *Just One More Chance*—HMV *This Little Piggie Went to Market*—Brunswick *A New Moon and an Old Serenade*—Decca
Stanley Black Orchestra	*A Little White Gardenia*—Decca

284

Frank Chacksfield Orchestra	*Blue Mirage*—Decca
Billy Cotton Orchestra	*Learn to Croon*—Regal *The Show Is Over*—Regal
Roy Fox Orchestra	*You Didn't Know the Music*—Decca *The Show Is Over*—Decca *A Little White Gardenia*—Decca *True Confession*—HMV
Geraldo Orchestra	*A New Moon and an Old Serenade*—HMV
Henry Hall and the BBC Dance Orchestra	*Twenty Million People*—Columbia *Moonstruck*—Columbia *Thanks*—Columbia *Cupid*—Columbia *A Place in Your Heart*—Columbia *The Show Is Over*—Columbia *The Morning After*—Columbia *It's Love Again*—Columbia
Jack Hylton Orchestra	*Just One More Chance*—Decca *Moon Song*—Decca *Learn to Croon*—Decca *"Too Much Harmony" Score*—Decca *In the Middle of a Kiss*—HMV *A New Moon and an Old Serenade*—HMV
Sidney Lipton's Grosvenor House Orchestra	*Cocktails for Two*—Decca
Joe Loss Orchestra	*Got to Dance My Way to Heaven*—HMV
Ken Mackintosh Orchestra	*The Crocodile Crawl*—HMV
Mantovani Orchestra	*Was It a Dream?*—Decca *Our Dream Waltz*—Decca
Ray Noble Orchestra	*This Little Piggie Went to Market* (see also Al Bowlly)—HMV
Jack Payne Orchestra	*Just One More Chance*—Columbia *Learn to Croon*—Imperial *The Day You Came Along*—Imperial *This Little Piggie Went to Market*—Imperial *A Place in Your Heart*—Rex *Make-Believe Island*—Decca
Savoy Orpheans	*True Confession*—Columbia

INDEX

(Italicized numbers refer to pictures)

287

Burns, Bob, 206
Burns, George, 133, 148–149, 153, 192, 265
Burt, Benjamin Hapgood, *56*
Burtnett, Earl, 198
Busse, Henry, 196, 279
Buzzell, Eddie, 81–82
"By the Light of the Silvery Moon," 82

Cagney, James, 101
Cahn, Sammy, *217*
California Melodies, 137
Calloway, Cab, 200, 279
Campbell, Jimmy, 177, 179–180, 190–191
"Can This Be Love?" 260
Cantor, Eddie, 12, 57, 59–62, 67, 77, 82, 85–86, 101, 124, 167
Cantor, Ida, 124
"Can't We Be Friends?" 259–260
Capitol Theater (New York), 75
Carbonaro, Gerard, *169*
"Carioca, The," 185
Carlisle, Kitty, 140, 142, 268, 270
Carmichael, Hoagy, 99, 206, 208, 251, 269
Carnegie Hall, 246, 267
"Carolina in the Morning," 34–35
Carroll, Earl, 12, *56,* 138, 140, 142–143
Carroll, Harry, 82
Carroll, Nancy, 97, 102, 104–105, 126
Carson, Jean, 257, 274
Carus, Emma, 14, 68
Casablanca, 17
Cassidy, Hopalong, 175, 269
Cavallaro, Carmen, 241, 279
"Cecilia," 72, 277
Century Theater (New York), 78
"C'est La Vie," 221, 276
Chacksfield, Frank, 284
Champagne for Everybody, 252
Champagne Waltz, 175
Chaplin, Charlie, 104, 242
Chappell and Company, 177, 179
Charisse, Cyd, 228
Charles, Milton, 92
Chase, Newell, 99, 108, 269
Chatterton, Ruth, 101
Cherkose, Eddie, 246, 269
Chevalier, Maurice, 101, 104, 125, 131, 137, 140, 271, 274

Chicago Theater, 92
"Chinese Lullaby," *217*
"Chloe," 189
Christy, E. P., 67
Christy, June, 274
"Ciri-Biri-Bin," 202
City Center (New York), 253
Clarke, Grant, 15, 42, *56,* 99
Clinton, Larry, 279
Clooney, Rosemary, 201
Clyde, Andy, *160*
Clyde, June, *45*
Cobb, Will, 16, 68
Cockles and Champagne, 256
"Cocktails for Two," 98, 141–145, 152, 182, 254, 264, 268, 274, 276, 278–282, 285
Cody, Lew, 12, 102–104, *163,* 179
Coghill, Walter L., *56*
Cohan, George M., 18–19, 68, 87
Cohen, Manny, 151
Cohen, Meyer, *56*
Cohn, Harry, 87
Cohn, Jack, 87
Colbert, Claudette, 100, 126
Cole, Nat "King," 228
Coleman, Emil, 40
College Humor, 134–136, 190, 207, 267–268, 270
College Scandals, 173, 269
Collier, Buster, 103
Collingeamin, Channon, *56*
Collins, Harry, *56*
Collins, Ted, 131–132
Colman, Ronald, 246
Columbo, Russ, 12, *45,* 93, 114–121, 138, *160,* 271
Como, Perry, 136, 199, 229, 267, 271
Confrey, Zez, 38, 270
Connolly, Reg, 177, 179–180, 190–191
Conrad, Con, 12, 22, 57, 88–89, 103, 116–118, 120, 179, 270
Conversation Piece, 178
Cooper, Gary, 126, 137, 237
Cooper, Jackie, 110
Coots, J. Fred, 12, 77, 82, 89, 122, 271
Copacabana, 209, 247–249, 269
Coronado, 203
Correll, Charles, 274–275
Cortez, Ricardo, 82, *162*
Coslow, Barton, 109–110
Coslow, Cara, 256, 262

292

Main-Wilson, Denis, *211, 212*
Major Bowes's Capitol Theater Family, 75
Make Believe Ballroom, 193–194
"Make-Believe Island," 222, 270, 277, 282, 285
Make Way for Tomorrow, 205
"Mammy," 94
Manfield, Marian, 282
"Manhattan Serenade," 81
Mankiewicz, Joe, 136
Mann, Joe, 125
Mannix, Eddie, 233
Mantovani, 103, 270–271, 285
Many Happy Returns, 153–154, *169,* 203, 268
"Maple Leaf Rag," 69
"Margie," 57, 60
"Marijuana," 144, 270, 276
Marjorie, 78
Marks, Gerald, *55*
Marks, Johnny, *55*
Markus, Fally, 83
Marquard, Rube, 81
Marsh, Howard, 78
Marshall, Dave, 278
Marshall, Henry, *56*
Marshall, Herbert, 12, 265–266
Martin, Freddy, 203, 270, 282
Martin, Mary, 147, 245
Martin, Tony, 269
Marx, Arthur, 248
Marx, Groucho, 12, 82, 248–249
Marx, Gummo, 248
Marx Brothers, 101, 248
Mary Poppins, 57
Maschwitz, Eric, 257
Matteson, Don, 279
Matthews, Jessie, 12, 177, 184–187, 268 –269, 276
Maxwell, Elsa, 246
Maxwell, George, *56*
May, Billy, 282
Mayer, Jerry, 232–233
Mayer, Louis B., 12, 231–233, 236–237
MCA, *see* Music Corporation of America
McCarey, Leo, 150
McCarron, Charles, *56*

McCarthy, Charlie, 192
McCarthy, Joe, 15
McGovern, George, *216,* 270
McLaglen, Victor, 140
McPartland, Marian, 276
Mehlinger, Artie, 83
"Memory Lane," 88, 116
Memphis Five, 40, 282
Menjou, Adolphe, 100
Menken, Helen, 82
Menuhin, Yehudi, *171*
Mercer, Johnny, 239, 241, 246
Meroff, Benny, 270
Merrill, Helen, 271
Merry Widow, The, 140, 156
Merry Wives of Windsor, The, 216
Mesta, Pearl, 244
Metropolitan Opera, 81
Meyer, George, 83
Meyer, Sol, 261–262, 264
Meyers, George, *56*
Midler, Bette, 144, 270, 276
"Midnight Music," 270, 282
Miller, Bob, 70
Miller, Glenn, 192, 198, 200
Miller, Ray, 40
Mills, Irving, 12, 38–42, 280
Mills, Jack, 17, 38–39, 41
Mills, Ralph, 227
Mills Music, 38–42
Mills Novelty Company, 227
Milton, Robert, 101
Miracle of Morgan's Creek, The, 238, 241
Miranda, Carmen, 247–249, 269
Missouri Theater (St. Louis), 92
"Mister Paganini (You'll Have to Swing It)," 156, 173–174, 206, 254, 270, 275, 277–278
Mistinguette, 78
Mix, Tom, 102
Mole, Miff, 200
Monaco, Jimmy, 15, *56*
Money Muddle, The, 260
Montesanto, Leroy, 283
"Mood Indigo," 41, 228
"Moon Song," 98, 132–133, *164,* 270, 275–277, 281, 285